MARXISM AND CHRISTIANITY
The Quarrel and the Dialogue in Poland

Józef Tischner

Translated by Marek B. Zaleski and Benjamin Fiore, S.J.

Georgetown University Press
Washington, D.C.

FOREWORD

"Great is my anguish. There are people whose religious timidity ordinarily causes the name of the Most High to stick in their throat and to flow from the pen with even greater difficulty. Nonetheless, in times of deep dissension they cannot renounce this name as the ultimate expression of thought. And so, allow me to close this letter with an ardent prayer: May God help our deluded and deceived country and point out the way to peace with itself and the world."

Thomas Mann wrote these words in 1937, in a period of national and personal distress; at the time when the University of Bonn, seized by the Nazis, stripped him of his honorary doctorate. Mann's attitude toward religion had been ambivalent and it took this encounter with a totalitarian dictatorship for God to appear on the pages of his books.

Many Poles have had a similar experience. Totalitarianism—every totalitarianism—is an attempt to reduce a human being to the status of an obedient tool; it is a continual attempt to inculcate in the public a mutual mistrust and fear. Totalitarianism teaches precisely this: "Thou shalt have no other gods but the Leader and his Party." Poles know that in a totalitarian world, meeting with God is always a form of spiritual resistance, and that the church will always be attacked by totalitarian rulers. The church, however, teaches that a human being may render unto Caesar what is Caesar's, but may kneel only at the altar of God.

I am somewhat abashed as I write these words. I wish to introduce the American reader to this book by the Reverend Józef Tischner, professor of philosophy, excellent writer, renowned pastor in Poland, and also my critic and friend. The source of my feeling is the "religious timidity" mentioned by Mann—how can one write without anguish about issues that are so personal and at the same time so widely known in my country? To people with different experiences, however, these matters are surely not so obvious.

I am not Catholic. I am not an apologist for Polish Catholicism. Nor am I finally an uncritical reader of Tischner's book on the "Polish shape of dialogue." Yet I believe that Polish Catholicism and its intellectual articulation are phenomena that deserve careful comprehension and keen consideration. In addition, this is a world of values for which I feel sympathy and respect.

According to a well-known stereotype, Polish Catholicism is rustic and primitive, anti-intellectual and shallow, ethnocentric and intolerant. It would be a frivolous lie to claim that such Catholics do not exist in Poland. It would be equally false, however, to argue that they dominate the Polish church. Tischner's book is a testimony of intellectual Catholicism, well rooted in Polish tradition, but simultaneously open to dialogue with the contemporary world.

Tischner is one of the most prominent and most restless spirits of Polish culture. His polemics with Thomism shook the Catholic church, while his polemics with Marxism stirred up the world of official Communist ideology. Defining himself ironically as the "philosopher of the dull-witted Sarmatians," Tischner assimilates a universal spirit into Polish culture, carries out dialogue with Hegel and Husserl, with Dostoievsky and Levinas, as well as with his compatriots. *Marxism and Christianity* is just a fragment of Tischner's work and should be viewed as an introduction to his other works, especially those included in the volume *Thinking According to Values*.

Marxism and Christianity: The Quarrel and the Dialogue in Poland should be read by everyone with an interest in Poland, Christianity and the real world of Communism. In it the reader will find information on Catholicism subjected to totalitarian pressure, as well as how this Catholicism, molded by the two great spirits, Cardinal Wyszyński and Pope John Paul II, defended itself from the destructive effect of Communist reality. This exhausting spiritual struggle of the Polish church is seldom understood; Tischner's book certainly contributes to this understanding.

The book also helps one to understand the nature of that totalitarian pressure. Tischner analyzes the content of Marxist doctrine and exposes the roots of its attractiveness. He quotes the arguments of official Marxism, juxtaposes them with the facts, and proposes his own interpretation. He shows with great precision how the Communist-defined "dialogue" with Christians came to be a smoke screen for the politics of atheism and repression. In opposition to this, he advances his idea of a different shape of dialogue. He carries on this dialogue. He summons the faces and words of Polish humanists; those of Czesław Miłosz and Tadeusz Konwicki, Jan Strzelecki and Leszek Kołakowski. He argues with them. Nonetheless, in these quarrels, passionate and sharp as they are, there is as much a brotherly gesture of meeting as there is polemic. Józef Tischner wants to be a loyal polemicist, open to the arguments of others, and he manages to do so.

Marxism and Christianity has become an essential book in the intellectual history of Polish Catholicism. In addition, it has become an important fragment of the polemics about the relationship between the church and the lay intelligentsia. The latter fact also indicates the way one should read this book, not as a definitive summary, but as a fragment of a conversation; a conversation that still continues. This dispute, which is becoming a *dialogue*, is still going on; we still participate in a conversation which is becoming a *meeting*.

This is not the place to report on the church–lay intelligentsia dispute. The dispute is accompanied by an unusual increase of religious practice in Poland. This in turn raises the temperature of the discussion among the opponents of totalitarianism, opponents with different biographies and pedigrees. The dispute about the chances of and threats to Polish Catholicism will be a component of Polish debates for a long time to come. But these debates confirm Miłosz's opinion that "Catholicism in Poland will be the soil, or at least the background, for all intellectual endeavors" and that "in it the promise of Polish cultural originality is contained."

Józef Tischner's book is a voice of such Catholicism. Within the sphere of the universal church, this voice has an original sound. One can find in it an attempt at a resolution of the universal and classic dilemmas of contemporary Christianity: the tension between the sacred and the profane, between politics and moral witness, between the theology of "conservatism" and the theology of "liberation", between the church of diplomacy and the church of apostolate, between a Christianity of conflict and a Christianity of dialogue.

Józef Tischner does not look for cheap agreement; he pronounces decisive and polemically provocative judgments. Certainly, he expects to meet with not a few polemics from Catholic integrists and Catholic progressives. Surely, people of other ideological orientations as well will dispute with him. In his time, this writer has listed his own polemic reservations. Both proponents and critics of this book, however, should remember that, among the categories present in Józef Tischner's philosophical reflections, the concepts of "dialogue" and "meeting" play fundamental roles; dialogue with the "other" and meeting with the one who is "different." For this reason a particular rigor is written into the polemics of and with Tischner—the rigor of brotherhood.

"Piety is a kind of wisdom," wrote Mann during the totalitarian night. What is the content of this "piety"? Somewhere, Józef Tischner has said, following Hegel, that the best that people can achieve is an active respect for the needs of other people, for the whole richness and diversity of human existence in the world. This respect is the basis of the harmony of plurality, the harmony of dialogue.

In this dialogue, both Polish and human, Józef Tischner's voice is among the most important and the most loudly resounding. May this voice help all those deluded and deceived. . .

Adam Michnik

From the Translators

Polski kształt dialogu—a book, a philosophical treatise, a description of and commentary on contemporary Polish history. All this is quite interesting for Poles, but why should it be of any concern for Americans?

Let us listen to the author, who in his recent interview in the Polish periodical *Kontakt* (48/4, 1986), said: "We Poles have many experiences with the fatherland. These experiences are not always verbalized. They are often silent events that we retain unspoken within ourselves without talking about them. We often speak in a language incomprehensible to Europeans. We speak in poetry that is untranslatable. In this sense I would defend Polish uniqueness, that is, I would defend the Polish heartache for the fatherland as something that brings us troubles, but for Europe it may be quite illuminating."

Indeed, *Polski kształt dialogu* is an illuminating book, and not just for the rest of Europe but for thoughful persons elsewhere in the world as well. In Poland, the centuries-old intellectual traditions of the nation and its Christian values were forced to confront an alien philosophy and the social system developed from it in the years following the devastating Second World War. The book's perspective sheds light, one is tempted to say, on the crucial element of dialogue between the Marxist and Christian philosophical positions. This element has more often than not been hitherto ignored by those who advocate, analyze or criticize Marxism, namely its ethical content or, to be exact, the poverty of its ethical underpinnings. Thus, the dialogue situations which the author describes are mostly on the ethical plane and their central point is neither economics nor politics—it is the human being, his dignity and his search for freedom.

Because of the sweeping nature of this dialogue, it has encompassed not only the experts, but virtually everyone in Poland—philosophers and ordinary people alike—all who make choices which affect human dignity and freedom. As the author puts it in the above mentioned interview:

"Choosing freedom is not a singular act. Freedom is a process, freedom is becoming oneself. This also means that the process can only be undertaken collectively. One cannot be free in isolation. One cannot be free when someone else is not free."

Here we reach the central point of the dialogue between Marxism and Christianity. For Marxism the human being is merely the product of labor, while for Christianity the human being is created by God in His image and uses labor as the road to the Creator God. Marxism proposes to liberate human labor, Christianity proposes to liberate the human being. As the recent history of Russia, Eastern Europe, Cuba, Vietnam, Cambodia, Nicaragua, Afghanistan, and Ethiopia demonstrates, Marxism has failed to keep its promise. Moreover, not only has it not liberated human labor but the process of its application has enslaved and even killed multitudes of human beings. In Poland, the dialogue has reached a point at which the question must be posed: "For what and for whom is Marxism still needed?" This question assumes particular meaning in the Polish context, where the principal representative of the people is a laborer with an image of the Black Madonna— Queen of Poland—in his lapel rather than a leader clutching a copy of Marx or even waving a gun. In this Polish context, the concepts of nation and fatherland have deeper and broader moral meanings than the pejorative and limited interpretations customarily assigned to them by the Marxist ideologues. Those moral meanings Poland shares with the rest of Europe and the world.

The author undertook the task of making "something that is mute speak on the same wavelength with the rest of European thinking." We the translators feel honored to have participated, in some small way, in the task of bringing the ideas of the author into the ongoing reflection of the even wider English–speaking audience beyond Europe. As part of the community of scientists and scholars and as members of the Solidarity and Human Rights Association, we are committed to the ideals of truth and human dignity, and we undertook the job of translation primarily as a call of conscience.

Our task was not easy but, looking at the neatly stacked pages of the manuscript ready to be sent to the publisher, we must admit that it was rewarding. We hope that our readers will enjoy the book as much as we did. Here we would like to acknowledge and convey our heartfelt thanks to all those who helped and encouraged us.

In the first place our gratitude goes to the National Endowment for the Humanities for awarding us a grant (RL-20750) to cover the expenses of research and manuscript preparation. No lesser thanks go to those of our friends who read various parts of the manuscript (Dr. Janice L. Schultz, Dr. Roger K. Cunningham), provided us with bibliographical references (Dr. med. T. Rymaszewska, Rev. James J. Shanahan, S.J., Mr. Wojciech Sikora, and Dr. Andrzej Załuska) and typed and retyped the manuscript (Mrs. Rozalind Forse). Last but not least we owe gratitude to *Editions Spotkania* (64, av. Jean Moulin, 75014 Paris, France) and their director Mr. Piotr Jegliński, and to the author Rev. Józef Tischner for authorizing the translation. We are grateful to Georgetown University Press and its director Rev. John Breslin, S.J. for encouraging us and offering us the opportunity to publish the translation.

To make the book more comprehensible to the American reader we give, whenever possible, titles of the English rather than Polish versions of works cited by the author. In addition, we provide explanatory notes for the persons, events and places mentioned in the text. In the case of persons, to avoid arbitrary selection, all names, including relatively familiar ones, are listed.

Finally, we would like to dedicate this translation to those who today and in the past paid a high price for their courageous participation in the dialogue—prisoners of conscience. Let this book bring them a ray of hope that they are not forgotten.

B. Fiore

M.B. Zaleski

May 1987

Introduction

A unique meeting of Christianity with Marxist socialism and the world being built by this socialism has been taking place in Poland for more than thirty years—a meeting of two contradictory concepts of bringing happiness to humankind. This meeting assumes a variety of forms and takes place on various levels. Sometimes it is called dialogue, but more often it is a quarrel, a confrontation, or a fight when one considers the tone that actually dominates the meeting. This meeting evokes broad interest. Today, Christianity and socialism gather in themselves the hopes of millions for the betterment of the human condition on earth. Christian and socialist ideas, especially their East European versions, appear to be contradictory. Christianity is a religion and teaches that a human being should believe in God and should, above all, strive for eternal salvation. Socialism, a social ideology, derives its inspiration from materialism and atheism and primarily calls upon human beings to care for their temporal existence. In Poland, historical circumstances[1] forced the two ideas to exist together and to chart the history of the nation. What has transpired from this meeting that has already lasted so many years?

When searching for an answer in the immediate past, we encounter two difficulties.

The first difficulty arises from the lack of proper distance and necessary objectivity. Everyone who lives in this country is somehow involved. Even the most ordinary people are not bystanders. This fact is reflected in the classification of history into specific periods. When did the dialogue really begin and through what stages has it passed? Such a question is posed by every historical reflection that attempts to reach a consensus on the principles of systematizing the historical material. Can agreement be reached between the opposing sides on the question of systematics? To a Christian, the most noteworthy moments are those that correspond to an attack against religion by indicating the beginning of a certain problem, and subsequently those moments that, by marking an end of a certain stage, testify to the invincible power of Christianity.

The "period of attacks" corresponds to the Stalinist era, the "period of success" coincides with the visit[2] of John Paul II[3] and the strikes of 1980.[4] Is the division into such periods binding for the Marxist too? Can the Marxist not reach for less spectacular criteria?

The second difficulty is connected with the first. To present the issue more clearly, let us use an example. Let us imagine a philosopher, Socrates,[5] who is imprisoned for political reasons. Let us further assume that we disagree with his philosophy and thus we wish to criticize it. However, we believe that his imprisonment is an open violation of the law. Do we have a right, while Socrates awaits a trial that might bring him the death sentence, to proceed with the criticism of his views? Should we not rather remain silent so our criticism will not be misinterpreted and thus will not contribute to an unjust sentence? The situation of Christianity in Poland resembled that of Socrates in his prison. Those who, in spite of everything, decided to criticize religion were putting themselves—perhaps involuntarily—in a dubious moral position. Such a critic might be suspected of abetting a dishonest trial. However, Marxism was in no better position. Trial judges called upon Marxism in rendering their decision. In this situation a criticism of Marxism meant an attack on the judges, while any, even the smallest, praise of Marxism meant some form of support for the trial. Neither the content of the discussion, nor the quality of the arguments used, nor the good faith of the disputants was essential; what was essential was the entire political context.

Thus we have a problem with the idea of scientific "objectivity." If "objective" means "uninvolved" or "bystander" then one must, even in Poland, refrain from writing about the dialogue between Christianity and Marxism. However, perhaps there is still another idea of "objectivity."

One can write a history not only from the position of a spectator but also from the standpoint of a witness. A witness is closer to history than a spectator. Perhaps the witness perceives things and events rather narrowly, but on the other hand, he has more direct access to them. One can be involved and still make reflections on the involvement. If such a reflection is an honest one, then objectivity here represents testimony—honest testimony. It is in this vein that I undertake the task of writing about dialogue. I admit that my point of view is limited. I am interested primarily in philosophy and, therefore, I place its problems in the foreground. Among philosophers there are some who are philosophically close to me as well as others who are distant. I do not hide it. It seems to me that only in this way shall I not only write about the issue, but also nurture it.

I am writing this introduction in the fall of 1980, while the book itself has been written over approximately three years, with the text changing repeatedly to catch up with events. Looking at the problem from this perspective, I must emphasize some essential points.

A specific feature of Polish dialogue is that it has not been a dialogue of a narrow group of experts—experts in Christian and Marxist thought—but was a dialogue of the entire nation. Virtually every inhabitant of this country participated in it. Each person at a certain key point in his life had to decide whether to baptize a child, whether to enroll a child in religious classes, whether to affiliate himself or herself with the Party, whether to participate openly in certain religious celebrations, whether to come out and greet John Paul II and display decorations in their windows, whether to join the strike of the summer of 1980. The period of the so-called "construction of socialism" was a period of certain duress; one had to make choices, one had to make decisions. This period did not so much create the possibility of choice—such a possibility exists in every democratic society—as actually force upon people the necessity of choice. Our times did not tolerate neutral people. Choosing meant giving testimony and both sides vied for the testimony. Each concrete decision was an act of consideration and an act of courage. One had to think through, discuss with friends, undertake some degree of personal risk. Risk was associated with every decision. No wonder that these times were conducive to the maturation of the people and the nation. The nation was maturing, I think that a greater maturity of the nation was the first obvious fruit of the controversy that was taking place. It disclosed itself in a particular way during the difficult days of the strike in the summer of 1980.

The key choice was between Christianity and Marxism. What did it actually mean? Let us start with Marxism.

Marxism in Poland ceased to be solely a topic of scholarly dissertations, the content of dust-covered volumes buried in library stacks. Increasingly, it became the essence of popular social consciousness. The process of the "construction of socialism" was accompanied by the process of "socialization" of society. Marxism was in the school textbooks, in newspapers, on radio and television, in the high schools, the universities, in hundreds and thousands of conferences which the Party presented to us from early morning to late evening. Can one wander in a fog and avoid getting soggy? Everyone got a bit soggy—some more, others less; some willingly, others unwillingly. The various socialist "dogmas" kept seeping into one's soul: the belief that the world is divided into two struggling camps, that in every society two social classes fight with each other for life or death, that the "base" determines the content of the "superstructure," that there is a proletarian internation-alism, and so forth. Some of the dogmas were valid permanently, while others changed with passing time. At one point it was believed that farming must be collective, that religion is "opium for the masses," but then somehow these beliefs dropped away. Marxism molded people to the essence of its doctrine, but people also modified Marxism to their own needs. Still, an unresolved question loomed over us. What is Marx-ism, really? What is socialism? There were those who put into these concepts only the loftiest social ideals. Marxism, they said, is a theory of struggle against the exploitation of labor, a theory of liberation of the human being; it is a thought that embodies the most beautiful ethical traditions of humankind. They still believed in Marxism, still assumed—despite repeated catastrophes—that the beautiful idea only failed to find sufficiently talented organizers. Socialism and Marxism became the ide-ology of certain social circles. There was still something in these concepts that attracted people. There are witnesses to this.

Christianity has a thousand-year tradition in Poland.[6] It too became an essence, not so much of scientific dissertations but of the faith of the people, of the self-knowledge of the nation, an indicator of the nation's ethical consciousness. Never in its history had the Polish church become an "opium for the masses." On the contrary, it was a factor in awakening the people from their slumber. It did not create a great theology but it gave rise to something more essential—religious thinking. The phenom-enon of religious thinking is all encompassing. It appears in literature, especially drama and poetry, and in painting; it is felt in the way history is perceived, in the entire Polish ethos. The church, after World War II, traveled a long road. Two figures of Polish Catholicism are symbolic of this journey—Stefan Cardinal Wyszyński[7] and John Paul II. The first was the author of the political concept of coexistence between the church and a Communist state. The characteristic feature of this concept was the principle of defending the basic ethical values that were threatened by state policies. The second figure was the author of the postconciliar renewal[8] of the church. The church gained enormous intellectual au-thority, it became a pluralistic church. People of different convictions found a niche in this pluralistic church, including those from the Left who were not tolerated by the Party. The moral and intellectual au-thority of the church grew constantly. In 1980, it did not have an equal opponent in Poland. While the Party lacked experts, the church had them in droves, in every field.

Thus, the alternatives were not equal. The nation was choosing ac-cording to values. What was its choice? No one could have a doubt in this regard. The choice was confirmed during the Pope's visit. The visit of John Paul II was an occasion for the nation to recognize its own communion. The nation saw itself. A nation that sees itself understands better its own dignity. All John Paul II's homilies delivered in Poland were about dignity. In 1980, this nation rose from humiliation. People said, "We are cleaning house." Such was the fruit of maturity in those months.

At the very same time we realized our necessities. Every choice is a choice of possibilities contained within certain necessities. The latter stood exceptionally clear before our eyes. What were the necessities?

The Christians realized that one cannot get rid of socialism in Poland. The Marxists saw that they too could not get rid of Christianity. We are doomed to an existence side by side within the borders of one and the same country. What transpires from these conclusions? I shall try to look at this question with the eyes of a Marxist who is not fond of religion, and with the eyes of a Christian who does not love Marxism.

Christianity is a Polish historic necessity. That is a fact. This being so, one must overcome fear in one's thinking. The church in Poland became an ethical force. This means that whatever it said, or did, was kept within the frame of ethics. It did not lead people to the barricades, it did not incite religious wars, in times of tension it poured water on hot iron. The church in Poland became a pluralistic church. If one puts all this together, another conclusion is reached; one must also get rid of fear of action.

Socialism in Poland also reflects historical necessity. We see this better today than yesterday. If this is so, the church cannot wish for nor aspire to a complete destruction of socialism. Maybe for some this seems sad, but such is our necessity, and only within it can the different possibilities outline themselves. Among them is the possibility of pluralism. The problem expressed: "If socialism, then what socialism?" concerns everybody. This is not exclusively an internal problem of the Marxists. Similarly, the problem, "If Christianity, then what Christianity?" is not an exclusive problem of the church. However, the answers to these questions are not arrived at behind a desk. Rather, real life and real history will fill the general concepts with a specific content. The postwar history of Polish Marxism and Polish socialism is quite equivocal. The original lofty ethos of the socialist idea collapsed several times and in some instances even bloodily. Until now we have dealt predominantly with economic and political socialism. Our experiences with it are not good. But perhaps there is still the possibility of experiencing ethical socialism. Has the primary ethos of the socialist idea, the solidarity of working people in the name of liberation from the burden of exploitation, vanished without trace? One must admit that in Poland, in the summer of 1980, in spite of the strikes and heightened social tensions, no one was shooting at workers. There were attempts to resolve difficulties by "po-

litical," that is, ethical means. The reasons and motives are less important. Looking at the issue as objectively as possible, it should be admitted
that this fact has an ethical significance. A good content has been written
into the history of the socialist idea. One must acknowledge this content.

On September 5, 1980, Stefan Bratkowski,[9] currently the chairman
of the reconstituted Association of Polish Journalists, commented on
the most recent history of the church:

> Let us consider; rapprochement with the people was made by the institution
> that not only for decades, but for many centuries was the personification and
> quintessence of feudalism in every respect: views, organization, customs. Even
> today not a few of its representatives forget that they are talking not to un-
> educated simpletons, but to equal citizens with their own common sense; not
> to children but to brothers. The church was returning from far away. However,
> it was capable of rooting out of its tradition the crimes of inquisitions, stakes
> and bloody murders in the name of faith, and a group of elderly men, each with
> his own ambitions and obsessions, was capable of electing a head of the church
> as if from a computer. I think it is a quite educating example since it proves
> that one can get out of a dead-end street. We must try too. [Probably from an
> unauthorized manuscript circulating around the country.]

I think that all who are responsible for the development of Marxist
and socialist ideas in Poland should realize a key truth: socialism will
either be an ethical socialism or it will not exist at all.

I look once again to the history of our dialogue and I ask: Was there
a dialogue or not? Unfortunately, in my opinion there was none. The
situation of Christianity resembled the situation of Socrates in his jail.
This essential context of the disputes altered the sense of the words
spoken, the polemics held and the clarifications given. A great lesson
remained: Where the arguing sides do not have full freedom, a "dialogue" is not and cannot be a dialogue. People speak but do not hear
each other.

What will happen to these "monologues" if one changes the context?

I think that if the context were changed, everything that has been
written until now could acquire a proper meaning. One could return to
the thoughts already spoken, to the propositions already made, to the
questions asked, and to the answers given. Perhaps in the dialogue ahead
no new words will be uttered, no idea will be advanced that has not
already been formulated. Still, a different context will return to these
ideas their proper sense. Returning a proper sense involves, first of all,
restoring a proper hierarchy of values. Until now the two movements
striving to bring happiness to humankind quarreled about their own
principles—about faith and nonfaith, matter and spirit, the power and
powerlessness of matter. Although, so far, no happiness has sprung

from these disputes, they have had some value. Is it not time to pose the question that flows from the heart of both ideologies: What can be done to help humankind? Both movements carry within them a colossal knowledge of human pain. Socialism considers primarily the pain of the working person. Christianity looks at the existential pain of creation exposed to a trial of despair, loneliness and hatred. It is something of a paradox that the meeting of these two movements increased rather than decreased human misery. Has the time perhaps come to reverse this tragic paradox? And are we perhaps the country in which the practice of reversing the tragic paradoxes will precede the theory?

Józef Tischner

November 1980

I.
The Struggle Over
the Content of
the "Superstructure"

1. The Situation in Polish Philosophy after World War II

The situation in Polish philosophy after World War II was determined by two basic factors: the political situation and tradition, the latter comprising the achievements of philosophy in the period between the wars. I shall touch upon each of these factors without claiming an exhaustive treatment of the topic, since the problem of a dialogue with Christian philosophy remains the principal object of interest here.

After World War II the helm of the government in our country was seized by an authority that—by its own admission—bases its practice on Marxist–Leninist doctrine and for a time on Marxist–Leninist–Stalinist doctrine. In our country, the basic means of production, i.e., everything which according to Marxist terminology constitutes the "base" of social life, became socialized or nationalized. The manner of exercising authority is called the "dictatorship of the proletariat." The forces ruling the country are aware that in the social reality of Poland, "remnants" of the old system still survive and that the new system finds itself under constant pressure from hostile forces; hence the need for strong and determined government. True, the new government controls the means of production; but there remains an entire "superstructure"—culture, morality, religion—in which the old meanings continue to hold their ground. Marxist–Leninist–Stalinist philosophy is the appropriate tool with which one not only can accomplish creative changes in the base, but can remodel the content of the "superstructure" as well. In a programmatic text concerning the aims of philosophy in the new period of history, one reads:

. . . We are faced with the task of combatting the contemporary, decadent philosophy of imperialism—the ideological weapon of warmongers; the task of combatting imperialistic, Anglo-American philosophy and sociology, that became the core of every obscurantist and genocidal doctrine; the task of combatting the diversionary ideology of social democracy, Vatican obscurantism, nationalism and cosmopolitanism—and to do this from a patriotic and internationalist position. . . . Our tasks are closely linked with the formation of a socialist nation in Poland, with the struggle to lay the foundation for socialism, the struggle for peace, for the Six-Year Plan.[10] The issues here, therefore, are dear to all patriots, to everyone involved in creative work, to the citizens of a socialist fatherland. Precisely in this do we, to a great extent, root our conviction that the tasks of the philosophical front-line in Poland will be accomplished ("Od Redakcji" 1951:15).

The philosophy of dialectical materialism ("dia-mat") became the official philosophy. It was introduced into the universities as a compulsory subject, and also entered the curricula of secondary and primary schools in various ways. This philosophy was presented as capable of explaining all the basic human problems, especially social problems. Dialectical materialism did not enter our culture as the result of the free choice of scholars but was launched and occasionally imposed outright by political means. Before the war, Marxist philosophy did not have even a single prominent representative in Poland. There were no Marxists in the universities and there were no Marxists among the authors of essays published in philosophical periodicals. Only after the war did the Marxists sprout up, like mushrooms after rain.

Tradition was the second factor that determined the postwar philosophical atmosphere of Polish philosophy. This tradition was fed by three principal streams: analytical philosophy represented by the so-called "Lwów-Warszawa School," the phenomenology of Roman Ingarden,[11] and neo-Thomism. A few words now on each of these.

The Lwów-Warszawa School concerned itself "predominantly with the analysis of concepts as a basic task that could be done precisely and scientifically. In its analysis of concepts the school considered their subjective and objective aspects, i.e., psychological and logical" (Tatarkiewicz 1948/50:366). The school traces itself back to Kazimierz Twardowski,[12] who before World War I gathered in Lwów a brilliant circle of disciples, open to various philosophical currents. Among his pupils were Kazimierz Ajdukiewicz,[13] Tadeusz Czeżowski,[14] Jan Łukasiewicz,[15] and Izydora Dąmbska.[16] Ingarden stemmed from Twardowski, but created a distinct school. Spiritually akin to the Lwów school were the Warszawa logicians: Stanisław Leśniewski,[17] Alfred Tarski,[18] and a string of their disciples scattered through Poland (in Kraków: Jan Śleszyński[19] and Leon Chwistek[20]). This current set for itself "partial, preparatory, and monographic efforts. It carried out an analysis of concepts, but set aside the work of philosophical syntheses. It formed an opposition to speculative philosophy but was not identical with positivism. It was more open than positivism, it prejudged neither the results, nor the limits of investigation, nor which of the competing positions would turn out to be correct. . . . The Lwów-Warszawa School owed its position to the fact that other, more ambitious trends that previously held sway in Poland did not bring the anticipated results" (Tatarkiewicz 1948/50:368).

Analytical philosophy considered more general philosophical conceptions, particularly in the works of Tadeusz Kotarbiński[21] and Ajdukiewicz. Because the polemic with Kotarbiński and Ajdukiewicz was to be a primary undertaking of Marxist philosophy, let us recapitulate the positions of these two authors, using Władysław Tatarkiewicz's[22] concise sketch.

Tadeusz Kotarbiński (born 1886), professor in Warszawa, interpreted concepts materialistically (*The Elements of the Theory of Cognition, Logic, and Methodology;* original title—*Elementy teorii poznania, logiki i metodologii*). He negated the existence not only of psychic objects but also of "events", "states of things", "relations", and "properties", i.e., all those notions that occupy the largest part of philosophical considerations. To him, these were only hypostases of concepts, abstractions. There is no battle—there are only fighting armies; there is no consciousness—there are only conscious bodies; there is no rain—only falling drops; there is no justice—only just judges. Conceptual difficulties and insoluble problems originate in the fact that we use words denoting fictions and, yielding to their suggestion, we take the fiction for reality, while in fact *only* things exist. This position . . . Kotarbiński called "reism" or "concretism". He also called it "pansomatism" to indicate that conscious beings are always corporeal beings. Moreover, he used the term "radical realism". He assigned this designation especially to the idea that the so-called content of consciousness, sensory qualities, colors or sounds, are also fictions. It is not true that, as critical realists would have it, we perceive colors, sounds and so forth, and then on that basis make conclusions about things; we perceive things directly (Tatarkiewicz 1948/50:370).

Ajdukiewicz (1890–1963) took language and its rules as the starting point of his investigation.

Anyone who does not answer affirmatively to the question whether every square is a rectangle would provide evidence that he or she does not understand the words "square", "rectangle", etc. The one who does not accept the principle of contradiction, and says that something may be and not be at the same time, shows a lack of understanding of the word "not". Judgments dictated by these rules are a priori judgments; they are universally valid and it is logically impossible to reject them.

Furthermore,

these rules thus lead to universally valid statements; but on the other hand, they introduce into the statements a factor of convention. The majority of the judgments of a given language (the "universal perspective of the language") depends not only on experience but also on the conceptual apparatus of the language. However, the latter is conventional, in part arbitrary. The result of this is *conventionalism,* not partial as in Poincaré,[23] but universal—"radical", as Ajdukiewicz called it. But conventionalism does not draw relativism behind it for, although various conceptual apparatuses are possible, it is impossible for a true judgment in one apparatus to be incorrect in another. Neither does conventionalism imply idealism since it does not follow that the universe recognized by us depends on the conceptual apparatus—it is only the "perspective of the world" that depends on the apparatus. A perspective is a collection of judgments about the world but is not the world itself. When we change the apparatus, we pose different questions to the world and consequently we obtain different answers; but the world does not change because of that. We are just observing a different aspect of it. Idealists create appearances of correctness for their judgment by using a language in which the discourse is about the cognition of the world and not about the world itself; in that language their utterances only apparently speak of the world. Therefore, conventionalism does not rebut realism, rather it limits empiricism. It is not true that assertions depend only on experience, since they also depend on language. Not only empirical statements are correct, not only those statements bear upon reality, and there is no reason for those alone to be considered scientific. Conventionalism does not imply reism or nominalism. The answer to the question of whether universals exist depends on the adopted language. In the reist language, there is no place for them since this language has names of only one type. But a language with many logical types is also possible, one in which multiple meanings might "exist" and in which one could speak of universal existences without contradiction (Tatarkiewicz 1948/50:370–71).

Ingarden (1893–1970) took hold primarily after World War II. Before the war, his phenomenology did not enjoy a broad understanding at all among people steeped in the atmosphere created by analytical philosophy. The situation changed radically after the war and especially after 1956, when Ingarden returned to the Jagiellonian University.

This active and multifaceted scholar was an ontologist and systematician in the period of Polish philosophy dominated by specialization and history; he belonged to the phenomenologist school when Poland gravitated toward positivism. He was a disciple of Husserl[24] but did not accept his idealism. Husserl saw in real objects intentional creations which are dependent on acts of pure consciousness and to which he ascribed absolute existence. Ingarden, on the other hand, arrived at a realistic understanding of the real world. . . . He set for himself the task of analyzing unequivocally intentional objects in order to confront them with real objects. Works of art would be objects of this sort. First he analyzed the works of literary art (*The Literary Work of Art*—original title: *Das literarische Kunstwerk*) and then others. This was an original path—through the theory of art to ontology. Although works of art have a basis in real objects like print or canvas, without which they would not have an intersubjective identity and thus would be inaccessible to their audience, they are nevertheless created intentionally by the artist and reconstructed and concretized by the audience. Almost incidentally, Ingarden developed a philosophical theory of art and aesthetics. Specifically, he demonstrated that in their structure works of art are always schematic and multilayered. . . . After these preparatory studies, Ingarden moved on to a full presentation of his ontological, epistemological, and metaphysical views in the work *The Controversy about the Existence of the World* (the first two volumes appeared in 1947 and 1948—original title: *Spór o istnienie świata*). In this work, he introduced a new method for resolving the controversy . . . via the analysis of the form of real objects. The application of this method led him to reject all forms of idealism but also to reject absolute realism which demanded primary existents from the world, while the world, as a temporary entity, is not a primary being. For this reason, in Ingarden realism was joined with creationism (Tatarkiewicz 1948/50:365–66).

From Ingarden's circle came Anna Tymieniecka[25] (currently in the United States), Danuta Gierulanka,[26] Andrzej Połtawski,[27] Maria Gołaszewska[28] (aesthetics) and the disciples (after 1956): Adam Węgrzecki[29] (philosophy of value), Władysław Cichoń[30] (also philosophy of value), Jan Szewczyk[31] (a current of the "philosophy of work" in Marxism), Władysław Stróżewski[32] (ontology, esthetics, history of philosophy) and this author. The works of Karol Wojtyła were under the unmistakable influence of phenomenology even though he did not study with Ingarden. This influence is also noticeable in Antoni Stępień[33] (Catholic University of Lublin) and Andrzej Siemianowski[34] (Theological Seminary in Poznań).

Finally, there is a third current that was also inherited from the interwar period—the current of Thomistic philosophy. One must mention here, above all, the Rev. Konstantyn Michalski,[35] who changed after the war from a historian of philosophy to a philosopher of history, a philosopher of the human person. Although he considers himself a Thomist, he nonetheless owes a great deal to St. Augustine.[36] Following in the footsteps of Augustine, he has attempted to bring closer to the postwar intelligentsia an understanding of the historical curve through which the world is passing. He wrote *Between Heroism and Bestiality (Między heroizmem i bestialstwem)*, a philosophical reckoning with the war, with cruelty and hatred, seeking in the cultural past of Europe the building material for tomorrow.

In his programmatic article, "Where Are We Going?", we read, among other things:

In the philosophy of history, too, appear the dreams that, along with rationalized thought, very often express the heartfelt desires of an author or even of an entire social group. If a Catholic today were to express his dreams, he would declare that, like St. Paul,[37] he longs for a new parousia,[38] a new revelation of Christ in history, through our hands and brains, our hearts and thoughts. Christ's parousia took place time after time, constantly renewing the face of the earth. We expect that, after the last world war, the face of the earth will be renewed not only through the release of atomic energy but above all through the appearance of a new world of social justice and love in order to become like God in all his attributes and perfections. We are afraid of the power of man without God's exceptional goodness. We are even afraid of justice without love, since justice might degenerate into cruelty. Poland again stands on the banks of the Odra and Nysa rivers[39] to fulfill a great historic mission on the recovered "land of the Piasts".[40] The one who wants to speak about the Polish myth for the near future will be drawn to our new lands. Maritain[41] speaks of a new type of Christian culture formed under the influence of our religion that resides, as it should, in the entire culture as immanently as God inhabits the universe created by him. Every Catholic in Poland fervently longs for Christ's parousia to take place from the Odra and Nysa through Polish work and the effort of Polish thought. Catholicism put on its banner the Thomist motto *genus humanum arte et ratione vivit* (the human species lives by art and reason). We live from the work of our hands and souls in order to climb ever higher, step by step; ever stronger through each new tool of thought and technology, but also ever better, ever close to God (Michalski 1964:32–33).

This article appeared in the first issue of the monthly *Znak*—a periodical of great value for our culture. The text not only exemplifies the author's broad interests, but also expresses the sense of responsibility of the Catholic intellectuals of those times for the fate of the country. Those intellectuals, among them Thomist philosophers more than the representatives of the other schools of thought, involved themselves in the concrete life of the nation by taking up quite openly the struggle for the content of Polish culture.

Lublin was the main center of Thomistic thought. Besides Lublin, many other centers evolved during the period between the wars. The greatest authority in the area of Thomism, especially Thomistic ethics, was Fr. Jacek Woroniecki.[42] Working in the same area as he were Rev. Piotr Chojnacki[43] (Warsaw), Rev. Jan Stepa[44] (Lwów), Rev. Franciszek Sawicki[45] (Pelplin) and others. After the war, there were Fr. Mieczysław Krąpiec[46] (Lublin), Rev. Kazimierz Kłósak[47] (Louvain Thomism, open to positive sciences), Zofia Zdybicka[48] (Lublin), Rev. Marian Jaworski[49] (Thomism akin to the transcendental version) and others. A unique place in Thomist philosophy is occupied by Stefan Świeżawski,[50] a historian of philosophy, who also writes works of a general nature. The beautiful style of his publications, their engaging profundity and broad culture, make him one of the most avidly read Thomists. His work, *Existence, An Outline of Thomistic Metaphysics (Byt, Zarys metafizyki tomistycznej)*, was one of the most popular philosophical works during the Stalinist period.

Into the philosophical atmosphere of those years, with the articulations just outlined, Marxism forced its entry with the intention of "fitting a superstructure to the base." It pushed in as the philosophy preferred, advanced, and not infrequently imposed. This does not mean, however, that Marxism was unattractive in itself, that it presented no cognitive and intellectual values. Marxism was the philosophy being promoted but it was not insignificant thought, not without its own power of attraction. Marxism was fascinating—whence this fascination? Certainly, it was not fascination with the purely formal or epistemological values of Marxist philosophy. Neither did it flow from a well-grounded knowledge of the type of philosophy Marxism represented. The sources of fascination lay deeper. Marxism proposed to our generation a particular ethos, before which one could not remain neutral. This ethos took its form in the imperative of an unwavering struggle to liberate human work from the yoke of exploitation. The practice of Marxism had a decidedly axiological character. In a sense the various strictly theoretical propositions of Marxist philosophy were of secondary importance—one could always improve them; the fundamental and absolute value was represented by a particular kind of ethical sensitivity to the problems of work. This sensitivity was at the root of Marxism and came to life in those who embraced it.

The primacy of the ethical outlook on Marxism over the strictly theoretical view will come forward once again when many, so far devoted Marxists will abandon Marxism. They will do so not so much because of "the holes" in the theory as because of the equivocal ethics to which Marxism had induced them.

Let us give one of the witnesses the floor. After the war this author took a radical turn—from the armed struggle against communism to its acceptance as his own ideology. Tadeusz Konwicki,[51] to whom we are referring, became for a time a representative advocate of "socialist realism" in literature. His writings entered into the canon of required readings on which graduation from a socialist high school depended. Subsequently, he took still another radical turn. This is what he has to say about his first "conversion":

It is necessary to remember that we were the vanquished. Behind us, in those forests of Wilno,[52] were the remains of a military disaster. We lost our war. I longed to find some place for all my naive anger. I could turn it only against myself and my own people. I searched for guilt in me and my people, more so because neither my people nor I were without guilt. Suddenly, the entire microclimate, that cocoon from which I emerged as a human being, became repulsive. Suddenly, daily prayer infuriated me, nightly dreams about Poland infuriated me—the Christ of the Nations,[53] the national gospel in the great romantic books infuriated me. I wanted immediately and demonstratively to smear the window pane that showed my entire past and my complicated lineage.

And at that time, through various people around me, Marxism made its appearance. Those people were quite like my former circles. Some were like frivolous jesters, others like anxious misanthropes, still others like feverish fanatics. But their talk was different. They quoted words of various bearded men who used to scare us as children. But these snippets, these *bons mots,* these slogans appeared to me extraordinarily accurate, very pertinent and exciting in their bare realism.

This was healing balm—this handful of wise interpretations of the world and of us in this world. This was a draft of spring-water—this drop of sound common sense. It appeared to be worth any price—even the daily price of a strangled memory (Konwicki 1976:77–78).

Marxism radiated. It radiated the hope of building a world more just than the world of yesterday. Agrarian reform, nationalization of industry, open access to schools, industrialization of a backward country . . . all this proved attractive. Works of the classic Marxist authors began to be published. Even if these works were not entirely true, their error was not easily perceived. To catch the error one had to have a trained eye, but the eye had nothing on which to train itself.

A unique situation developed. Representatives of university philosophy—analytic philosophy, semantics, reism, or phenomenology—did not consider Marxism as a philosophical adversary, as an alternative to their own philosophy. Actually, in private, they despised Marxism. They did not attack Karl Marx,[54] perhaps they did not even read him. From time to time, they signalled their kinship with Marxist thought—for example, the reists emphasized atheism as a common horizon of the two philosophies. Generally, however, their hidden contempt for Marxism evolved into a posture of detachment from the nation's moral and ideological conflict. Young enthusiasts of philosophy admired the architecture of their teachers' thought, but often held against them their *désintéressement.* It is certainly paradoxical that a frontal attack on Marxism was launched by—the Marxists themselves. It is another matter that this attack would not have elicited such deep repercussions had there been none of those other trends on the periphery of the country's cultural life. Although no one in Poland attacked Marx and his successors directly, the example of honest and responsible thinking was nevertheless attractive and contagious, on its own merits.

Some neo-Thomists undertook an attempt at polemics. Some argued against the theoretical principles underlying the construction of the new order; they demanded respect for individual rights and also the right to private property. Others disputed with dialectical materialism, with atheism, with the Marxist interpretation of religion and Christianity. The polemic here was a form of self-defense. Christian thinkers made up in a way for the neglect of the interwar period when, apparently not realizing the existing danger, they essentially knew nothing about Marx, Marxism, and socialism, and did not want to know. They also assumed a posture of contempt. They did not create at that time any institute for the study of socialist thought; they neither wrote nor translated any in-depth analysis of the phenomenon; they satisfied themselves with a few not very profound platitudes. Polish interwar Thomism shaped minds on such a level of abstraction that no one felt a particular need to pay attention to what was under one's nose. They more readily argued over realism and idealism, rationalism and fideism, the possibility of applying a structure of logic to theology, than over the shape of history. The change in interest came only after the war. At that time, and on a scale greater than before, they began to transplant onto Polish soil Maritain's ideas of "integral humanism" and the personalism of the school of Emmanuel Mounier.[55]

Numerous writers have attested how unprepared the Polish postwar intelligentsia was for a confrontation with Marxism. Let us quote Czesław Miłosz:[56]

The pressure of the state machine is nothing compared with the pressure of a convincing argument. I attended the artists' congresses in Poland in which the theories of socialist realism were first discussed. The attitude of the audience toward the speakers delivering the required reports was decidedly hostile. Everyone considered socialist realism an officially imposed theory that would have, as Russian art demonstrates, deplorable results. Attempts to provoke discussion failed. The listeners remained silent. Usually, however, one daring artist would launch an attack, full of restrained sarcasm, with the silent but obvious support of the entire audience. He would invariably be crushed by superior reasoning plus practicable threats against the future career of an undisciplined individual. Given the conditions of convincing argument plus such threats, the necessary conversion will take place. That is mathematically certain (Miłosz 1953:12).

Actually, Marxism could sink into the social consciousness like a warm knife into butter. If, in spite of this, it did not do so, this was for several reasons. First, Marxism appeared in Poland under the banner of Soviet thought; it was simultaneously Leninism and Stalinism. As such, based on the principle of "proletarian internationalism," it painfully wounded patriotic feelings. A conflict developed between the national consciousness of the Poles and the internationalistic consciousness superimposed on them. Soviet socialistic internationalism was from the very beginning suspected of being a veiled form of Russian imperialism. There were attempts to resolve the controversy about patriotism on theoretical as well as practical grounds. On the ground of theory they advanced a thesis about the building of a new culture—"a culture national in content and socialist in form." The ambiguity of this thesis was obvious. The thesis became fatally univocal through censorship and repeated "purges" in the party. Again and again the victims of the latter were alleged to be advocates of "nationalistic deviation" (among others, Władysław Gomułka).[57] Marxism, which helped in justifying these practices, assumed the character of an ideology bent not only on socialism but also on sovietization.

Even sharper and broader opposition was elicited by the attacks on religion and the church. Marxism did not understand and was not even in a position to understand the nature of Polish Christianity. The Polish church did not associate its interests with those of capitalism, but with the struggle of the nation for freedom and independence. The attack of Marxism against Christianity only deepened these ties. The church proved to be the only heir and protector of a thousand-year-old national culture, the spokesman of the struggle for freedom, tolerance, and national sovereignty. Polish Marxists had no other choice but to create a new, Polish version of Marxism. They did not create anything of the sort. Why?

2. The Common Trait of the Marxist Critics

A particular "unmasking" strategem toward a given philosophical current was the characteristic trait of Marxist polemics of those times. It was not sufficient to carry out a purely "objective" analysis of a text. It was also necessary (and strictly speaking, primarily so) to show what place in the "superstructure" a given trend occupied ("objectively"). This place was measured by its distance from the center established by the philosophy of dialectical materialism. Dia-mat was progressive; the other currents were more or less regressive, depending on how far they were from dia-mat. Kotarbiński was closer to dia-mat than Ajdukiewicz, but Ajdukiewicz was closer than Ingarden and, especially, Thomism. In spite of this, the most common indictment against these and other philosophical currents was the charge of "idealism." What was the theoretical basis for lodging such an accusation?

The following text by Friedrich Engels[58] served as the basis:

Did god create the world or has the world been in existence eternally? The answers which the philosophers gave to this question split them into two great camps. Those who asserted the primacy of spirit to nature and, therefore, in the last instance, assumed world creation in some form or other—(and among the philosophers, Hegel,[59] for example, this creation often becomes still more intricate and impossible than in Christianity)—comprised the camp of idealism. The others, who regarded nature as primary, belong to the various schools of materialism (Engels 1941:21).

The dualistic division of philosophical currents created an illusion of the dialectic (thesis-antithesis). In addition, it was convenient; it allowed everything that was not Marxism to drop into one basket, "idealism."

Another distinction was also important: the subjective and objective significance of a given current. A philosopher, representing a given system, could "subjectively" believe that his approach was correct and even progressive, but only Marxism, armed with the dialectical method of interpreting history, knew "objectively." Marxism proceeded with its opponents as one deals with the mentally ill; an insane person has delusions in which he or she "subjectively" believes, but only a doctor knows and can show the patient what those delusions are "objectively."

What was the basic effect of applying those methods? The effect was a *political interpretation* of philosophical phenomena. There are no "apolitical" phenomena in philosophy. Each philosophy either serves or interferes with the building of the system. One who wants to remain on the sidelines actually also stands in the way. In a programmatic article in the scholarly journal *Philosophical Thought (Myśl filozoficzna)*, we read,

For a nation fighting for peace and the Six-Year Plan, ideological problems lie at the very center of interest. Under these circumstances, the ideological struggle assumes fundamental importance. Without rooting out the remains of bourgeois consciousness; without combating bourgeois political, legal, moral, philosophical, and esthetic views; without the victory of new views and the constant strengthening of new institutions responsive to the needs of the socialist base; in a word, without the constant development of a socialist consciousness, a socialist nation cannot become definitively crystallized ("Od Redakcji" 1951:15).

The dualistic character of the stratification of philosophical currents was but a segment of the dualistic mode of interpretation of all social phenomena and human attitudes. There were no neutral literary works; every work, if it did not serve socialism, interfered with it. The same was true of films and painting. The cultural sphere was only an expression, however, of the attitude of the creators of culture. Here, three postures seemed particularly significant: reactionary, progressive, and opportunistic. Thus, one who was not "for" was in every case and irrevocably "against." Could a Marxist think differently? It was not an easy thing at all. To think differently, one had to oppose Engels, to change one's view on the essence of the dialectic, to read in a personal way the logical course of history. In short, one had to deny Marxism. Opposition in the light of such a classification of cultural phenomena could come only from opponents of Marxism. There was no way to arrive at such attitudes from the principles of Marxism itself.

3. Polemic with Kazimierz Ajdukiewicz

The task of this critique fell to Adam Schaff[60] himself, chief editor of *Myśl filozoficzna*. Schaff was aware of the responsibility that he undertook. The object of his attack was not only Ajdukiewicz but the entire Lwów-Warszawa school. Concerning Ajdukiewicz, he wrote:

He was a disciple of Twardowski, just like Kotarbiński, Czeżowski and others. Like the majority of the representatives of the Lwów-Warszawa school, he was involved with the so-called minor philosophy, limiting himself to a variety of minor contributions in specialized areas, especially logic and the methodology of science. Nonetheless, his views included the quintessence of the position of the Lwów-Warszawa school, whose representatives were bound together by an understanding of semantics, leading inevitably to conventionalism. In a "purified" form, as it were, we find these views squarely in Ajdukiewicz. In his works, we do not have to uncover the idealistic semantics and conventionalism from under a layer of more or less complicated philosophical views as is the case, for example, with Kotarbiński. Ajdukiewicz is a conventionalist *tout court* and a *radical* conventionalist. His line of development is clear and unswerving. Ajdukiewicz was a conventionalist during the interwar period and for all intents and purposes has not changed his position up to the present. From all this we see that an analysis of Ajdukiewicz's views allows us to grasp the essential links in the polemic with the entire Lwów-Warszawa school (Schaff 1952:209-10).

But why is it necessary to carry on a polemic with this school? Is this an ordinary dispute of one philosopher with another, or is the issue perhaps somehow different? Schaff writes:

Around the Lwów-Warszawa school a certain myth was formed with which intellectual circles, especially those at universities, surrounded themselves. As a result, a clearly detached and esoteric doctrine could exert a broader influence on forming the image of our science and of the minds of our intelligensia, and in this way—indirectly—have broader social repercussions. This influence—in our opinion, a negative one—is precisely one of the essential reasons why we are concerned with analyzing the school. This "mythology" evolved in two main directions. First, it was proclaimed and believed that the Lwów-Warszawa school is the embodiment of scientific precision, that it finally banished all metaphysics and irrationality from philosophy. Accordingly, it was asserted that its theses should lie at the root of all scientific endeavors; that it provides a scientific methodology for the various disciplines. Naturally, those who believed such assertions indignantly rejected the charge of idealism laid against the school. Second, it was declared and believed that the Warszawa school created an original philosophy that constituted the fruit of Polish thought; and a special attempt was made to show that the various "achievements" of "the most modern" philosophy—neopositivism—had been borrowed from Polish thinkers (Schaff 1952:210).

Thus, the main motive for the attack against the school was the fact that it conquered the minds of the Polish intelligentsia. The issue was to "adapt the superstructure to the base." The quoted text says it quite clearly: the philosophical struggle is a struggle for power. The issue in the polemic is to prove that Marxism has a greater right to rule minds than other philosophies. Only Marxism is a scientific philosophy, a philosophy of progress and a philosophy that blends patriotism with internationalism without falling into the extremes of nationalism and cosmopolitism. The political nature of the polemic is beyond question.

We cannot refer here to each and every point of the critique. Let us note only those which without mincing words speak about the political repercussions of each philosophical system and aim at "unmasking" the system of appearances surrounding a given idea. "Representatives of the Lwów-Warszawa school certainly believed in what they proclaimed. However, Marxism teaches us to make an assessment not according to what people say and think, but according to what objective social role is played by their achievements, their deeds, the views proclaimed by them" (Schaff 1952:211). Thus, during the trial of philosophers before the tribunal of history, there can be only one reliable witness—a Marxist.

What does a Marxist have to say about the views of the "school"?

First, it is not true that the Lwów-Warszawa school created some sort of strictly scientific philosophy that is a negation of metaphysics and irrationalism. Rather, it is true that the philosophy of the Lwów-Warszawa school is in its basic outlines—despite the individual deviations of its particular representatives—a philosophy of idealistic semantics and conventionalism; thus, it is a subtle and refined variant of idealism and is, therefore, deeply contradictory to the postulates of scientific precision. The appearances of precision and scientific character might have their source only in the language used by the school in its philosophy (the language and technical apparatus of mathematical logic) as well as in the claim of bringing precision to linguistic terms—a claim which the school's representatives realized successfully but converted from a technical tool to an aim in itself. A basic feature of idealistic semantics is the conversion of the thesis that language should be not only a *means* for philosophy but also an *object* of study, into the thesis that language is the only object of study, that semantic analysis is a particular method for untying knotty problems about a world view in philosophy. Such an approach to the problems means the unjustified idealistic absolutizing of language and its detachment from the process of reflection on objective reality in our thinking.

Second, it is not true that the philosophy of the Lwów-Warszawa school was a sort of original product of Polish philosophical thinking. Rather, since its inception (Twardowski) and throughout its entire existence, it was an aggregate of various influences of bourgeois Western philosophy. The school was characterized by an exceptionally cosmopolitan image (in the sense of groveling before every "bit of novelty" from the West). The fact that individual representatives of the school enriched the arsenal of neopositivism by certain "discoveries," a fact repeatedly underscored by Ajdukiewicz as the contribution of Polish philosophy, indicates only that the philosophy of the Lwów-Warszawa school intertwined into a single whole with a certain reactionary current of the bourgeois philosophy of the imperialistic period—the current called logical empiricism or neopositivism, of which it was a variant (Schaff 1952:212).

Here are some other interesting excerpts from the article:

The division into Marxist and non-Marxist philosophy is in our epoch the deepest, the most essential, the logically primary division in the sphere of contemporary philosophy. This division is a contemporary form of the division of philosophers into the hostile camps of materialism and idealism. Dialectical and historical materialism is today the *only* possible, consistently materialistic philosophy. The reaction of the bourgeoisie to dialectical materialism and the revolutionary movement of the workers is to strengthen and promote idealism in its various forms. The form of idealism selected by the bourgeoisie in its struggle—extreme or moderate, open or camouflaged—depends on the concrete conditions of place and time, on the ideological needs of the bourgeoisie, on the character of the ideological consumer whom it addresses- -in a word, on the strategy and tactics of class struggle of the bourgeoisie.

The so-called semantic philosophy is one of the variants of this idealistic reaction to the revolutionary workers' movement and its philosophy, one of the "antidotes" to dialectic materialism. One must admit that this is a particularly refined, camouflaged idealism and because of that, more difficult to recognize and unmask. In this, under concrete historical circumstances and in a concrete environment, lies the social function of this philosophy.

The bourgeoisie, in its economic and political struggle against the proletariat, does not limit itself at all to one method and by no means does it always use the method of open conflict. It acts similarly when waging an ideological struggle. Here, too, the bourgeoisie uses various methods, resorts to various resources, tries to sow confusion among the ranks of its opponents, in order to more easily strengthen the bourgeois positions in ideology. For the bourgeoisie, it is not decisively significant which current of its ideology wins, but that in the end victory belongs to the bourgeois, anti-Marxist ideology (Schaff 1952:213-14).

And further: "The 'palette of colors' of bourgeois philosophy is diverse and rich: from open religious obscurantism to a refined and camouflaged form of idealism in the guise of semantic philosophy. The aim and social function remain the same—opposition to Marxism, opposition to the working class, defense of bourgeois ideology" (Schaff 1952:214).

The main thesis of this critique was: in Ajdukiewicz we encounter radical conventionalism. Radical conventionalism originates from the concept of "world view": " 'a world view' depends on the selection of a language and this selection is arbitrary" (Schaff 1952:255). "We now understand the 'Copernican mentality' of radical conventionalism. It consists in the idea that by changing the conceptual apparatus, a person 'creates' a world and truth; creates it unconsciously or consciously" (Schaff 1952:242). But just so: "Conventionalism is one of the subjective-idealistic currents of the degenerate bourgeois philosophy of the imperialistic epoch. Radical conventionalism is a particularly acute and reactionary form of conventionalism, so much more dangerous because it masks its essential content by the formal baggage of scientific language" (Schaff 1952:242).

But this is not all. Ajdukiewicz's philosophy is even more menacing because it may pave the road for religion (this accusation was particularly characteristic since representatives of the Lwów-Warszawa school took a deliberately neutral stance toward religion and did not recognize metaphysics as a science). Schaff writes:

It should be stated that from the radical conventionalism of Ajdukiewicz one can derive a number of more interesting and unexpected conclusions, for example, that a religious position is justified. Let us carry through the speculation according to the directives of radical conventionalism. The world view depends on the selection of language and this selection is arbitrary. Since the language thus chosen is complete and nontranslatable to other languages, however, one must conclude that the position of religion, under the condition of sufficient precision and formulation of its language, is unassailable; it cannot be overturned on the grounds of the language of religion, and it is untranslatable to other languages. In this way a defender of any given position whatsoever becomes transformed into a monad without windows. Such a monad cannot penetrate into the interior of other monads but it is also safe from penetration by them from the outside.

Did Professor Ajdukiewicz ever say anything like this? Did he want to defend obscurantism? No, but these conclusions nonetheless flow from his own doctrine—socially reactionary conclusions, conclusions allowing the defense of all sorts of obscurantism, giving license to the dilution of any real conflict by speculating about words. Is this philosophy not convenient for the bourgeoisie? Is this philosophy not an assault—totally independent of its author's intentions—on the position of science? (Schaff 1952:255-56).

Schaff includes in his critique several charges which the school had already encountered earlier and with which it had struggled under the rubric of clarifying its own position. But these charges were not the most important. The most important one is that the philosophy of the Lwów-Warszawa school is a bourgeois philosophy, contrary to the interests of the proletariat and favorable to imperialism. Today, these charges appear comical or even downright absurd. But at that time they were not. They were serious charges, since first, it seems, those who used them believed in them and second, they were a form of the "unmasking on behalf of the authorities" who were to draw practical consequences from them. The authorities did draw consequences—the authors attacked were usually deprived of university chairs. Even today, the purely psychological process which led to this kind of accusation remains to be explained. But this interests us less.

(The dispute between Schaff and Ajdukiewicz continued: see K. Ajdukiewicz, "On the Question of Prof. A. Schaff's Article about My Philosophical Views," *Myśl filozoficzna* 2, 1953; and A. Schaff, "On the Question of an Evaluation of the Philosophical Views of K. Ajdukiewicz," *Myśl filozoficzna* 3, 1953.)

4. Against Tadeusz Kotarbiński

The position of Kotarbiński, creator and advocate of materialistic "reism," was in many aspects akin to dialectical materialism. Nevertheless, it did not find favor in the eyes of the dialectical materialists. Bronisław Baczko[61] became the critic of Kotarbiński's views. In his critique, all the previously mentioned elements of the Marxist way of thinking find expression.

Baczko writes:

The decisive event in the history of our nation—the liberation of Poland by the Soviet Army and the establishment of the structure of a people's democracy—was also the decisive fact in the history of scholarly learning in Poland. The Polish nation entered a new stage of its development—the process of building socialism. The process of transforming our nation into a socialist nation is taking place. In the People's Poland, perspectives of development hitherto unknown to our history opened themselves to scholarly learning. Philosophy, in particular, ceased to be the domain of a narrow group of bookish scholars. Marxist philosophy became the property and acquisition of the multimillion-strong masses, a critical ideological weapon in the process of forming a new socialist nation. The world view of the Marxists developed and took root in Poland through the struggle with obsolete ideological remnants of idealism. For these reasons also, the front-line struggle with idealism and its remnants in Polish philosophy is one of the battlegrounds on the ideological front line (Baczko 1951:247).

But, can one consider Kotarbiński—the creator of reism—an "idealist"? Yes, since Kotarbiński's reism is associated with conventionalism. Even materialism cannot save Kotarbiński from the charge of "idealism."

Baczko writes:

The subjective intentions of the author of a given system should not be identified with the objective function and repercussions of this system. These two aspects not only do not overlap but often are divergent. In the evaluation of a system, however, it is the objective role and not the subjective intention that is decisive. It is thus in the case of nominalism also: a conventional interpretation of nominalism is certainly not the intention of Professor Kotarbiński; surely, his only intention is a desire to preserve the anti-idealistic edge of nominalism. Objectively, however—independently of anyone's intentions—contemporary neonominalism is inseparable from conventionalism, and is exploited by subjective idealism for an idealistic interpretation of science.

In Kotarbiński's neonominalism too, metaphysics (in the Marxist sense of the term, i.e. antidialectic) clearly stands out as the essential mark of reism. One must state once again that the materialistic elements of a reistic concept most often constitute metaphysical materialism, a materialism that oversimplifies and impoverishes the whole of this complex reality that is in perpetual motion, and in particular, the complicated dialectical process of cognition (Baczko 1951:266-67).

And further:

The same applies to the analysis of the thesis of pansomatism propounded by Kotarbiński. The materialistic element of this thesis consists of underscoring the close connection between consciousness and the body, and the consequent negation of any soul outside of material bodies. On the other hand, the pansomatic thesis does not give a universal answer to the basic question: which is primary—matter or consciousness? Professor Kotarbiński treats this basic question as a problem of incidental and secondary importance. His numerous pronouncements, however, clearly reveal an incorrect view on these matters, some sort of variant of panpsychism or psychophysical parallelism, and open wide the gates for all kinds of idealism (Baczko 1951:267).

The author of this critique also protests against Kotarbiński's social views. He describes them as "individualism" and "cosmopolitan elitism," while "individualism and cosmopolitan elitism were . . . expressions of the fears of the masses, the imaginary fears of the intelligentsia, fears instilled by the bourgeoisie" (Baczko 1951:284).

The calls for liberation advanced by Kotarbiński and applied to university life are assessed in the following way:

Before the war, when the *Sanacja*[62] regime's obscurantist ideology ruled the universities, when every voice of socialist thought was stifled—the battle cry of absolute freedom of discussion and critique was directed against the growing Fascism in the universities. But against whom and in whose defense is today's slogan of "absolute freedom" of discussion advanced? Freedom for whom and in the name of what? Should we grant freedom to undermine the socialistic world view to the same young Fascist gentlemen who before the war were breaking skulls with brass knuckles, who were throwing inkwells at Professor

Kotarbiński? Can we grant freedom also to the agents of foreign imperialism who make use of every chink to attack our system, to undermine the system, power and independence of our fatherland? In what name does one grant them freedom—in the name of an abstract slogan that they will exploit in order to undermine the real freedom and achievements of the Polish nation? Should we, in the name of an abstract slogan of freedom, give a free hand to the impassioned enemies of our nation's freedom? (Baczko 1951:288).

Finally, there is a global assessment:

Kotarbiński's philosophical and social views were the starting points for an evolution toward dialectical materialism, toward the rejection of anachronistic, liberal individualism. Naturally, this required overcoming the remnants of idealism. What a positive role such an evolution could play—and after all can still play—in the process of change taking place especially among our scholarly intelligentsia. How much it could help in overcoming the remnants of liberal idealism among our creative intelligentsia.

Unfortunately, however, such an evolution has not yet taken place; as a whole, as a system, Kotarbiński's philosophical and social views remained peripheral, and fenced themselves off from the ideological changes that occurred and are occurring in our reality, in our scientific scholarship, among our intelligentsia. The logic of events, the logic of development cause these views increasingly to play the role of a brake, of an obstacle to further development of our scientific scholarship and our intelligentsia. Polish philosophers, however, are confronted with the task of overcoming these ideological obstacles and brakes, the remnants of idealism in our scientific scholarship. The task of overcoming ideological obstacles on the path to the further development of our intelligentsia brings and will bring ever-increasing contributions to the great work of the struggle for peace, and for the Six-Year Plan, the struggle for the future of our fatherland (Baczko 1951:289).

5. Assessment of the Philosophy of Roman Ingarden

In those years, phenomenology did not play as big a role as the Lwów-Warszawa school did. No wonder, then, that polemics with phenomenology did not occupy the foreground of Marxist philosophy. Nonetheless, it too received attention from Tadeusz Kroński,[63] also noted as the prematurely deceased expert on Hegel's philosophy. He wrote a review of the book, *The Controversy about the Existence of the World,* which was published in *Myśl filozoficzna.* This review appeared when Ingarden no longer lectured at the Jagiellonian University. It is difficult to suppose that this review caused Ingarden's removal from the university, but in any case it became the theoretical justification for that removal.

Here is the beginning of the review, entitled "The World in the Shackles of Ontology":

Ingarden's *Controversy* certainly does not belong to those contemporary idealistic books whose reactionary character is so shrewdly guarded by various devices and tricks and is so artfully cloaked in the most sophisticated scientific terminology that to expose it requires a lengthy and complicated process of argumentation. Here at least we are *en plein idealisme.* No tricks, no terms pretending to be scientific. Simply stated, Descartes[64] has put the existence of the world in doubt and since then no one has overcome Cartesian skepticism in a manner satisfactory for Ingarden. Again, we must place a question mark over the world's existence. Clearly, the problem of the world's existence is a burning one and it must be solved scientifically. Obviously, the solution can be reached only by idealistic speculation. Ingarden takes no notice of the experience and practice of humanity as a whole. He is called upon to solve "the problem" of whether or not the world exists. In his head lies the key to this great "mystery". He neither sees nor understands how utterly ludicrous his chosen topic is. But let us be careful and sparing with humor. As dry and devilishly pedantic as Ingarden's reflections appear, his book, like any philosophical book, has its objective social repercussions, it expresses something, it fights for something (Kroński 1952(1):318).

That introduction alone indicates the level of the polemic with Ingarden. It must be a political level. In this discussion it will be important to distinguish what Ingarden's phenomenology is "objectively," as opposed to what it is "subjectively," i.e., how Ingarden himself regards it.

Kroński writes:

The two volumes before me represent an attempt to overcome Husserl's idealism and an introduction to studies that are intended, in a supposedly non-idealistic way, to present anew and solve the problem of the world's existence. Well, when an idealist comes to us and says that "actually" he is a realist and has evidence for the existence of the world *outside of consciousness,* we ought to listen to him. However, we should remember that in such a case we must be doubly careful. Confronted by an idealist who accuses his friend [that is, Husserl—J.T.] of idealism and offers us "the world," we must particularly remember the words Laocoon spoke to the Trojans as a warning against the wooden horse cunningly left by the Greeks on the seashore: *Timeo Dannaos et dona ferentes*—"I fear the Greeks even when they bring gifts" (Kroński 1952(1):319).

Kroński's review presents the antecedents of Ingarden's thought and characterizes his writings. He lingers at some length over *Controversy.* He characterizes Ingarden's "ontology" as a pathway to "metaphysics." He observes that the value of ontology will be revealed only when, with its help, one reaches metaphysics. But Ingarden does not demonstrate this transition. What does this mean?

The author of *Controversy* never and nowhere betrays that he knows what a metaphysical experience is, while this "experience" is supposed to be a guarantee of the usefulness of ontological investigations. Metaphysics is supposed to be the gold-backing of the ontological currency of *Controversy.* Ingarden's banknotes bear the rather clear imprint: "The cashier will exchange these notes for gold, if such exists", while it is known that the cashier has no such funds. True or false, backed or not, ontological currencies are still being exchanged in the capitalist countries. The verification of philosophical banknotes cannot be limited simply to determining that the gold covering them does not exist (Kroński 1952(1):323).

By this analogy, therefore, Kroński makes an appeal for subjecting Ingarden's system to a control verification in addition to that based on the phenomenological method. What should such a control be?

The end of the review speaks of it:

Ingarden is a writer absolutely bereft of political imagination. He never understood at all the political meaning of the sudden renaissance of objective idealism in the Germany of Kaiser Wilhelm's last years and in the Germany of the Weimar period.[65] Nor does he understand that by moving from the position of objective idealism against subjective idealism he does not come closer to science. Similarly, as an objective idealist Ingarden does not thereby become closer to us for "attacking" the subjective idealist Husserl. Neither does Husserl acquire anything in our eyes by being "attacked" by Ingarden. There is no "better" or "worse" idealism—each is equally bad. Which form of idealism becomes ideologically dominant, which form in a given moment becomes the most aggressive, depends solely on the objective conditions of the times.

What significance does Ingarden's book have today? Very little. All that can be said at this time about *Controversy* is that it is an idealistic book, poorly conceived and badly edited. In writing his *Controversy*, Ingarden probably thought little about his potential readers.

Ingarden's book is a glaring example of the sterility, degeneracy and bankruptcy of contemporary bourgeois philosophy (Kroński 1952(1):331).

6. *The History of Philosophy* by Władysław Tatarkiewicz

In 1950, the third volume of *The History of Philosophy* (*Historia filozofii*) by Tatarkiewicz was released in a small edition available only to libraries and high-ranking scholars. How did the Marxists of those days assess this book and its contribution to Polish culture? Again, Kroński wrote the review.

Here is a general evaluation:

The History of Philosophy by Tatarkiewicz is methodologically erroneous and as such cannot serve the People's Poland today. The bourgeois handbook of history of philosophy is not a prewar dictionary, e.g., Polish-German, which "after all" can teach something today even if it is outdated and does not contain all the "words". But a dictionary teaches facts, namely, that "badly" in German is *schlecht.* Does the handbook by Tatarkiewicz teach facts? Superficially, yes. But in history generally, hence also in the history of philosophy, facts do not arise at random but form a cohesive entity. The idealist writer who treats facts outside the frame of history and then forms arbitrary constructions with them falsifies reality to a greater extent than if he had done this through an error here or there in dates or references. For a particular event Tatarkiewicz selected and assembled facts in a way that distorts the true sense of the entire development of philosophy. In reality this development has two periods: before Marx and after Marx. Marxism is the turning point in the history of philosophy. "Marx and Engels created a new philosophy, qualitatively different from all previous philosophical systems, even the progressive ones", as Zhdanov[66] said. Marxism assimilated all the progressive achievements of humanity; the rise of Marxism made possible the objective progress of learning.

Marxism was the first ideology of an oppressed class, the proletariat, in whose interest is the infinite development of learning, unlimited by any conditions. . . . Failure to understand the pivotal character of Marxist philosophy unavoidably leads to a distortion of the entire development of philosophy. For Tatarkiewicz, Marxism is just one of the possible currents, "isms", drowning in the waters of the idealistic school. For scientific methodology, the history of philosophy is a history of the struggle between materialism and idealism. For Tatarkiewicz, materialism is merely one more possible "posture". For Marxist methodology, philosophical views are ideological expressions of class struggle, regardless of the historical conditions of their origin. Marxism treats philosophical phenomena in close relationship with the conditions of their development. For Tatarkiewicz, the development of philosophical ideas takes place in abstract space.

The methodological errors of Tatarkiewicz lead to a total distortion of the sense of the facts being described. With his choice the center of gravity moves into idealistic doctrines, social views become almost totally neglected. The achievements of Polish thought are almost totally eliminated, and Russian philosophy is totally omitted. In the articulation of facts, Marxism is placed on a level with other systems. These two errors—ignoring Polish and Russian thought and treating Marxism as one of the philosophical schools—are the consequences of the author's methodological idealism, above all, of immanentism in the treatment of facts of philosophical history. The handbook by Tatarkiewicz is also insufficiently instructive from the point of view of the information itself (only minimum space was devoted to materialistic philosophy and the development of the dialectic was almost totally ignored). It is not only an idealistic but also a cosmopolitan handbook. Whatever the author's intentions, his handbook to a great extent contributed objectively to the dislike with which the Polish intelligentsia treated Polish and Russian philosophy.

A handbook of the history of philosophy that is going to be used by students and society at large must be based on the principles of Marxism–Leninism, that is, it must present the development of philosophy as it was and is in reality: as the history of the genesis, rise, and development of the materialistic point of view. It follows that this handbook must refer to particular views in close connection with the historical circumstances of their origin. It must present philosophical problems in a concrete manner and consider them in close connection with the lives of nations. Since the philosophy constituted the pinnacle of development of pre-Marxist thought, the handbook of the history of philosophy should assign to it a central position in its discussions of nineteenth century currents. In a Polish handbook of the history of philosophy, one cannot, of course, omit Polish philosophy without regard for the fact that today it is the object of special studies.

A handbook of the history of philosophy is neither a dictionary nor a grammar which can be used always and everywhere, regardless of historic conditions. Each historian of philosophy is simultaneously a methodologist of his or her discipline, each is therefore a philosopher—materialist or idealist. Thus, either by starting today from the principles of dialectical materialism he gives us a vision of the past that corresponds to the truth, or starting from idealistic positions he offers a false vision (Kroński 1952(4):270-71).

No comments on this text are needed.

In summary: I purposely have used a large number of citations to give the atmosphere of those times more clearly. There is something depressing in that atmosphere. Everything indicates that the authors of the cited texts acted in good faith. They did not write under duress but of their own free will. At the same time they had eyes to see but did not see, they had ears to hear but did not hear. They did not know what they were doing. They themselves admitted this later.

One is struck by the deeply rooted conviction that the political struggle in which the writers participate has the character of the highest ethical imperative. This is the summons of history. They are the voice of this summons. At the same time, however, one is astounded by the simplicity with which they divide the world around them into two parts—the one demonic and the second well-nigh angelic: there, the bourgeoisie; here, the proletariat. The bourgeoisie are not only powerful but also perfidious, as evidenced by their capacity constantly to find new forms of idealism simply in order to destroy materialism. The proletariat, with their Party at the helm, are saintly, innocent and, above all, courageous. In the end, proletarian simplicity always wins out. By demonizing their enemies in this way, did not they themselves succumb in a way to subconscious fears? They thought of the world and divided it in the same way as a person concealed in a hiding place. For a person in hiding, an enemy lurks behind every bush, in every alley, in every shadow cast by a tree. This enemy, however, is not visible to everyone. One must have good eyes to see him. The eyes of a Marxist equipped with the dialectical method were able to discover opposition where others saw only differences, and hostility where only neutrality and even a sort of sympathy dwelt.

Marxist teachers of philosophy, by discovering enemies in this way and taking pride in their capacity for keen vision, were in a way overcoming in themselves a sense of inferiority. They were demonstrating that they are forces as necessary as the military and police, but to be called on a bit earlier than the latter. They wanted to be the light of a new political system and its Party. They believed that they were irreplaceable in this function. In this way they erected an edifice of their fictitious greatness. If we want to apply to their activity their very own distinction between "subjective" and "objective," we could say that, regardless of "subjective" convictions, they "objectively" performed a function in the system close to that of informers.

II.
The Highways
and Byways
of Marxism
from a Polish
Perspective

7. On the Essence of Marxist Philosophy

In the case of Marxism, a question emerges that one usually does not pose with respect to other philosophical movements: What actually is Marxist philosophy? Marxists themselves have treated Marxism differently during its more than century-long history. One might write a dissertation just about the ways in which Marx's thought has been taken by its successive proponents. For some, Marx's philosophy was primarily a certain way of interpreting the history of mankind; for others, it was an economic theory of social life; and for still others, it was an example of the proper employment of positive science for building an integral, progressive world view for humanity. What then is Marxism?

I must admit at the outset that for me the correct answer is as follows: Marxism is primarily a philosophy of human labor. Acceptance of this answer as true is somewhat arbitrary on my part, especially since I am going against the opinions of many Marxists. It seems to me, however, that in accepting this point of view, we elucidate for ourselves a basic problem—the question of the mainspring and underpinnings of Marxism's success in the contemporary world. Marxism understood as a philosophy of labor does not, strictly speaking, have an equal competitor. Just posing the problem at the period of the increasing exploitation of work guaranteed its success, and even more so did the attempt to solve the problem. Marxism makes the problem of the exploitation of work the central issue of its thought. No other philosophy of those times did this on a comparable scale. It is not surprising then that Marxism attracts the attention and hearts of those who cannot come to terms with evil. At the same time, however, the sources of the subsequent crises for Marxism become understandable to us. In the world of real socialism the question of exploitation moves to a second plane; Marxism moves from the position of critic to an apologetic posture; instead of criticizing the existing world, it begins to justify this world. But social evil by no means disappears; it even increases. Seeing this powerlessness of Marxism to deal with the social expolitation brought about by socialism, many Marxists abandon Marxism. As the ethical motive of the exploitation of labor was once the rationale for their joining Marxism's camp, so now the very same motive becomes the reason for their leaving it.

A dispute over the essence of Marxism surged through Poland in 1967–69, and was accompanied by student unrest in the universities.[67] One should point out, however, that the disturbances of that period were not at all expressions of this dispute. Different theories, different problems moved the youth of those times. Nevertheless, the time in which the dispute took place made an imprint on it. At that time, Szewczyk, a pupil of Ingarden, rigorously defended the thesis that Marxism is a philosophy of labor. Here is a fragment of his lecture from that period, excerpts from which were published in the periodical *Philosophical Studies* (*Studia filozoficzne*).

What key word can one find in Marx that would open for us a mental pathway to the essence of Marxist philosophy? I can now say, with complete responsibility, that the word and the idea behind it is labor. Marxism, as it entered into the history of philosophy and into the history of self-liberating work, extricated itself from Hegelian philosophy and established itself as an independent and completely separate doctrine from the moment when the young doctor of philosophy named Marx began to concentrate his attention on labor and to suspect its role in human life and in the course of universal history. Marx transformed himself from a Hegelian into the creator of Marxism when the working power of purposeful and productive human activity revealed itself very clearly and sharply to him as the primary driving force of human history, in contrast to the "absolute idea" in history upon which Hegel speculated; and when the real course of human labor appeared to him as the basic and central problem of history.

Human labor initially was enslaved as a blind element, truly unconscious of its own power and role, subjugated to other derivative forms of human activity that actually depended on it. With passing time, labor became increasingly aware of itself, of its power, that exploded in bloody revolts, mass slaughters, and earth-shaking upheavals. But in time, labor subjugated all other activities of human life and molded them, where necessary, by sheer power for its needs and aspirations. Labor, whether in the form of a craft *sensu stricto* or of military craft, constitutes the only real source of the forces that create and drive history. Thus, labor revealed itself as the central topic and term in the field of modern philosophy thanks to the genius of Karl Marx, who unveiled its tragedy and martyrdom and also its greatness and sublimity. The philosophical, Marxist concept of human labor is the only common denominator of all the other basic categories of Marxism. In this respect, Marxism must be defined in human history as an original and authentic philosophy of labor itself. The meaning of Marxism is at the same time the meaning of labor as it extends throughout the history of humanity. Labor must rediscover in itself this unifying meaning in order to achieve self-control, i.e., freedom (Szewczyk 1969:64).

This viewpoint on Marxist philosophy brings out concepts and theses concerning the nature of human labor, i.e., a concept of the raw material of labor (matter and materialism), of the way people organize themselves in the process of work, of the exploitation of labor, etc. Materialism, the dialectic, the theory of the exploitation of labor, become the integral components of Marxism. All other concepts of Marxist philosophy are more or less derivative.

Let us turn our attention to the idea of materialism and to the idea of the dialectic. Martin Heidegger[68] writes appositely: "The essence of materialism does not consist in the assertion that everything is simply matter but rather in the metaphysical determination according to which every being appears as the material of labor" (Heidegger 1976:220). Heidegger's remark conveys the essential meaning of Marxist materialism. This meaning consists not so much in the assertion that everything is matter or that only matter is a self-dependent being, but in the treatment of the whole of existing reality as the raw material for labor. What is matter? Matter is the universal raw material for labor. What does it mean to say that only matter exists? It means that nothing exists that would not be the raw material for work. Thus, God does not exist since if he existed he would constitute a limit to all-encompassing and omnipotent work. For the same reason, the soul with its innate, constant properties does not exist. In Marx's materialism, the idea of labor unveils its final consequences. Thanks to his philosophy, the history of humanity can become an object of human labor. Human beings can transform not only the reality of the surrounding corporeal world but also the reality of history. In a human being, labor is work conscious of itself. Self-conscious labor becomes self-existing, independent. It can govern itself. And labor that can govern itself also governs its future. Marxism is the philosophy that bears witness to the first large-scale liberation in history of the concept of labor from the burden of other concepts. This is linked with the discovery of its might. All boundaries of labor can be crossed by self-conscious labor, particularly the boundary drawn and concealed by the fact of exploitation—the internal falsehood of labor. To abolish exploitation means causing labor to be fully labor. For such labor there are no bounds—everything is its raw material, as we shall see, even the working person.

The idea of the dialectic is linked with the idea of labor. Marxism uses dialectical methods. But why? Because work itself has a dialectical structure. It is, above all, the relationship of human beings to raw materials that is dialectical, and then the relationship to other human beings in the process of labor. The raw material is the antithesis for a working person (the thesis). As a result of the process of labor, a synthesis develops in the form of the product of work. Thanks to labor, the world around human beings changes. The human beings themselves also change. This change goes so far and reaches so deeply that we may say that labor directly creates the human being. The human being created in the process of labor and thanks to labor is per se a synthesis of its own work and that work's product. A human being constructs a car and then the car constructed by the human being "creates" a new person. "Labor humanizes the ape," Engels would say. The dialectic of labor also permeates interpersonal relationships. These relationships depend ultimately on the status of the tools of labor. The status of the tools determines whether people work privately or gather in various commonalities and work together. The owner of the tools of labor, and consequently also of the product of labor, has essential significance. Between the possessors of the tools of labor and the possessors of the power for labor, there is a relationship of dialectical antagonism—of unity and, at the same time, of struggle. Classes of exploiters and classes of the exploited develop. The struggle between them is the basic motor of history. Because of that, the dialectical method is the only appropriate method to describe social life and historical progress.

In the further development of Marxism, the dialectical method was also used to study natural (biological) processes, primarily by Engels. He wanted in this way to begin a dialogue with the positive sciences and move Marxism closer to the then fashionable positivism. Following Engels, other Marxists also began to discover a dialectic in biology, chemistry, and physics. In this way, they proposed a new interpretation of Marxism as a world view capable of elucidating the basic riddles of being. With time, "Marxism of the world view" will come into conflict with the "Marxism of Marx."

8. Alienated Labor—Exploitation of Labor

If labor is the basic factor creating the human being as a human being, any disfiguration of labor, any falsification of labor, any unfulfillment also indicates the falsification and unfulfillment of human beings. The problem of labor was understood by Marxism as a basic issue of anthropology. But during and after the period of the great industrial revolution, the general falsification of human labor became evident to everyone. The exploitation of labor reached an extent till then unrealized. The problem of labor became a basic social issue. Under those circumstances, it could not but become an issue in philosophy as well. Philosophy cannot narrow itself to mere description and elucidation of the world, it must strive to change the world. Without a radical change of the existing world, further progress of humankind is impossible. Hence, the significance of the problem of exploitation of labor. One must recognize objectively: no thinker before or after Marx gave such prominence to the problem of exploitation as did Marx.

What is exploitation of labor according to Marx? To this question the young Marx gave an answer different from that of the mature Marx. This problem is one of the most burning issues of Marxism. The resolution of the problem of exploitation influenced the taking of revisionist as well as dogmatic positions within Marxism. We must look at this more closely because otherwise we will not understand the proper meaning of the disputes about Marxism that are taking place in Poland.

The young Marx classified all forms of exploitation under the concept of "alienation," "estrangement." This concept comes from Hegel's philosophy but Marx changed its meaning. To Hegel, "alienation" was essentially a positive phenomenon; the human spirit in the process of historical development passes through the stage of "alienation" wherein it comes into conflict with itself, like a lazy pupil who is forced to study. Subsequently, however, the spirit discovers that the sense of alienation was only apparent, that the new world in which it found itself is also its world, a "familiar" world; the lazy student starts to enjoy his studies and become himself again. In this way the spirit matures, overcoming recurring experiences of estrangement. Marx changes the meaning of the concept of alienation. Alienation, for him, is every situation in which a human being finds himself "outside of his being" and becomes "foreign to himself," a situation in which what he is stands opposed to who he is. Alienation, then, is something negative. For a human being to be able to develop, alienation must be abolished. But alienation exists, it has even become a social phenomenon. In industrial society working people feel estranged from themselves during the execution of their work. This estrangement continues beyond work. In a capitalistic industrial society, human beings are not themselves.

Marx lists several forms of alienation. Here are some of them:

(a) Alienation through the worked product. He writes:

The worker becomes all the poorer the more he produces, the more his production increases in power and size. The worker becomes an ever cheaper commodity the more commodities he creates. With the *increasing value* of the world of things proceeds in direct proportion the *devaluation* of the world of men. Labor produces not only commodities; it produces itself and the worker as a *commodity*—and this in the same general proportion in which it produces commodities.

This fact expresses merely that the object which labor produces—labor's product—confronts it as *something alien,* as a *power independent* of the producer. The product of labor is labor which has been embodied in an object, which has become material; it is the *objectification* of labor. Labor's realization is its objectification. In the sphere of political economy this realization of labor appears . . . (as *the loss of realization* for the workers; objectification) as *loss of the object* and *bondage to it;* appropriation as *estrangement, as alienation.*

And further: "The *alienation* of the worker in his product means not only that his labor becomes an object, an *external* existence, but that it exists *outside him,* independently, as something alien to him, and that it becomes a power on its own confronting him. It means that the life which he has conferred on the object confronts him as something hostile and alien" (Marx 1964:107-8).

(b) Alienation through the very kind of work performed. Marx writes:

Labor is *external* to the worker, i.e., it does not belong to his essential being; that in his work, therefore, he does not affirm himself but denies himself, does not feel content but unhappy, does not develop freely his physical and mental energy but mortifies his body and ruins his mind. The worker, therefore, only feels himself outside his work, and in his work feels outside himself. He is at home when he is not working, and when he is working he is not at home. His labor is, therefore, not voluntary, but coerced; it is *forced labor*. It is, therefore, not the satisfaction of a need, it is merely a *means* to satisfy needs external to it. Its alien character emerges clearly in the fact that as soon as no physical or other compulsion exists, labor is shunned like the plague. External labor, labor in which man alienates himself, is a labor of self-sacrifice, of mortification. Lastly, the external character of labor for the worker appears in the fact that it is not his own, but someone else's, that it does not belong to him (that in it he belongs, not to himself) but to another (Marx 1964:110-11).

(c) Regarding alienation from humankind, Marx writes: "As a result, therefore, man (the worker) only feels himself freely active in his animal functions—eating, drinking, procreating, or at most in his dwelling and in dressing-up, etc.: and in his human functions he no longer feels himself to be anything but an animal. What is animal becomes human and what is human becomes animal." And further: "Man is a species being . . . also because . . . he treats himself as the actual, living species; because he treats himself as a *universal* and, therefore, a free being" (Marx 1964:111). But particularly in capitalistic systems this becomes impossible: "Estranged labor turns thus: . . . 3. *Man's species being,* both nature and his spiritual species property, into a being *alien* to him, into a *means* to his *individual existence.* It estranges from man his own body, as well as external nature and his spiritual essence, his *human* being. 4. An immediate consequence of the fact that man is estranged from the product of his labor, from his life activity, from his species being is the *estrangement of man* from *man.* When man confronts himself, he confronts the *other* man. What applies to a man's relation to his work, to the product of his labor and to himself, also holds of a man's relation to the other man, and to the other man's labor and object of labor" (Marx 1964:114).

The institution of private ownership of property developed as a result of the various forms of alienated work. "Through *estranged, alienated labor,* then, the worker produces the relationship to this labor of a man alien to labor and standing outside it. The relationship of the worker to labor creates the relation to it of the capitalist (or whatever one chooses to call the master of labor). *Private property* is thus the product, the result, the necessary consequence, of *alienated labor,* of the external relation of the worker to nature and to himself" (Marx 1964:116-17).

However, there is in Marx himself yet another concept of exploitation. It appears in *Das Kapital,* a work of the mature Marx. Here, exploitation does not refer to a feeling of alienation but to the basic laws of political economics. Marx distances himself from Hegel and writes in the language of classical English political economics, thereby showing, with the very language of that system, the true face of capitalism. Just as in the *Manuscripts* capitalism is shown to be contradictory to the human essence, so in *Das Kapital* it proves to be a system that is contradictory in itself.

For Marx, the ideal is the full development of the forces of production. But exploitation, which is a manifestation of precautionary care for the interests of capital, is an insurmountable obstacle to this development. What is exploitation in *Das Kapital*? In this instance, let us give the floor to the *Philosophical Encyclopedia* (*Philosophisches Woerterbuch*) that concisely summarizes the essence of the matter.

Exploitation is a social relationship between human groups which occupy opposing positions with regard to the means of production. Exploitation is always the exploitation of human beings by human beings. Exploitation is generally a result of the fact that the owners of the means of production gratuitously usurp someone else's labor for themselves (the surplus value and also, in particular historical situations, part of the proper value). Exploitation arises when the development of the social forces of production permits the emergence of surplus valuation. Through his theory of surplus value, Marx discovered the essence of capitalistic exploitation. Accordingly, the positions of various groups of people with respect to exploitation define their corresponding social classes. The circumstances of exploitation condition class antagonism and consequent class struggle (Klaus and Buhr 1964:176).

A surplus value is, as we certainly know, the unpaid labor of the worker. A capitalist pays workers only what covers the cost of restoring their working power (or at least, tries to pay only this much) and the remainder he keeps for himself. Such a remainder is always available because, due to technological progress, the costs of production decrease.

What is to be done to abolish exploitation understood in this way? It is sufficient to organize social life so that the surplus value will return to the pockets of the workers. First of all, one should abolish private ownership of the means of production. If the means of production are in the hands of workers, then exploitation will be abolished, and along with it the antagonistic social classes and their struggle as well. Socialism is supposed to achieve precisely this.

The two concepts of exploitation led to numerous disputes among Marxists. "Dogmatic" Marxism agrees with the "mature Marx," while "revisionist" Marxism follows the "young Marx." The polemic about the "young Marx" turned out to be one of the most basic philosophical and political disputes within Marxism. This polemic was connected with the question of whether or not the exploitation of one human being by another existed under socialism. Spokesmen for dogmatic Marxism, especially the so-called "Stalinists," held that under socialism exploitation does not exist. Josif Stalin[69] wrote: "In the socialist system, which so far has been realized only in the USSR, the basis for relationships of production is common ownership of the means of production. Here, there are no longer exploiters and exploited. The manufactured products are divided according to work, following the principle, 'He who does not work, does not eat.' Here, mutual relations among people have the character of social collaboration and socialistic mutual assistance among the workers, and are thus free of exploitation. The relations of production here correspond completely to the status of the forces of production since common ownership of the means of production strengthens even more the social nature of the process of production" (Stalin 1949:512). Schaff had a different opinion. As we saw, Schaff was initially a supporter of Stalinism, but later (after 1965) he was one of the acknowledged leaders of revisionism. He wrote in one place: "Alienation also occurs in socialist society. And as such it is both an ordinary, not yet subdued relic of the past, as well as a phenomenon quite organically and persistently associated with the conditions of the new system. In any case, the problem does exist and must be an object of reflection and real concern" (Schaff 1965:193).

The issue of the essence of exploitation leads us right into the nucleus of Marxism as a philosophy of work. Let us analyze this issue somewhat more closely without abandoning the Polish perspective, for in Poland, this issue bore particularly interesting fruit.

9. The Dispute about Alienation

Leszek Kolakowski[70] writes: "In Paris in 1844, Marx was engaged in composing a critique of political economy in which he attempted to provide a general philosophical analysis of basic concepts: capital, rent, labor, property, money, commodities, needs, and wages. This work, which was never finished, was published for the first time in 1932 and is known as the *Economic and Philosophical Manuscripts of 1844*. Although merely an outline, it has come to be regarded as one of the most important sources for the evolution of Marx's thought. In it he attempted to expound socialism as a general world view and not merely a program of social reform, and to relate economic categories to a philosophical interpretation of man's position in nature, which is also taken as the starting-point for the investigation of metaphysical and epistemological problems" (Kołakowski 1978:132). This text appeared for the first time in Polish only in 1958. Its first edition in 1932 immediately evoked many controversies. Should one consider the "young Marx" a "Marxist"? Can the ideas developed by him here be shown to be consistent with the hitherto well-known and avowedly essential framework of the thought of the author of *Das Kapital?*

Where did these questions come from? Let us focus our attention on the problem directly associated with the matter of exploitation.

The concept of exploitation understood as alienation contains a necessary assumption that determines its meaning: a human being is a being that possesses in itself its own essence. Alienated work is work that remains in conflict with the essence of a human being. Thus, the theory of exploitation assumes a particular theory of human beings, that is, a particular anthropology. This assumption disagrees with the basic thesis of Marxism which emphasizes that everything is raw material for labor, including the essence of a human being. By being a product of common labor, the essence of a human being cannot be some kind of absolute norm for that labor.

This assumption also conflicts with a text by Marx himself known as the sixth thesis on Feuerbach.[71] "Feuerbach resolves the religious essence into the *human* essence. But the human essence is no abstraction inherent in each single individual. In its reality it is the ensemble of the social relations. Feuerbach, who does not enter upon a criticism of this real essence, is consequently compelled: (1) To abstract from the historical process and to fix the religious sentiment (*Gemut*) as something by itself, and to presuppose an abstract—isolated—human individual. (2) The human essence, therefore, can with him be comprehended only as 'genus,' as an internal, dumb generality which merely *naturally* unites the many individuals" (Marx and Engels 1959:244-45). This text clearly declares that the essence of a human being is outside the human being. People are those particular beings that have to acquire their essence. A horse is a horse because of the species to which it belongs; the essence of a horse is in the horse; likewise for the essence of stones, water, trees. But people are particular beings; their essence is outside themselves in the "totality of social relationships." Human beings become human beings when they enter ever deeper into societal life, especially when they take a place in the system of production; when they become owners of the means of production or are just the possessors of work power. One is thus compelled to express the concept that anthropology cannot be a proper basis for a theory of exploitation; rather, the theory of exploitation as a component of a general theory of socioeconomic life must be the basis for anthropology.

On the theme of the concept from the *Manuscripts,* Lucien Sève[72] writes: "This theory is based . . . on the failure to recognize the basic principles of historical science (in particular, the determination of the form of social relations by the nature of the productive forces) and fundamental concepts in scientific economy (value, labor-power, surplus-value, etc.). Although they mark an important stage in the change from the old, humanist, speculative point of view to the new, historical and economic, scientific point of view, a large part of the analysis in the *1844 Manuscripts* is still upside down, has still not been set right side up in a materialist manner" (Sève 1978:67).

At a certain point, the dispute in Poland about alienation assumed the character of a political dispute, centered on Schaff's book, *Marxism and the Human Individual* (*Marksizm a jednostka ludzka*). At the time, Schaff was the principal representative of Marxist orthodoxy in Poland. As a member of the Central Committee, Schaff stood guard during the Stalinist period over the proper development of Marxist ideology in the universities. His *Introduction to the Theory of Marxism* (*Wstęp do teorii marksizmu*) had several editions and was the main textbook of Marxism.

General opinion ranked him among those responsible for the errors and deviations of cultural policy during the Stalinist period. His book, *Marxism and the Human Individual,* constituted a clear expression of a radical switch from Stalinism to "revisionism." Disputes over the book and its author accompanied the university student protests of 1968. At that time, Schaff lost his position on the Central Committee. Although it is difficult to recognize him as the spiritual leader of the revisionist movement in Poland at that time (a position that belongs more properly to Kołakowski), nonetheless in those days he played a rather important role as a theoretician.

Schaff's book appeared under unique circumstances. After 1956 (following the famous "Polish October"),[73] there was in Poland an increasing interest in existentialism. Many who until then had been enthusiasts of Marxism experienced frustration. The young sought a more suitable philosophy for themselves. Then came the discovery of French existentialism. Some works of Jean Paul Sartre,[74] Albert Camus,[75] and Simone de Beauvoir[76] (predominantly novels, essays, plays) were translated. The discovery of the *human individual* followed—the human individual as an autonomous being important for itself, for whom society is not at all a joy but rather a torment (there is Sartre's famous saying, "hell is other people"). In this confrontation, Marxism proved to be an empty philosophy. It does not give existential answers since it does not pose existential questions. It is interested in the individual only insofar as he or she can or cannot work. Schaff tried to remedy this deficiency. He began to see in Marxism the rudiments of a philosophy of the human individual. From this perspective, he read the *Manuscripts.* The concept of alienation served as the center of his critical reflections. But his conclusions proved devastating for the current ruling system; socialism did not abolish exploitation, it only altered its character.

It was commonly known that in the *Manuscripts* there is hidden the kernel of a sort of philosophy of "the human individual." But this text was not recognized as the work of the mature Marx. In the case of *Theses Concerning Feuerbach* (1845) (*Thesen über Feuerbach*), the situation was different. Despite their sketchiness, they became from the very beginning a part of the basic canon of Marx's writings. Thus, when Schaff referred to the *Manuscripts,* no one protested very strongly, but when he referred to the famous sixth thesis on Feuerbach, voices of protest arose, all the more so since Schaff "stretched" its translation a bit. By a paradoxical coincidence, the dispute about the translation of "the sixth thesis" became one of the primary political controversies of that period.

Let us recall the fragment of the sixth thesis that is of interest to us: "But the human essence is no abstraction inherent in each single individual. In its reality it is the ensemble of social relations." The question arises as to what the word "it" refers. Does it refer to the "essence of a human being" or to "a particular individual"? If "it" refers to "a particular individual," as Schaff interpreted the thesis, this means that Marxism is, at least in embryonic form, a "philosophy of the human individual" (like existentialism). If "it" does not refer to "a particular individual," then Marxism remains a philosophy of socialized work. Then all the problems of an individual—problems of happiness and unhappiness, feelings of guilt, love, fidelity, conscience—appear to be secondary. People should step out of their personal world and discover their *social* essence in work toward the common good, in the struggle for a better future for humanity, in preparation for the revolution.

Critics of Schaff demonstrated that his interpretation of the thesis is erroneous. They also attempted to prove that a compromise with existentialism is de facto the author's personal compromise with bourgeois ideals. Szewczyk wrote: "Marxism is like a piece of red cloth out of which one may make either a banner for socialism or a cushion under one's bottom" (Szewczyk 1965:11). It was pointed out to Schaff that he devalued all the social institutions in which the people of our country live—the state, the Party. The Central Committee debated Schaff's work. Summing up this debate, Zenon Kliszko[77] said, in part:

> The main theoretical and political flaw of Comrade Schaff's work lies, in my opinion, in the fact that he eliminated from his considerations the Party and its role both in developing the theoretical thought of socialism and in shaping the practice of building socialism. Comrade Schaff mentioned the Party only superficially and in an essentially negative way. He writes concretely about our Party only in the context of the accusation that it does not duly combat anti-Semitism. It should be stated that this accusation represents a falsification of reality since the phenomenon of this kind of economic, social or political discrimination does not exist in our country. Under these conditions, formulating such an accusation, as well as blaming the Party for not fighting anti-Semitism, might indicate only a lack of political responsibility (Kliszko 1965:12).

This, however, does not solve the key issue. What is the relation of the "mature Marx" to the "young Marx"? What place in Marxism should be allotted to the concepts from the *Manuscripts?*

It was a generally accepted view among Marxists that there is continuity between the concepts of the young and the mature Marx. Various texts pointed to this continuity, above all, the text of *Das Kapital* itself. Here is a selection from it: "On the one hand all labor is, speaking physiologically, an expenditure of human labor-power, and in its character of identical abstract human labor, it creates and forms the value of commodities. On the other hand, all labor is the expenditure of human labor-power in a special form and with a definite aim, and in this, its character of concrete useful labor, it produces use-values" (Marx 1936:54). The distinction of the two aspects of labor—"abstract work" (e.g., work on an assembly line, where the worker's entire function is reduced to the performance of one and the same operation) and "concrete work" (e.g., the work of an artist, who not only spends "working power" but also expresses himself through his labor)—goes back to the views presented in the *Manuscripts*. Marx was concerned that a worker should be able to labor according to the model of concrete work so that in his labor a worker's individual personality could be expressed, as opposed to working according to the rules of "abstract work," which is nothing more than the simple "expenditure of working power."

Kołakowski characterizes these concepts as follows:

The fundamental novelty of *Capital* consists in two points which entail a wholly different view of capitalist society from that of the classical economists with their labor theory of value. The first of these is the argument that what the worker sells is not his labor but labor-power, and that labor has two aspects, the abstract and the concrete. But this view is itself the final version of Marx's theory of dehumanization, first sketched in 1843–44. Exploitation consists in the worker selling his labor-power and thus divesting himself of his own essence: the labor process and its results become alien and hostile, a deprivation of humanity instead of a fulfillment. In the second place, having discovered the dual nature of labor as expressed in the opposition between exchange-value and use-value, Marx is able to define capitalism as a system in which the sole object of production is to increase exchange-value without limit; the whole of human activity is subordinated to a non-human purpose, the creation of something that man as such cannot assimilate, for only use-value can be assimilated. The whole community is thus enslaved to its own products, abstractions which present themselves to it as an external, alien power. The deformation of consciousness and the alienation of the political superstructure are consequences of the basic alienation of labor—which, however, is not a "mistake" on history's part but a necessary precondition of the future society of free beings in control of the vital process of their own lives. In this way, *Capital* may be regarded as a logical continuation of Marx's earliest views; and this continuity is attested by his reference, in the Afterword to the second edition of Volume I (1873), to his criticisms of Hegel "almost thirty years ago," i.e. no doubt to the *Manuscripts* themselves (Kołakowski 1978:264).

The discovery of continuity between the young and the mature Marx is only one problem. The second question is: What is "concrete work"? What does it express? If it expresses the essence of a human being, then one must ask: What is this "essence"? How is this essence possible in light of the fact that a human being is "the most pliable material"? Without developing a full anthropology, the answer hangs in a vacuum.

But, acceptance in a human being of some sort of "nature" or "person" indicates a crack in radically understood materialism and a retreat from the ideal of a "philosophy of work."

In this context, Sève's work, *Marxism and the Theory of Personality* (*Marxisme et théorie de la personalité*), deserves particular attention. This book is one of those few contemporary Marxist works that do not hesitate to pose the issue of exploitation as the main problem of Marxism (the majority of Marxist textbooks do not devote *even a single word* to this problem). Sève declares himself in agreement with the continuity between the young and the mature Marx and at the same time claims that Marxism cannot dispense with a philosophy of the human being. Sève wishes, however, to base this philosophy on a scientifically understood psychology of personality. The psychology of personality discloses the richness of human beings and describes the "capital of their talents." On the basis of these discoveries, one may try to define exploitation as the contrast between the sum of talents possessed and the work performed. One who would force a deaf-mute to sing, for example, would certainly perform an "act of exploitation." Let us examine this view more closely.

A significant trait of Sève's views is that in his studies of the phenomenon of exploitation he does not step outside the sphere of the consciousness of exploitation. I am exploited when I am conscious of being exploited; there is no exploitation where there is no feeling of exploitation. The psychological experience of exploitation is an experience of some sort of conflict (perhaps contradiction—the author is not sufficiently precise on this point) between how I feel and experience myself and what I am doing. The conflict pervades the personality of a human being and deforms spontaneous development (broadened reproduction or expanded replacement). Exploitation does not occur here outside the limits of human consciousness and does not influence it as docs the psychoanalysts' subconsciousness. Exploitation reverberates in human self-knowledge, filling it with various forms of suffering. When, however, we try to understand better where the poles of this alleged conflict lie, we see that Sève's otherwise extraordinarily interesting concept dissolves in ambiguity.

We find at least four answers:

(1) Exploitation is the conflict between the "concrete" and the "abstract" work of human beings. Concrete work is the "determinate expression of the ability of a living individual"; abstract work is the "simple expenditure of working power." Exploitation, as we see, begins earlier than the moment of payment for work. The onset of exploitation is the moment at which the workers are forced to sell their working

power alone to the employer, regardless of the capabilities and preferences that constitute their personal richness. The level of compensation is measured by the level of the simple restoration of their working powers and not by the need for broadened reproduction (expanded replacement) of their potential.

(2) Exploitation is the conflict between "concrete" and "abstract personality." This answer is in line with the preceding one, provided the hypothesis that "concrete personality" is a direct consequence of "concrete work" while "abstract personality" is a direct consequence of "abstract work," is true. But this is not at all obvious. The author then speaks about "dichotomized" personality. He writes: "The concrete personality first presents itself as an ensemble of personal, indeed interpersonal, nonalienated activities, unfolding as self-expression; but, without examining here the historical process of which it bears the scars, the general rule of capitalist society is that the concrete personality is both cut off from social labor and essentially subordinated to its products, i.e., to the abstract personality, which more or less severely besets it, assails it, overwhelms it and crushes it, not only from without but from within" (Sève 1978:341-42). In contrast, abstract personality participates in socially productive work. Such a work is no longer considered a free, independent expression of concrete personality. This leads to "dichotomization" or "separation and partitioning between its different sectors of activity" (Sève 1978:362).

(3) Exploitation is the conflict between the totality of the abilities of a personality (store of ability) and the available working time. This formula is especially dear to the author since it ties in with his proposed model for studies of the structure of personality. Besides, this formula originates in projecting onto personality the basic conflict in capitalism between the level of productive forces and social relations. The author writes: "The necessary correspondence of use-time with capacities defines the internal psychological requirements of the individual's development" (Sève 1978:357). The way in which time is utilized by a human being is dictated by the structure of social relations. The utilization of abilities means the "broadened reproduction" of personality, that is, its multilateral development (in contrast to simple reproduction, in which only regeneration of the energy expended in work takes place).

(4) Exploitation is the conflict in the perception of ownership: that which is mine, my own, becomes someone else's, foreign to me. Exploitation is selling oneself, it is the renunciation of autonomy. For the consciousness of exploitation to develop in exploited human beings, they must have the consciousness of "owning themselves." If one hypothetically liberates human beings from the consciousness of owning themselves, the necessary basis for their feeling of being exploited would

likewise disappear. Nowhere does Sève clearly formulate such an answer to the question of the essence of exploitation, but several proposed descriptions of exploitation clearly indicate that nowhere else but precisely in disturbances of feelings of ownership should one see the essence of exploitation, and the liquidation of exploitation lies in the removal of these "disturbances." Sève writes, for example, that the dichotomization of personality will disappear when "social work becomes the *personal* work of a human being" or when an individual "*appropriates for himself* the productive forces in the process of social work," and also when one abolishes at least the "legal separation of an individual from productive forces." Thus, the significance of exploitation would be its indirect confirmation of feelings of ownership in human beings.

Sève's propositions are exceptionally valuable since they permit an examination of the phenomenon of exploitation through the prism of its immediate victim, and the unveiling in it of all the anomalies to which compulsory work leads humans. Nowhere else in philosophical or psychological literature do we find works treating the issue of exploitation so incisively and honestly. Sève's propositions are, undoubtedly, pioneering with regard to psychology. They may be a starting point for broad experimental studies on the structure of the exploited personality. Because of their pioneering nature, one should not be surprised that the propositions contain a number of equivocations which need to be eliminated if the concept being defended is going to provide effective tools to unmask exploitation.

A question arises: What is the relationship between the objective exploitation of personality and the subjective consciousness of exploitation that the author attempts to depict? Is the dichotomization of personality merely an accidental derivative of exploitation or does it also belong to the essence of personality? In other words, in each case when an individual displays signs of dichotomization, do we have the right to assume that this individual is a victim of exploitation? And conversely, when someone shows no symptoms of dichotomization, does it mean that exploitation has not laid hold of him? Should the psychological description of exploitation replace or only supplement the objective description given in *Das Kapital?* And if it is a supplement, then to what extent?

The issue of dichotomization requires even further determination since, after all, the dialectical vision of reality itself allows for the vision of a person as a deeply dichotomized being. What is the relationship between the dialectic of the development of human beings per se and the dialectic of exploitation? Perhaps the former can be identified with the latter? Perhaps as exploitation cannot exist without work, work too cannot exist without some exploitation? Or perhaps the dialectic of work has nothing in common with exploitation, since exploitation attempts to introduce into the core of the dialectic of work a disturbance in the form of the logic of maximal gain with minimal investment.

In the descriptions of the dichotomization of personality, Sève often refers to the concept of "ability" and even to the concept of "needs." At the same time, however, he forcefully emphasizes that there are no innate abilities in human beings and that a characteristic of human need is its susceptibility to "unlimited reproduction." These axioms make incredibly relative the proposed criteria for distinguishing exploited work from liberated work. Furthermore, they readily expose these criteria to degeneration. Could not a situation then arise in which some sufficiently beneficial capital fund (e.g., state capital) would strive to eliminate from human beings their former needs and replace them with new ones, while saying that it does so in accordance with the idea of "broadened reproduction"? (This means, for example, the elimination of the need to own land privately in favor of the need for state property.) Where then should one seek criteria of true progress in the development of personality?

There is another important point: the entire description of the exploitation of work by Sève, and also to a great extent by Marx, neglects the elementary fact that exploitation is not only a disturbance inside the human personality but, above all, a disturbance of the relationship of one human being to another. If this fact is overlooked, we risk the error of solipsism in our treatment of this issue. Exploitation is always a tragedy in the immediate sphere of contacts between human beings. It is one of the most radical ways of falsifying of these relationships. As such, it does not touch so much upon the distribution of products as it does directly upon the sphere of the human ethos, which includes not only the distribution of products but also every exchange of information. Deprived of its ethical aspects, the concept of exploitation loses most of its power to act upon the oppressed as well as upon the oppressor, mobilizing the former for a just struggle for liberation and unmasking the moral self-delusion in the latter.

The issue of alienation and alienated work assumed importance in the Marxist literature of the 1960s because it became obvious that the concept of exploitation as the appropriation of surplus value by a capitalist cannot explain the presence of the exploitation of work in a socialistic system. Theoretically, in socialism, the entire surplus value returns directly or indirectly to the worker's pocket. But this is only in theory, for in practice it is appropriated by the state which assumed all the basic functions of the classic capitalist. Economic exploitation of the workers reached hitherto unheard of proportions. The state monopoly of work made any successful worker resistance against exploitation impossible. Trade unions, instead of defending workers' interests, became passive tools of exploitation. The wages of the vast majority of workers do not exceed the requirements for fulfilling the elementary needs of the species.

The gap between the living standards of the working class in "capitalist" countries and the standards in "socialist" countries became dramatic. In this situation, the entire effort of Marxist philosophy and socialist ideology goes into obscuring the picture or changing its message. Thus, one speaks of the ruinous effects of the capitalist economy on the socialist one, in spite of the fact that the latter was developed precisely to make such an influence impossible. The various "benefits" of the socialist system are stressed excessively, but the same or similar phenomena in the opposing system are ignored. Above all, the entire problem of exploitation is eliminated from the exposition of Marxism as if this problem had no role at all to play in this philosophy. In the currently obligatory curricula of Marxist philosophy in the universities, the treatment of exploitation has been omitted. It is said of Marxism that it is the "philosophy of a scientific world view"; that it is a "consistent struggle with idealism"; that its aim is "the all-around development of the human being"; that it gathers in itself "the most ingenious trends of the thinking of humanity"; but it is not said that Marxism is a philosophy of work—work that is falsified internally and externally.

There is yet another way of ignoring the crux of this problem. One may, on the one hand, say that "Marx in his later works on economics not only did not negate the theory of alienation, but enriched it" (Wójcik 1978:92), but on the other hand, one may use such an equivocal concept of alienation that in practice its abolition is postponed indefinitely. Then one will say that although socialism is indeed an important step toward this end, the goal before us is still clouded. To achieve it, one needs the full victory of the socialist revolution, the abolition of the state, the introduction of socialism in the whole world. Let us contemplate the following words: "A great deal has changed since Marx and Engels created their projections of the future. We have had new experiences; today we evaluate the tempo and possibilities of the desired social changes more realistically. Socialism was to be built under conditions different from those anticipated by classical Marxism; the construction of communism turned out to be a more complex and slower process than Marx and Engels, and even Lenin, imagined." What do these words mean? Do they not perchance mean that we find ourselves again at the starting point? And a few lines further: "Social practice will also decide which of the ambitious projections of the future by Marx and Engels will be realizable and to what extent. Today, an arbitrary pronouncement in these matters would be far too premature. The fate of the Marx-

Engels teaching about revolution in the context of socialist countries should give us a great deal to think about. Can one exclude the possibility that, after the final solution by socialist countries of the problem of the abundance of goods, other aspects of the theory of communism will also disclose their considerable attractiveness?" (Wójcik 1978:329–30). Let us note the words: "The fate of the teaching about revolution in the context of the socialist countries should give us a great deal to think about." But do they not do so? And the words ". . . after the final solution of the problem of the abundance of goods . . . other aspects of the theory of communism will disclose their considerable attractiveness." This means after the solution of the problem that has already been solved elsewhere! All this breathes an air of deep skepticism. One is amazed by one thing only: "A new synthesis of experiences and the charting of the path of further social development can be accomplished only by a new generation of Marxists." Precisely, Marxists. Faith in the ability to reproduce this species of philosophers is indeed impressive.

When speaking of exploitation, one thing must not be forgotten. Not only did socialism not solve the problem of exploitation as originally understood, but it became itself a source of new forms of exploitation of one human being by another—exploitation that is less "economic" and more "moral" in nature. Thus, exploitation constantly drives human beings into a state of moral conflict with themselves. The basic affliction of socialist human beings is moral rather than physical; it is the feeling that their otherwise sincere good will is time after time misused for aims that have nothing to do with this good will and which often are even contradictory to it. If the classic form of exploitation primarily concerns the work of human beings and consists of the manipulation of its fruit, then this new form is a direct manipulation of human beings themselves, their attitude toward others, toward themselves. Socialized human beings discover time after time that their entire lives follow a course below the "normal level" of human life, due to an inability to exercise their proper rights and to execute the duties entrusted to them. Their right to the truth is canceled, their feelings of personal dignity are taken lightly, their personal freedom suffers limitations. The societal life in which they participate is surrounded by various mysteries. They devote most of their time and energy to satisfying their most elemental, almost animal needs. They suffer from an excess of needless, empty tasks, and from a constant lack of time. They live in a world of the propagandistic lie. And this situation does not improve at all, but in many respects intensifies and becomes more complicated.

To describe the essence of the moral exploitation of one human being by another, the economic, political, and even strictly anthropological conceptual categories must be left behind. Since this concerns a condition of moral nature, ethical concepts must be employed. However, Marxism lacks such concepts. Christian philosophy and theology make use of such concepts. No wonder, therefore, that Christian philosophy has made and continues to conduct an ethical evaluation of the processes of socialization. In this way, it brings reason to bear on these processes to some extent. Can one be surprised that this rational analysis is simultaneously a sharp critique of these processes?

10. Concerning the Dispute about the Essence of Human Beings

Is Sève's position on the essence of human beings the only example of a Marxist solution to this problem? There are critics of this concept. Let us examine one of those critiques. Let us also examine another concept close to that of Sève, but formulated independently of his and in accordance with the popular view of Marxism. Janusz Kuczyński[78] represents the former, while Włodzimierz Szewczuk[79] represents the latter. Kuczyński attempts to overcome the extremism of Sève's position from a view of the human person as both an independent and a creative being (*homo creator*). Does he succeed? Szewczuk does not have such aims. He is convinced that the interpretation of the essence of human beings as "the entirety of social relationships" represents the definitive solution to the mystery of human existence. Thus, we have two mutually contradictory positions to deal with. Still, there is something connecting them: they have in common a fear of the concept of a human being as an independent substance or a generally self-existent being—a concept akin to that of Christianity.

Where, in Kuczyński's opinion, is Sève's mistake? It consists of "absolutizing one of the 'strata' of human beings, and this subsequently leads to locating the essence of human beings . . . outside of human beings. [Sève], while rightly emphasizing the significance of the study of relationships for science, notices neither the problem of the interiorization of 'the entirety of social relationships' in the psyche, and above all in consciousness, nor the connections, internal to human beings, between their somatic and psychic structures. Granted, these connections are mediated by social relationships but to a large extent they also have their own autonomous dynamism" (Kuczyński 1976:253–54). Kuczyński's interpretation tries to avoid these extremes and aims to take greater account of the autonomous character of human beings. Is this really true?

Kuczyński, following the conceptual path of "consequent dialectics," distinguishes in human beings three "strata," each of which is itself characterized by its own specific essence (from Lenin[80] the author knows that an object may have multiple essences). Thus, "the essence of the human body is its 'spirituality,' i.e., its particular 'psychic condition'; the essence of consciousness, the attitude toward the world; the essence of 'the entirety of social relationships,' the dialectic of struggle and reconciliation" (Kuczyński 1976:236).

Thus, the human being is a unity of three strata. The question arises: which of these strata is the most basic? Or conversely, which "essence" characterizes human beings in the most "essential" way? Here is the attempt at an answer:

Thus, the essence of human beings . . . is an attitude toward the world that is formed through physical, corporeal, and sensory contacts repeated billions of times, generalized in the psyche, mirrored in *theory,* in consciousness, and realized in the praxis of the *entirety of social relationships.* Hence, it is likewise a formal determination, relational and not substantial; the essence of human beings is a relationship. But this relationship is understood here not only as a relationship between A (a human being) and B (the world) but also as a quality, trait A. More succinctly, the essence of human beings is a *relationship* to, . . . that has a material basis and a psychic codetermination. . . . Thus, the essence turns out to be a trait. . . . The essence of human beings—in another colloquial or "literary" sense of the word "essence"—is nonidentity, crossing into, *tilting toward.* . . . The essence does not rest in the static center of this existence, but in the movement, in the constant drive to break through the physical and psychic limits of human existence. Therefore, the essence of human beings is not the self-preservation that determines an animal and instinctive way of existence, but the striving toward a continuous transcendence of themselves (Kuczyński 1976:251–52).

Does this concept really differ from that of Sève?

Before we answer this question, I want to ask something else. On which and what sort of experiences does Kuczyński want to base his solution? What method does he employ? He speaks of a dialectical method. But how does this "dialectic" look in practice? First of all, the author does not look for some key, decisive experience through which one might demonstrate the error of opposing solutions. There is no mention here of any experience. The approach is the following. First, we match the two opposite concepts that we consider to be "extremes." Then, we make of them a "thesis" and an "antithesis." In the very concepts of thesis and antithesis there is extremism, i.e., error. To avoid the error, we seek a "synthesis," in which extremism is abolished and the "true nucleus" of the original concepts is preserved. In the case of the essence of human beings, the "thesis" is represented by the substantialist concept of the human soul as proposed by Christian philosophy. The "antithesis" is represented by Sève's concept in which human beings are deprived of their strictly internal essence. (Sève, as we shall see, calls human beings an annex to socioeconomic relationships.) Obviously, in this situation, "synthesis" can only be a concept that will place human beings in the sphere of their own existence, but at the same time will say that this essence consists in a relationship of human beings "toward something." Can one object to this method? Can one cavil at the "golden mean" of a third interpretation? Obviously, one cannot. One must say, however, that the conclusion was determined from the start by the very method of setting up the opposites. First, obstacles corresponding to the abilities of the athlete are erected and then triumphal victory is proclaimed. In this method, the point is not truly to learn something but to sidestep something safely.

Let us now look at the concept itself. What picture of the human being do we see?

We disregard semantic paradoxes such as, for example, "essence proves to be a trait." Let us read carefully: a human being is "to a great extent an autonomous dynamism," is a "tending" toward . . . , is "nonidentical with itself," is (if we take it from the side of essence) devoid of the drive for "self-preservation." There is in it some distant echo of Heidegger. In both we are directed toward something that actually transcends the human being. But in Heidegger the issue does not end with that; his human being is interested in his "own existence," is interested in achieving authenticity in the face of death, is interested in being and remaining himself or herself.

Kuczyński says nothing of the sort. The human I? This is only an appearance of identity, an illusion of self-existence. Human beings are "to a great extent autonomous dynamisms." After that, however, they are "nonidentical with themselves," directed outward, to fight and make peace, make peace and fight. Does not this strange *homo creator* demand too much alienation? Does not the essence, that is, a "relationship," direct human beings toward only one thing—not being themselves? In summary, there is only one difference between Kuczyński's and Sève's human being—the latter is an unattainable ideal for the former.

Szewczuk's concept does not raise any further doubts. Here it is:

An animal is born almost totally preformed. Human beings come into the world without a ready-made program for living in social conditions. They learn this program gradually and with difficulty. Their differentiation from the animal world does not depend on a sudden, self-activating beginning of pulsation in them, in their interior, of some kind of conscious tendencies displaying specifically human content. Rather, the differentiation rests on the fact that, by growing into human relationships, by undertaking human activities that they learn from society, by beginning to manipulate objects, shape objects, and then produce new objects, they begin to be conscious beings, human beings. Human beings begin creating themselves by remaking the nature of which they are part. This ingenious discovery of Marx overturned the traditional concept and created a new sociohistorical group of the human being. Human beings are not and cannot be ready-made earlier than their real historical existence. The social conditions of life create human beings and their personalities, they shape their value systems and modes of valuation, their life styles. They shape the entire *interior* of an individual. Changing sociohistorical conditions change human beings. The meaning proposed here and in Marx is that the human being is the "entirety of social relationships" (Szewczuk 1962/66:422–23).

I think that the initial thesis of the radical philosophy of work has been confirmed: a human being is raw material, only raw material, and as much as raw material is. Work can humanize or dehumanize. One who has power over work has power over human beings. We are at the heart of socialism.

11. Problems of the Base and Superstructure— Historical Determinism

Marx directed particular attention to the role played in humanity's history by the development of the tools of production. He concluded that development of these tools, i.e., the broadly understood productive forces, is the main driving force of historical development. The production relationships depend upon the state of the tools of production. Upon the production relationships depend the class system of society and, as a further consequence, the whole culture as well; hence, law, ethics, religion. The authors of the *Philosophical Dictionary,* published in East Germany, write:

The materialistic interpretation of history assumes that the social relationships into which people enter in their practical lives and which in their entirety constitute a given society, can be divided into material and ideological relationships. The first are formed upon the material process of production and reproduction and represent the primal, first, defining relationships that form the economic base of a given society—its economic structure. On the other hand, ideological relationships shape the superstructure of this base. The base, then, is the entire set of production relationships that correspond to the state of development of the material production forces. The superstructure, corresponding to this base, is the complex of legal, moral, and philosophical views, as well as the corresponding political, legal, and other institutions (state, political parties, social organizations). The base and superstructure remain in dialectical relation to each other (a dialectic of base and superstructure). In each social formation, the base leads to the emergence of a corresponding superstructure. The superstructure emerges from the base but at the same time it actively influences the base, to strengthen or alter it. In the final analysis, however, the nature of the superstructure and its efficiency is determined by the base which underlines it (Klaus and Buhr 1964:198–99).

An antagonistic situation takes place in the base. For example, characteristic for capitalism is the conflict between the status of production forces and production relationships (the social character of production forces versus the private nature of property). This situation causes the emergence of antagonistic classes and evokes a class struggle. In this struggle, the "class interest" of the human being is always decisive. And so the base, in determining for human beings their place in society, gives a direction corresponding to their consciousness. In all moral conflicts, they will be unable to pass the boundary of class interest (class consciousness). In short, their consciousness will be determined by their existence ("existence determines consciousness").

The concepts of base and superstructure belong to the key conceptual apparatus of Marxism. They serve Marxism in its critique of other philosophies, in the critique of religion as well as of morality and culture. This critique has, as we have seen, a particular character. When analyzing a view critically, it is not enough to demonstrate, on its merits alone, that it is an erroneous view, but one must also show whose interest this view *objectively* serves. The critique here has the character of a political unmasking. Even the most beautiful words about the loftiest ideals turn out to be just slogans when they are recited by the capitalist who "sucks the blood from the working people." Paul Ricoeur[81] called Marx a "master of suspicion." The mastery of Marx was supposed to have disclosed itself in his successful exposé of the "false bottom" of bourgeois morality. Marx unmasked the spurious religiosity, spurious morality, and spurious virtue of the bourgeoisie. He demonstrated that this is morality only as long as it serves the interests of production.

Simultaneously, however, these concepts centered attention on the role of the human individual in history. In what does determinism of the base consist? Does the action of the base abrogate the freedom of a human being? Is it possible for the human being to oppose the base? What are human beings in relation to the base and the superstructure: Are they themselves, with their culture, ethics, morality, merely the "superstructure of the base"?

Controversies over the nature of the base and superstructure played a key role in the history of Polish Marxism. They were in any case a reflection of controversies that were also taking place outside Poland. Their aggravation occurred at the time of the famous "October 1956." The polemics with the Stalinist understanding of the nature of the base and superstructure were at that time associated with the general de-Stalinization of our culture. Let us try now to present the main lines of those polemics. As Schaff's name was the most important in the disputes about alienation, so the name Kołakowski was particularly important for the polemics about the base and superstructure. Kołakowski was one of the main advocates of Stalinist Marxism, but subsequently became the spiritual leader of Polish revisionism. The evolution of his views is very illuminating. By examining this evolution, we shall be able to observe the slow decomposition of the concept of the base and superstructure in Marxism.

Let us begin with the extreme formulation of the issue, as found in Stalin.

(a) Historical determinism in the understanding of Stalin

Stalin writes: " . . . Changes in production and its development always begin with changes in the sphere of productive forces and, above all, with changes and development of production tools. Production forces are therefore the most volatile and revolutionary factor of production. First, the production forces in a society change and develop and then, depending on those changes and in accordance with them, there is a change in the production relationships between people—the people's economic relationships. . . . One should emphasize that production relationships cannot lag too far behind the development of production forces and be in disagreement with them. Production forces can fully develop only when production relationships are consistent with the character and state of the production forces and when they open a broad area for the development of the production forces." And a bit further: "New production forces . . . develop not as the result of purposeful, conscious activities of the people, but spontaneously, unconsciously, independently of the people's will" (Stalin 1949:508 & 514).

In this passage, we find a germinal explanation of the mechanism of the Stalinist policy toward culture. First of all, it says that the superstructure is totally delineated by the relationships that exist within the base. Stalin says directly that the superstructure "reflects the base": "The spiritual life of a society is a reflection of objective reality, a reflection of existence!" (Stalin 1949:502). The only possible dissonance is a temporal one: the "superstructure" might not keep pace with the changes in the "base," e.g., religious beliefs may persist for some time in a world freed of class exploitation, even though they are nothing more than reflections of the world of exploitation. But in this case, one must accelerate the maturation of the "superstructure." A properly executed cultural policy can bring it about that the superstructure will be better suited to reflect the relationships in the base. In literature, for example, one must advance "socialist realism," which faithfully represents the base. Stalin reduces the human being's role in history to a minimum. When the proper time comes, many can "stumble upon" the idea of making an electric bulb, of releasing atomic energy, etc. The role of the ingenious individual is in this case minimal.

(b) A critique of the Stalinist view

After 1956, the renaissance of Marxist thought brought radical criticism of the oversimplified picture of the relationship between the base and superstructure. Even Stalin protested against the oversimplification of the theory in his article on linguistics, in which he excluded language from the base-superstructure relationship. Nonetheless, religion, science and jurisprudence still remained within the superstructure. This critique, on the one hand, was based on the texts of Marx himself and, on the other hand, constituted Stalin's own expansion of the concept. Here are some examples of the critique of Stalin's views.

First of all, attention is drawn to the third thesis on Feuerbach in which Marx concisely but unequivocally points to the decisive role of human beings in shaping the base. A human being is not merely an "appendix" to the base, but is its particular creator. Here is the relevant text: "The materialist doctrine that men are products of circumstances and upbringing, and that, therefore changed men are products of other circumstances and changed upbringing, forgets that it is men that change circumstances, and that the educator himself needs educating. Hence, this doctrine necessarily arrives at dividing society into two parts, of which one is superior to society (in Robert Owen,[82] for example). The coincidence of the changing of circumstances and of human activity can be conceived and rationally understood only as revolutionizing practice" (Marx and Engels 1959:244). This thesis is not entirely clear. What is clear, in any case, is that Marx opposes the naive materialism that makes human beings the passive material for history. Conditions are changed by people. The educator must be educated. Conspicuous in this is an idea, not fully developed, of the elevation of human beings as the fundamental production force above other forces.

In Poland, an article by Edward P. Thompson[83] had great importance. He first quotes a text of Marx's *Capital* (Vol. 1) and then provides his own commentary. Here is Marx's text: "We propose labor in a form that stamps it as exclusively human. A spider conducts operations that resemble those of a weaver, and a bee puts to shame many an architect in the construction of her cells. But what distinguishes the worst architect from the best of bees is this, that the architect raises his structure in imagination before he erects it in reality." Then Thompson's commentary: "At root the Stalinist does not recognize this central fact. When he reads that men 'set in motion' their heads, he conjures up a picture of men butting their heads against trees, or jerking them about as they lift weights. He conceives of the 'economic base' as made up of *things*— ploughs, spinning jennies, shipyards—to which men are appended, and which they affect only by technical innovation. . . . But the Stalinist forgets that the 'economic base' is a fiction descriptive not of men's physical-economic activities alone, but of their moral and intellectual being as well. Production, distribution and consumption are not only digging, carrying and eating, but are also planning, organizing and enjoying. Imaginitive and intellectual faculties are not confined to a 'superstructure' and erected upon a 'base' of things (including men-things); they are implicit in the creative act of labor which makes man man" (Thompson 1957:60–62).

But such a view of the "base" alters its essence. If the "base" is also the moral and intellectual existence of human beings, the opposition between the base and superstructure is nonsense. What was the "base" becomes the superstructure and vice versa. The mind, as the fundamental production force on which depends the state of the tools in society, is shown to be the true creator of history.

In this same vein are the views of a team of Czech and Slovak Marxists who try to provide a Marxist theoretical justification for the scientific-technical revolution into which the industry of developed countries has currently entered. Their work, published in Polish, was highly significant. They discovered that human beings are the main production force and that this is due to the science that human beings practice. Science ceases being a constituent part of the superstructure, and instead becomes the very core of the "base." The future of humanity depends on science. We read: "Since the progress of science and technology is to a large extent dependent on the *level of man's creative powers,* and so on the development of man himself, we are faced here with a new element in economic growth, and, in the entire history of our times—an element revealing the secret of the present scientific and technological revolution. At a certain stage in the advance of modern civilization, the most effective means of multiplying the productive forces of social and human life is inevitably found to be the *development of man* himself, the growth of his abilities and creative powers—the development of man as an end in itself" (Richta 1969:43).

Compared with the others, the most advanced revision of the Stalinist concept of the base and superstructure is that by Kołakowski. I have in mind those of his works published in Poland while he still lived there. Their influence on the convictions of young intellectuals was exceptionally strong. One must, therefore, say a few words about them.

Kołakowski's essay, "Historical Understanding and the Understandability of the Historical Event" ("Rozumienie historyczne i zrozumienie zdarzenia historycznego"), was published in 1967. The essay's general tone is skeptical; none of the methods of historical cognition, including Marxist methodology, allows us to recognize the true sense of the course of history. Concerning this sense, we are taught only through an act of faith. But the act of faith does not reveal anything; it only ordains the sense. Kołakowski writes: "That act of faith is certainly needed by people, . . . the greatest events actually accomplished in history assumed that act of faith, it was a mental precondition for them. This faith is therefore creative and fertile, though we should not delude ourselves in thinking that it is anything other than merely faith, and especially that it is a conclusion elaborated out of historical raw material. Since the time of the Enlightenment, philosophers have elevated their beliefs to the rank of science; today, it is proper to relocate this alleged science to the level of faith. I am not saying 'degrade,' I am not saying 'elevate,' I am saying 'locate on the level of faith' " (Kołakowski 1967:236–37).

From Kołakowski's text, it becomes obvious that the entire conceptual apparatus with which Marxism tried to understand human history is, in fact, an articulation of faith and not the result of a scientific analysis of the state of things. This means the entire apparatus, thus also the concepts of the base and superstructure. The history of humanity is incomprehensible; also incomprehensible are the relationships between the "base" and "superstructure."

(c) The present situation

The result of the above-mentioned critiques of the Stalinist view of the relationship between the base and superstructure should have been a total rejection of the concepts of the base and superstructure by Marxist philosophers and Marxist students of humanism. This, however, has not been the case. These concepts are still held and still constitute an axis of the Marxists' teaching on historical materialism. The general tendency of this teaching is clear: the point at issue is to demonstrate the key role of material production forces in history and to devalue the role of human beings. One may argue the range of the concept "base," but one must always insert into it material productive forces. This formulation of the matter entered into the required Marxist philosophy textbooks in the universities, and into studies in the fields of literature and history. This formulation shapes the younger generation.

Bohdan Cywiński[84] wrote accurately about the ideological consequences of the spread of the base and superstructure categories among university and even high school students:

Careful analysis of the contents of school curricula and textbooks permits us to isolate the leading theses of the doctrine imposed on students and to demonstrate the manner in which they were presented in the teaching of history and the history of literature.

(1) Historical narration is consistently subjugated to the Marxist thesis proclaiming that the total history of human society is determined by the process of the development of production relationships and their consequences in the form of socialism. It is reflected in the way that the knowledge of historical events is arranged, in the construction of models of particular epochs, in the explanation of their consequences, and also in the commentary on particular events and description of particular societies (from ancient Egypt to modern European

states). It is also reflected in the application of the same scheme that sees the source of every phenomenon in its socioeconomic background. The extreme exaggeration of the role of this certainly essential, but not at all solitary, factor fundamentally distorts the student's view of history.

(2) In the typical descriptions of societies, class structure is given as the only essential indicator of their form. The specifics of race, nation, religion, civilization-cultural zone, etc. are always treated as marginal and secondary factors for an "understanding of the emerging historical canons". Accordingly, the specifics and facts of history are pushed aside. In the description, a universal scheme dominates which, in its application to various historical realities, levels away the richness of different societal organisms in favor of a uniform stereotype.

(3) A stereotyped view of a society described primarily as a class structure automatically distorts the view of actual historical forms. The human being, the individual personality with its passions, drives, and a full range of motives of individual action, largely disappears from the textbooks. Such a person is replaced instead by a representative of a given class who usually acts with a mind toward class interests (regardless of his conscious, declared motives). This interpretation brings to life two major stereotypes that persist through all of history (hence, they are actually ahistorical): the exploited and the exploiter. On the one hand, these stereotypes arouse in the student's consciousness a blend of the characteristics of the Egyptian fellah, slave, early medieval tenant farmer, serf, and twentieth century peasant up to the PKWN Manifesto[85] and agrarian reform; on the other hand, they call up a blend of the traits of the landowner from antiquity through the Middle Ages, the Poland of knights and nobility, the nineteenth century, up to prewar estate holders. Here are some representative stereotypes: the proletarian, burgher, bourgeois, capitalist, magnate, and finally, the priest of any religion. The richness of individual historical persons is reduced to the set-dance of these few figures passing in fixed patterns, dressed quite carelessly in historical costumes.

(4) Class struggle is the basic social dynamism in the textbooks; international conflicts move to a second plane as less essential from the viewpoint of the readability of "historical processes". Other motives of conflicts (cultural or religious differences, the concept of dynastic politics, state interests, strategic alliances, geopolitical conditions) are seldom and superficially analyzed as complicating the application of the generally accepted scheme (Cywiński n.d.:5–6).

Cywiński calls attention to still other distortions of the world picture which are somewhat derivative from those mentioned above. He formulates several essential conclusions. Here is one: "Finally, one should draw attention to the intrusive thesis, never fully spelled out in the curricula or textbooks, that must emerge from this type of historical vision. This is the thesis of the determination of human beings, their psyche, views, moral and conceptual stance, through the historical, economic-social conditions in which they live. The whole of history seems to confirm the words of Mayakovsky:[86] 'The individual is zero, the individual is absurd'. In reading textbooks, one has the feeling of the total nonautonomy of the human person versus the society, class, or laws of historical development as dictated by Marxist doctrine."

Thus, "poisoned humanism" has a definitive task to accomplish; to disarm the individual before the prevailing power of history.

Summary: I hope that I am not mistaken if I say that after the war Marxism became, for many, a particularly attractive philosophy and ideology for the following reasons. (a) It embodied a theory that described the essence of the exploitation of work and the ways of abolishing that exploitation. (b) It showed the human person as a being deeply integrated into the social organism and sensitive to its global needs. (c) It emphasized the key role of material factors and forces in the formation of history, subordinating to them everything in the nature of an idea, faith, or myth. These three components of Marxism became the three factors for socializing the society that had been so tragically tested by the war. Postwar society turned out to be more susceptible to the slogans of socialization than one could have expected. The need to rebuild the country, to subordinate private to public interests, the defeat of the lofty summons to independence and patriotism—all this favored the crystallization of "realistic" attitudes. One had to save from a burning house whatever was possible, even at the cost of compromising one's own conscience. The society became all the more socialistic as it believed more deeply that the question of the exploitation of work was already a thing of the past; that human beings become themselves to the extent that they are integrated into a collective of work; that the key to an understanding of the conceptual, moral, or religious behavior of human beings is whether and how they fulfill their basic needs.

At some point, however, though no one knows for sure when, it became clear that socialization is a violent assault against the human spirit. The pressure of socialization met a response of protest—the protest of individuals and of society. It became clear that the fundamental theses of the philosophy and ideology of Marxism do not correspond to reality, but rather create its illusion. The social exploitation of work not only has not been abolished but has actually increased under new forms. Full integration into a collective of work appeared to be impossible because of chronic organizational errors in the system. Second, socialization threatened people's basic rights, especially the right to freedom. The view that "existence determines consciousness" took deep root in society with relative ease—a view that we have seen to be most controversial on the theoretical level. Since the keys to "existence" were in the hands of the state, this view bore the fruits of a spurious loyalty to the state: "one must not bite the hand that feeds one." Loyalist posturings multiplied, people joined the Party, but the Party composed of such members no longer had an appreciable ideological significance.

In summary, socialization had to end in mutiny. The mutiny of the intellectuals, however, was not at all the same as the mutiny of the workers; its forms of expression were different. We may say that the basic feature of this mutiny was the separation of the "superstructure" from its "base." Instead of creating works of culture suitable to it, the "socialist base" began to produce works that were critical and in open opposition to the system. "Existence" ceased to determine "consciousness"; rather, consciousness began to strive to revise thoroughly the entire sphere of "socialist existence."

What is interesting in this situation is that in Poland the clear absurdity of the theory and the obvious disasters in the practice of socialization did not lead to a deeper revision of Marxism but rather to its rejection. During the three decades in question, no version of "Polish Marxism" developed in our minds—a version, that is, in which specific Polish experiences of the people and their history would be considered. The theory of capitalistic exploitation was not supplemented with a theory of socialistic exploitation. Neither was the theory of economic oppression supplemented with a theory of national oppression. What was written on the matter was just a shy attempt, not a decisive position on the problem. The entire issue of patriotism turned out to be a nut that could not be cracked. On the one hand, various "patriotic associations" were organized, while on the other, those suspected of "nationalism" were jailed. A particular trait of Polish national heroism—whether on the pages of literary works or in history—was the feeling of internal human identity, a feeling of being oneself, a feeling of personal dignity. Nothing of these experiences was encompassed by Marxist anthropology. The socialist hero of work was characterized by a poverty of interior life. In the end, the very concept that "existence determines consciousness" proved to be an illusion. Economic dependence on the state, which acted as the main employer, did not lead to deeper spiritual bonds with it, but resulted in the formation of a whole system of pretended loyalty toward Marxism, socialism, the Party. But this fact escaped the attention of the Marxist philosophers. They did not perceive its source. They were only capable of accusing the people of equivocation.

It seems to me that, in Poland, a truly deep revision of Marxism could have occurred in the name of Marxism itself. To accomplish this, it would be sufficient to look more incisively at social life, to sympathize more deeply with the working man. But such a revision did not take place. Why? Was this because the Party did not permit it? One who goes to ask the Party secretary's permission in matters like these is not a philosopher. I think that the lack of revision proves something else.

Marxism as a method of comprehending the world exhausted its theoretical possibilities. Instead of sharpening the Marxists' view toward reality, it directed it toward something entirely different—toward an illusion or appearance of reality.

III.
Dispute with
Christian Thought and
Attempts at Dialogue

12. Polish Shape of Dialogue

To understand correctly the process of socialization in a country with a thousand-year Christian culture, one must start by grasping the sense of hope expressed by Marxism, the hope which Marxism tries to defend, and with which it attempts to lure the tired and often starving masses.

A human is a being who needs some hope in order to live. People live by various hopes. Some hopes direct people toward God, some toward another human being, still others appear along the lines of a person's attitude toward the world of objects, things, matter. Each of these hopes contains in itself a promise of some kind of salvation for human beings. Hidden in each, therefore, is some idea of human suffering, with some consideration about which of many kinds of suffering constitutes the greatest misery for the human being. Which of the three hopes is, according to the Marxists, a fundamental hope? In other words, which hope should one realize in order to start to improve the world, to make human life in this world truly worthy of the human being?

Marxism, as we know, radically negates supernatural hope. It declares itself on the side of atheism and by doing so breaks all bonds with Christianity. Supernatural hopes are utopian; they separate the human being from real life, from the struggle for a better tomorrow; they force acquiescence to exploitation by promising eternal reward for temporal suffering. They preclude a true, scientific cognition of the world or the full conquest of it. As to the hope connected with a relationship with other people and to the pain of misunderstanding by another from whom this hope stems, Marxism silently accepts that the realization of this hope is contingent on the realization of the hope to conquer the world of social relationships, production forces, and material elements. When we conquer the forces governing social life, when we become more familiar with nature and subjugate it, when private ownership of the means of production disappears, then interpersonal antagonisms will disappear too. War will become obsolete. Exploitation, hatred, and envy will pass away. If human beings had enough food and shelter, and did not have to fear their fate in society, the occasions for their mutual disagreements would disappear. The tragedy of human beings is that when they are hungry and have no place to live, they cannot avoid fighting with each other. But when they fulfill their basic needs, the prospect of mutual agreement lies open to them.

Albeit unknowingly, Marxism performs drastic surgery on human hopes. Its result is the establishment of a new ethical horizon for mankind. The limit of this horizon is the earth—*terra*. There is no other heaven for human beings but the earth. The relationship to the earth is the major problem for human beings. The human being must rule over the earth, its natural forces, and the social forces of production. Because of this domination, new, unexpected energies will be released from both matter and human beings themselves. People will become full human beings and the earth will be their fatherland. The ethical horizon of Marxism is an earthbound, "terraistic" horizon and the hope of socialization is a "terraistic" hope. It understands human beings exclusively as creatures capable of operating with rational force, i.e., labor, and due to this proficiency, able to feel ever more deeply "at home" on the earth.

Naturally, not all Christians realized how deeply Marxism penetrates into the structure of the human personality. Many grasped only what could be seen on the surface: lofty slogans that resembled the Christian ethos and ideals. The expansionist nature of this ideology disclosed itself gradually. Nevertheless, Polish Christian thought and religious teaching came forward with a critique and protest. The main current of the polemic, without a clear and conclusive designation, moved toward the defense of the Christian ethos of hope.

The problem of human, religious, and national hope became a central issue. In reality, the issue was always the same—the defense of the Order of Hope, the defense of every human hope, natural as well as supernatural. Polemics with the doctrine and practice of "terraism" were essential components of this defense.

Let us take one step forward to shed more light on the problems to be discussed. At issue was, above all, the defense of supernatural—strictly speaking, religious—hope. What does this mean? This means that one had not only to defend hope against the theoretical attacks of materialism and atheism, but also to defend the very *right* of a human being to have this hope. I underscore the words, "the right to hope."

The defense of supernatural hope is one thing; the defense of the right to this hope is another. Marxism and the ideology of socialization, in considering religion as a phenomenon unworthy of a developed human being, in removing Christians to the margin of social life, in suspecting them of obscurantism and regression, indirectly put in question the moral right itself to religion, to life according to religion. The act of religious faith became an act tolerated with difficulty. From this stems the need to defend the ethical basis of religiosity, to defend the right of human beings to the choice of a supernatural hope. Naturally, the defense of the right to hope did not supplant attempts to provide a rational basis for the hope itself. These attempts are taking place today in every society, whereas the need to defend the right to have such a hope became peculiar to a society being socialized.

Moreover, Christianity tried to demonstrate in various ways the primacy of interpersonal hope over the hope of conquering the forces and elements of the earth. Human beings must be reconciled with other human beings, they must trust other human beings, they must remain faithful to them; only then will they be able to rule wisely and justly over the earth's riches. One who chooses the opposite path may easily become a thief of someone else's goods. Moreover, such a person basically lives by the spirit of capitalism that also sacrifices the rights of human beings in favor of ruling the world. This particular trend of Christian thought on human hope has also not been clearly articulated. Despite this, the trend has been operative—operative in the fight for respect for human conscience, for concord in the nation, for unity in the family. The church tried to build bridges between people, to establish harmony among classes, groups, factions. The virtue of fidelity was an object of particular concern—fidelity to tradition, to the ancestral faith, to the history of the nation. The call, "Betray not the human being" became the characteristic feature of church teaching in a socialist context.

An earthly hope was also at the center of Christian attention. When the process of socializing the country began in earnest in Poland, Christians were practically cut off by the new authorities from responsibility for remodelling socioeconomic relationships. The entire field of the relationship of human beings to the earth—whether understood as nature or as society—became the object of attention from Marxist experts on the functioning of production forces. Christians were allotted the role of "supporting ally." An ally is one who helps the main force to realize its goals, one who in no way questions those goals, one who acknowledges that the main force carries the burden of responsibility for the cause. In exchange for this help, an ally receives certain protection from the one whom it serves—protection limited according to the general usefulness of the help in the fight. Christians in principle rejected the proposition of such an "alliance" (with the exception of the "socially progressive movement PAX"). On their own, they took up the concern for temporal existence. They left to the Marxists a concern for those things that the Marxists themselves considered to be of primary importance—production forces, the functioning of factories, and repayment of an ever-growing indebtedness to capitalists. Instead, at least in some circles, Christian concern was concentrated on culture, on the ethical "framework" of social life, on the historical identity of the nation. Christians did not intend to take possession of political authority in the country. Thus, they did not constitute a strictly political opposition to the government. Rather, the object of their concern was the way in which the Communists exercised authority. Christians tried to subject this exercise to ethical control. Without a decisive declaration for or against socialization, Christians and the church justified or refused ethical justification for concrete actions of the authorities.

This is, in my opinion, the deepest meaning of the dispute about hope that has gone on in our country for over thirty years. The fight for hope was simultaneously a fight for the human being. Each current wanted to have the human being exclusively to itself. But to have this exclusive possession, it was necessary to show human beings an ethos suited to them. The picture of each ethos was different and the differences could not be erased. One had to choose; to be either on this or that side. This does not mean that people who differ must immediately take up arms. Weapons could not resolve anything here. One had to convince the adversary rather than coerce him. Nonetheless, the atmosphere accompanying the convincing was not idyllic.

The Christians' polemic against Marxism was mainly on the ideological plane, a dispute with the ideology of terraism. Here are some points from that dispute.

The differences in the basic horizons of hope led to differences in the perception of the *value of the human being*. Both Marxists and Christians said "the human being is the highest value," but these words had different meanings. Socialism's world of basic values is different from that of Christianity; thus, the value of the human being is different in each of these worlds, even though in both, the human being is "the highest value."

In socialist ideology, human beings are the most perfect "production force." Their value is a value within the horizon of production forces. The proper gauge of the nature of human beings is their work. This work creates not only the world that surrounds them, but also the human beings themselves. The ultimate goal of work is to subjugate the forces of nature and the forces that move the history of humanity, forces considered from the angle of the human needs that grow as the result of that very work. However, human beings cannot work alone but must unite with others to increase their strength and efficiency. We live in an era of the social division of labor. Thus, only the "socialized human being" truly counts—the human being who is a component of a larger "collective." Owing to this association with the collective, the human being becomes freed of individual limitations, becomes a social production force. Only then is the human being who he truly should be. The human being is the highest value, but only within the horizon of social work and only due to social work. The human being is a particular kind of force, capable of ruling over the forces that propel history and over the elements of nature. The ideal of humanity in socialism is always the "champion of work." The hero of socialism is located on the axis human being–earth, within an axiological horizon that encompasses the ideal of efficient production forces.

For Christianity, the value of the human being is achieved within a different ethical horizon. The hero of Christianity is located on the axis human being–human being and ultimately, human being–God (ultimately, because in fact this second relationship is implicitly contained in the first one). First of all, one must notice that the fundamental dignity of the human being is revealed to us through the story of the Son of God, and in particular through his death by crucifixion. The value of human beings resides deeper than in the value of their actual or even potential work. Nor is it based on the association of an individual with a collectivity. The individual existence of a person is a value in itself. For this individual existence and for its salvation, the Son of God endured death on the cross. The measure of human dignity is not work but sanctity. Work is such a measure only to the extent that it is a component of sanctity.

For the most recent history of Christianity in Poland, the sanctity of Father Maksymilian Kolbe[87] has assumed a particular significance. Father Kolbe, in the concentration camp at Oświęcim[88] (Auschwitz), gave his life to save a fellow inmate unknown to him. Father Kolbe's heroism is revealed through the fact that he valued the life of his neighbor more than his own. Thus, by his act of sacrifice, he definitively transcended the level of values around which the ethical efforts of the heroes of work in a period of socialization are concentrated. Father Kolbe's deed shows us not the value of work, but the values which work should serve. It unveils a sphere of values that gives meaning to all of human life. In this way, it also demonstrates the true order of human hopes. Faith in God is not synonymous with turning one's back on the temporal problems of human beings; it is in no way a kind of "opium," but is the way to the deepest involvement in the struggle for a better world.

Thus, in both perspectives, the human being constitutes the highest value, but in spite of the same–sounding slogan, the essential meaning is different. For Christianity, the entire Marxist vision of human dignity is in fact a masked form of its degradation.

Against this background, during the entire thirty-year period in Poland, a more or less open dispute was taking place, a dispute over the interpretation of the history of the fatherland. Marxist ideologues reading the Polish past have seen in it primarily movements of large masses of people fighting for their daily bread in an abiding condition of oppression and hunger. The hunger for bread must have been, in their opinion, the major hunger of the Poles. Masses of people and hunger for bread, hunger for bread and masses of people—this was the basic viewpoint on Polish history. All else, if mentioned at all, was something secondary. The great national and religious individualities disappeared from Marxist historiography and their historical role was minimized. The core of the Polish past, the history of Polish moral heroism, escaped the Marxist vision of Polish history.

It was different with the church and the writers who stayed within the orbit of Christian influences. In the history of the nation, they felt as if they were in their own milieu. Boldly and directly, they assimilated for new generations all the greatness and prostration of the Polish past. The greatness brought encouragement, the prostration served as a warning. The church celebrated the thousand-year anniversary of the baptism of Poland, showed the figure of St. Stanisław (bishop)[89] as an advocate for the cause of moral order in the state, recalled the blessed Queen Jadwiga[90] as the reformer of Kraków University,[91] referred to the solemn vows of King Jan Kazimierz[92] in Lwów,[93] took pride in Paweł Włodkowic's[94] treatise on tolerance, associated itself with Mikołaj Kopernik,[95] referred to the idea of Poland as the bulwark of Christianity, honored the deeds of the Commission of National Education,[96] remembered the heroes of the uprisings,[97] celebrated the anniversary of regaining independence [November 11, 1918], recalled the Polish beginnings of Wilno University,[98] was at the tombs of Jozef Piłsudski,[99] Wincenty Witos,[100] Władysław Sikorski,[101] and at all the places where even the smallest traces remain of the Polish struggle for independence and freedom. Christianity paid homage to the people and in this way tried to educate them.

These gestures, however, represented something still more. In the dispute about the meaning of the Polish past, ethos was also an issue. Referring to the nation's heroic tradition, Christians placed themselves, as it were, in the light of that tradition. They regained the feeling of their own dignity, derived from the dignity of those whose deeds they continued. The ideologues of socialism, for whom the true history of Poland began after World War II and the true history of the world after the October Revolution in Russia, and who did not know what to do with certain fragments of their own past, had nothing truly worthy of respect to offer in this area.

Only from this vantage point can one grasp the proper meaning of the dispute over the *nature of the human being,* which has been carried out in Poland with varying intensity since the advent of socialization.

Marxists defended the ideals of collectivism. They claimed that the essence of the human being is outside the human being, in the entire web of social relationships. Human beings in and of themselves are only matter, and hence, essentially of the same nature as the surrounding world. The human being as a material being is the most flexible matter for work. Work humanizes the ape and then makes of the human being a full human being. The socioeconomic "base" determines the sphere of human freedom. The freedom of the human being is ultimately reduced to the understanding of necessity and to using that understanding to foster the growth of power and production.

The theses of the Christian philosophy of the human being opposed these assertions. It was said that the human being is a person and thus a self–existing substance, having within it its own human essence. The body of a human being is permeated by spiritual elements, thanks to which the human being is an ethical existence. A human being's work is an expression of the person, an act of the person, but it does not create the person. Work does not determine the dignity of a human being, but human dignity determines the value or lack of value of the work performed by human beings. A human being is a being who can rise above the conditions of the base and direct the development of the production forces.

To substantiate their concepts, each current referred to the achievements of contemporary thought. For Marxism, these references usually ended unpleasantly. References to existentialism elicited the accusation of revisionism. References to phenomenology, to positivism, to hermeneutics, led to a departure from Marxist orthodoxy. As a result, after many years of Marxist philosophical indoctrination, Marxism actually became the ideology of some teachers and professors in the chairs directly dependent on the Party, but in the broader humanistic education, especially at the universities, nothing was left of Marxism but the label. It was different with Catholic thought. The postconciliar period brought an extraordinary revival of philosophical and theological discussion. Christian thought embarked on a broad dialogue with the positive sciences, reached out to phenomenology and hermeneutics, drew life from the ideas of existentialists, made use of positivist methodology. No one raised obstacles to this. Against the background of a severe paralysis of Marxist thought still struggling and searching for self-identity, Christian thought had the attraction of wide-open horizons.

For Marxism and socialist ideology, the ultimate goal of the politics practiced by the Party and the socialist state is the liberation of the working people of the world from the yoke of exploitation. From this comes the *primacy of politics* over ethics. Owing to the lofty goal, the entire political activity of the Party somehow automatically acquired, in the eyes of socialist ideologues, the character of the highest ethical activity. Politics became synonymous with ethics. Whatever appeared to be politically necessary had to be accepted as ethically good. In this context, political compromises ceased to be something bad and became a moral necessity imposed by the situation. Party people sometimes said that one had to tolerate and even collaborate with Stalin since by overthrowing him, we would overthrow socialism itself and the cost of beginning the construction of socialism from scratch would be greater than the "errors and deviations" of Stalin. They also said: We Communists have the courage to take upon our consciences the sins of the revolution, sins from which our happy children and grandchildren will absolve us. Where there is political necessity, there is no sin.

The primacy of politics over ethics, or rather the recognition of politics as the highest type of ethical activity, was not clearly stated. Rather, something quite the opposite was being stated, the superior character of socialist morality. When, however, one inspects more closely the meaning of the words "socialist morality," it always comes down to the same thing, the recognition of political obligations as absolute ethical obligations. This explains the Party's far-reaching tolerance of those who with its approval and on its orders committed various "abuses" with the aim of defending the Party's rule. There never was a trial of those who ordered the firing on workers during the "December" events[102] on the coast. There were, however, trials of those who, as Party members, committed financial abuses. Politics acquitted and politics accused.

The question of the relationship of politics to ethics never became, because it could not become, a theme of public discussion, in spite of the fact that it was one of the most burning issues during the period in question. From the viewpoint of Christian ethics, the Communists who ruled the country applied the principle: "the end justifies the means." Even though Christians considered this principle to be erroneous, they did not submit it to open criticism in relation to the practice of socialization. Rather, they resolved concrete issues by trying to determine what in a given case is politics and what is not. The ideologues of socialism strove to expand the range of the concept of politics to such an extent that nearly all aspects of social and political life would fall under it. Thus, for example, politics encompassed not only the issue of Poland's independence but also, for a certain period, the tight trousers and long hair of the young people.

The church's activity went in the opposite direction. In essence, the church, as it claimed, did not meddle in politics. It wanted to be faithful to the ethical point of view. But this point of view encompassed the entire social life. For this reason, the church spoke of politics. It spoke of the problems of exercising authority, of the rights and duties of citizens, of the conditions of independence, of the ethical aspects of international alliances. It did so not from the angle of the economic effectiveness of authority but from the angle of the ethical principles of its way of functioning.

In this connection, the declaration of Poland's episcopate to the episcopate of Germany in 1965[103] appears particularly characteristic. The episcopate of Poland, on behalf of the entire nation, forgave the Germans all the trespasses committed against the Poles in the past and asked the Germans for a similar forgiveness of Polish trespasses against Germans. This letter stirred a political storm in Poland. One of the sharpest accusations against the letter bellowed: The bishops were meddling in the affairs of politics. The bishops tried to explain: The issue is not politics but ethics, the issue is the practical application of the commandment to love one's enemy. A similar position was taken by numerous letters from Poland's episcopate to the government on matters of schooling, upbringing, culture, religious freedom. Basically, the church did not question the system of state alliances in which the Polish government involved itself. However, it focused attention on the ethical conditions for the rectitude of those alliances.

Let us now consider the matter of the relationship of one human being to another. This relationship is described in Marxism with the help of the dialectical principle of the struggle of opposites. What does this mean practically? It means that the primary solidarity of one human being with another does not result from some "nature" of the human being but is a consequence of the struggle of opposing forces: first the elements of the earth and subsequently other people, the owners of the means of production. The relationship connecting one co-worker with another appears as the model of interpersonal relationships. Where does that relationship come from? It stems from struggle, from the need for self-defense, from consciousness of a threat, e.g., of hunger or unemployment. When the threat disappears, when in general the need for work disappears, the communion of co-workers is threatened by disintegration. The interpersonal ethos of socialism is the ethos of "people in hiding."

When we look at the record of the past three decades, we see how the enemies kept changing. They were the agents of imperialism, the remnants of the owners, salivating reactionary dwarfs, nationalists, neofascists, kulaks,[104] clericalists, Zionists, revisionists, dogmatists, teddyboys, bunglers, opportunists, bureaucrats, sloppy workers, etc. Interestingly, these adversaries were always treated as relics of the past. In general, the Marxists did not admit the possibility that the enemy of socialism might be someone who was created by socialism itself.

But maintaining the atmosphere of a hiding place in a country unifies its inhabitants only up to a certain point. Then something quite the opposite happens. A mutual distrust grows among the inhabitants of the stronghold; suspicion increases and with it, division among the various social groups; the external enemy becomes an internal one. One of the most crucial problems of daily life comes to be the problem of truth and falsehood; to be oneself or to pretend. In contemporary Polish, there is the expression, "to do a number on someone." This expression reflects succinctly the situation of a human being in the world of growing socialization. It means to manipulate another human being in such a way that he or she in good faith behaves according to the principles of current politics. The human being lives on the border of certainty and uncertainty. One constantly hides something, is afraid of something, is ashamed of oneself. But because everyone is equally afraid and suspected, an individual does not see the possibility of rebellion. One is unable to leave one's hiding place.

On this level of existence, the contrast between the ethos of Christianity and the ethos of socialism appeared most vividly. The church insisted that the first exigency for a human being is love for his fellow human being. Love does not come from fear of a presumed adversary but is an expression of human nature. One must overcome the atmosphere of a state of siege. There is no danger so threatening that it could break down a believer, truly "they cannot kill the soul" (Mt 10:28). The fundamental right of each human being and of the nation is the right to the truth, to full information; censorship is contradictory to a person's rights. Each human being carries his or her own internal truth within, his or her own calling; fidelity to oneself is simultaneously fidelity to God. The basic charge of Christians is the protection of human authenticity, even when this authenticity seems to be contradictory to the gospel; authenticity is freedom and freedom is a necessary prologue to morality.

The words of the church were accompanied by the practice of the church. This practice consisted of creating occasions for leaving the hiding places, for showing one's face publicly. This was, among others, the meaning of the church-organized pilgrimages and other big religious celebrations. They provided the people an occasion for revealing internal truth, for giving testimony to religious faith, for mutual strengthening in faith, and also for establishing bonds of strictly religious understanding with other people. To the thesis advanced by socialist ideologues that religion is a private matter for human beings and thus a matter that should be hidden in oneself, the church replied that it is a basic right of a person to proclaim faith publicly and consequently to order one's whole life according to that faith.

One more point of dispute requires underscoring: the Marxist principle, applied in practice, of the primacy of practice over theory. The sense of the principle was approximately as follows: to find out what matter really is, what sort of thing social reality is, who is a human being, it is not enough to examine those realities passively; rather one must trigger them into motion, submit them to molding, act upon them, and allow them to act on us and on each other. The truth of what is clay is revealed when a pot is made of clay, but also conversely, when in spite of our efforts no living organism issues from clay. Truth is the result of the test of forces—human forces with external forces and also human beings with their own forces.

The Marxist theory of truth could serve as justification for the social tensions that arise time after time, often consciously provoked by the Party. The nation was pushed into a process of incessant experimentation. If it worked, good; if it did not work, that means we were wrong. Try first, think later! From that came the conviction that the Communists "back off only when facing force," which often appeared to be the case. When the faithful were building a church without permission, the authorities tried to object, impose fines, raze what was erected; but in the end they backed off in the face of an excited crowd. Did this occur only in the face of force? Apparently not; the authorities also did this when confronted with their own theory of the primacy of practice over the detached objectivity of pure science.

In connection with such a formulation of a criterion of truth, the scientific and philosophical currents that opted, through an appropriate cultivation of science, for a classic though variously modified idea of truth had great significance in the polemic with Marxism. To the thesis that truth has a class character, they counterposed a science that developed from accepting the fact that truth has an absolute character. The truth either is truth for all or it is the delusion of an individual or collective subjectivism. The science that developed in this spirit, by virtue of the fact that it was and what it was, hence, without engaging in an open polemic with Marxism, overthrew the myths of an era of socialization.

The myth of Ivan Michurin[105] and Trofim Lysenko[106] was blown away; the myths accumulated around the achievements of Ivan Pavlov[107] were dissolved, the theory of the base and superstructure collapsed, various theories of economic development, humanistic concepts, etc., were shattered. The issue of ethos, in this case the ethos of science, was poised on the razor's edge. Marxism found itself in the shadow of suspicion that it serves to preserve Party rule, that instead of exposing social evil, it justifies it and in this way preserves it. Scientists were faced with a difficult choice: to accept or reject Marxist methodology. Many of them were choosing compromise; they declared respect for Marxism but then, under this label, developed different methodologies. This made even more questionable the ethical aspects of practicing Marxism.

What seems to be the final result today of the practice of dialogue as sketched here? I think that the main result can be grasped in two basic points. The first deals with the answer to the question: What is Marxism for Christians, for the faithful who lived and still live in a society exposed to world-centered socialization? The second point touches upon the question: What is Christianity in the world of Marxism?

What is Marxism when seen through the prism of the contemporary and historical experiences of Christianity? One thing must be underscored: Marxism and the ideology of socialization, completely independent of the intentions of those who supported them and whom one cannot suspect of a total lack of good will, were pilloried on the ethical charge of providing theoretical justification for acts of cruelty. Those acts of cruelty are not simply by-products of the theory but to a certain degree they are its consequence and even its completion. Let us summarize what we have said: Marxist political atheism questions not only the existence of God, but also the right of human beings to possess supernatural hope. A direct consequence of this is the struggle with religion. If work creates the human being, if it opens the fundamental ethical plane of human life, then the "hero of work" must be an ideal for the human being of socialism. If the struggle for the liberation of work is the highest ethical task, then political evaluation must be accepted as ethical evaluation. Why, therefore, should the political processes and all the acts of coercion that are meant to consolidate and broaden the rule of communism be evil? Agreement that interpersonal relationships are ruled by the principle of opposites leads to the development of an atmosphere in the country of "people in hiding." In this situation, why not introduce censorship, control, police, if these will "defend the achievements of socialism"? The police system of socialism and the police system of capitalism, it is said, are not the same because each serves something different. Practice is a criterion of truth, which means that one may and must exert pressure on people so that they adapt themselves to the demands of history taught by the infallible Party. Marxism proved to be a theory capable of justifying the practice of coercion and cruelty. This was a threatening matter. Cruelty found historical justification. And if in Poland, in spite of everything, there was less cruelty than in Cambodia, Vietnam and other Asiatic countries, it was only because Christian traditions were alive and strong in that country.

But not only this. Viewed through the prism of the history of Christianity and through the prism of the experience of cruelty, Marxism showed itself to be one version of European neopaganism. Paganism in Europe was never totally defeated. The analogy between Marxism and paganism is clear. The Marxist conviction that the main source of human suffering is the earth revolting against human beings and that the conquest of the earth is a primary goal of humanity brings to mind the pagan faith in which earthly forces acquired a sacral character and sorcery was a means of ruling over the earth. In Marxism there is no more *sacrum*, and sorcery is replaced by technology, but the basic structure of the relation to the earth is the same. For Marxism, the value of a human being is the value of the human species, hence, just as in the pagan *politeia*. True, instead of "species" one says "collective," but in daily life it amounts to the same thing. From this comes the cult of the state, of the Party, and above all, of the leader who, standing at the top, sees the most. A love of one's enemies lies outside the reach of a dialectical mind and outside the reach of the psychic capabilities of the proletariat brought up in Marxism. Proletarians love only those who love them, just as, according to the gospel, pagans do. The open cult of power—force of nature, productive force, class power, economic power—is transformed into a strange tolerance of tyranny "in the name of the interests of socialism." Terraistic philosophy at a certain point becomes terroristic philosophy. From the theory that the human being was created from earth, Marxism derives an ideology that tries to bind the human being to the earth. Marxism has not solved the issue of the relationship of one human being to another; rather, it locked people up in a huge hiding place, developed a bureaucracy, and ordered people not so much to love as to control others. Did we not observe something similar within the great state powers of the pagan era? (In *Captive Mind*, Czesław Miłosz also points to the pagan genealogy of Marxism).

To say that Marxism is a version of neopaganism, is at once to define the task of Christians toward Marxism. This task is essentially a *missionary task*. I do not think that Christians in Poland, with the exception of the few who live in blissful separation from the life of the country, have any illusions in this respect. The basic program of the church in Poland has been evangelization. The main effort of priests has been directed toward catechization. All other tasks, programs or propositions of dialogues either derived from this or grew not so much from the spirit of the Christian apostolate as from the spirit of political tactics.

However, we also claimed that Marxism and the ideology of socialization grew in Europe from Christian inspiration. One must understand well those people who became Marxists in Poland. One must understand those who tried to act under the banner of Marxism. Something in this Marxism fascinated them in spite of everything. Marxism promised them something, offered them something. What? Marxism was a philosophy that wanted to build a society without the exploitation of one human being by another. Marxism had excellent slogans on its banners. Who could remain indifferent? Marxism carried some hope and one cannot always govern one's hopes. Could one not believe that, in the situation in which Poland found itself, one could do something good for Poland only through alliance with Marxism and the Party? Perhaps for many, it was not an ideal alliance but one—or at least so it seemed—that created a real platform for action in the country and for the country. At a certain moment, however, it turned out that the basic intention of Marxism, a world without exploitation, had not been realized, and that it never will be achieved under this scheme. But the need for its realization remained; the need for a new hope emerged. Who will assume responsibility for this hope? Who will undertake the task of an *ethical* critique of the existing world, a world so perfectly justified with the help of the classic declarations of Marxism?

13. In the Circle of Ethical Problems

To understand the ethical dimension of Marxist philosophy, one must consider this dimension on several planes: on the plane of ethos, i.e., with respect to the ethical sources and inspiration of Marxist philosophy, on the plane of seeking ethical systems as close as possible to both Marxism and the demands of the moment, and on the plane of real societal life with respect to the ideals and personal models that Marxism advanced and justified. Such a multifaceted presentation of Marxism has the advantage that it not only demonstrates its complexity and heterogeneity but also exposes to public view the sources of this state of affairs.

(a) The Ethos of Marxism

I shall repeat once more what I said before: Marxism, understood as primarily a philosophy of work, was born from the revolt of human beings against the exploitation of human work and this fact decides its ethos—the basic ethos that, however, is generally neither defined nor described more precisely. This revolt would certainly not be possible without the nearly twenty-century-long tradition of Christianity in Europe that sensitized people to the value of social justice. But at the same time, Marxism, from its very inception, became a philosophy directed against Christianity. The anti-Christian or even patently pagan streak of Marxism expresses itself in the call to use coercion for the realization of social ideals, i.e., to ignite a revolution. Marxism in principle agrees with the application, in certain circumstances, of the thesis "the end justifies the means" that is foreign to Christian ethics. On this point, Marxist ethics comes into conflict with Christian ethics. Using coercion to achieve just ideals negates those ideals. The one who achieves justice by means of coercion, by the very act of coercion abolishes justice. The ethos of Marxism seemed unacceptable to Christianity. In reality, it was a continuation of the pagan cult of tyranny.

This was expressed on many levels, but above all—and this is particularly characteristic—on the level of political activity. The sphere of political life acquired increased importance. It turned out that for Marxism there is no area of life that does not have a political character. Economic, cultural, religious events and even the successive fashion fads arriving in the country have a political character. It was a sign that politics assumed the character of ethics and ethics the character of politics. This is understandable. The highest goal of socialism—the worldwide elimination of the exploitation of work—was both an ethical and a political goal. Therefore, anything that opposed just political aims had to be recognized as contradictory to the principles of ethics as well, and conversely, anything that fostered political aims had to be taken as ethical. If an alliance with a particular state fostered the liberation of workers, the alliance was something ethical; if the liberation of workers was fostered by breaking an alliance, then to break it was considered ethical. Most ethical was the very existence of socialist states. Henceforth, the interests of socialist states could be considered not only as political interests, but also as a basic ethical postulate.

These principles were declared with sufficient clarity to remove any doubts about them, but at the same time they were not enunciated too often, since they were somehow uncomfortable. In university textbooks on Marxism, we read:

The next elements of socialist morality are norms which are closely connected with ideology, politics and future ideals. Those norms include the principles of the moral condemnation of exploitation and approval of a system of social justice. Important here is the principle of an involvement on the level of ideas in the contemporary struggle underway for the future shape of human societies. The principle of broadened responsibility is associated with the principle of involvement on the level of ideas, responsibility then not only for private matters, but also, and perhaps above all, for general social concerns. For a general characterization of the norms specific for socialist morality, one may cite Lenin's formula, according to which that behavior is moral which hastens the victory of socialism (Jankowski 1971:619–20).

In another anthology devoted totally to the problems of ethics, we read clearly: "Thus, communism in Marxist ideology is not only a historical necessity to be foreseen as the inevitable consequence of the development of social production and of the status of class conflicts, but communism is also a *moral ideal*. It has moral justification, it is an arrangement of social relationships in which—to put it most generally—the most humanistic postulates formulated by socialist ideology come to be realized" (Michalik 1973:255). And further:

In the epoch of socialist revolution and of the emergence of the foundations of a socialist society, in the epoch of fervent struggle for the victory of socialist principles of government, for solidifying the social character of ownership of the means of production, and finally for the victory of socialist ideology in the consciousness of people, the class content of Marxist ethics occupies the forefront among its basic assumptions. Lenin emphasized this when he formulated his well-known principle of socialist morality. According to Lenin, the ethics of communism is that which serves the destruction of the former, exploitation-based society and the unification of all workers around a proletariat that builds a new society of Communists.

From there come two simple conclusions:

Marxist ethics emphasizes . . . the principal unity of politics and morality [and] the means of coercion—as being necessary in a given situation for the victory of the revolution—are thus indispensable *constituent components* of this ethics. Revolution does not justify "evil means," but assumes definite means— armed conflict, coercion, terror—all of which constitute, in a given situation, necessary elements of the struggle for realization of the highest ideals of the revolution. They are the only way to oppose the actually existing forms of social evil. The aim, in such a formulation, is the totality composed of the means employed for its realization; the moral value of the aim can be measured by the moral value of the means and vice versa (Michalik 1973:256–64 *passim*).

However, the principle of the equal importance of political and ethical evaluation was not obvious to all Marxists. In the post-October reckoning, it was recognized as one component of the Stalinist ideological deviation. A demand arose to return to the common human sources of morality, a desire was expressed to submit the practice of building socialism to the principles derived from that morality. At that time, a sharp attack on Stalinism by Thompson was published in the periodical of the Central Committee. In this attack we again find a fragment devoted to the above-mentioned identification of politics with ethics. The author, having in mind the political trial of Trajczo Kostov[108] in Bulgaria and Vylko Czervenkov's[109] involvement in it, writes:

We feel these actions to be wrong, because moral judgments do not depend upon abstractions or remote historical contingencies, but arise from concrete responses to particular actions, relations, and attitudes of human beings. No amount of speculation as to intention or outcome can mitigate the horror of the scene. Those moral values which people have created in their history, which writers have encompassed in their poems and plays, come into judgment during the trial. As we watch the counsel for the defense spin out his hypocrisies, the gorge rises, and those archetypes of treachery in literature and popular myth, from Judas to Iago, pass before our eyes. The fourteenth-century ballad singer would have known this thing was wrong. The student of Shakespeare knows it to be wrong. The Bulgarian peasant, who recalls that Kostov and Chervenkov had eaten together the bread and salt of comradeship, knows it to be wrong. Only the "Marxist–Leninist–Stalinist" thinks it was—a mistake (Thompson 1957:57).

The above-mentioned text was published in 1957, whereas the earlier quotes [on pp. 84–85] are from the years 1971 and 1973, testifying dramatically that at this later point nothing in Marxism has changed. If one believes Thompson, the "Stalinist" identification of politics and ethics still persists. It is still too essential for the practice of socialization and its roots reach too deeply into the core of the Marxist system of thought.

For the sake of fairness, I shall add one thing: Thompson's protest occurred only when the principle of Marxist ethics turned against the Marxists themselves.

(b) Attempts to renew the theory

Marxist philosophical literature tried and still tries to revise the revolutionary and simultaneously totalitarian ethos of Marxism by calling directly upon Marx or upon other common human ethical experiences. Obviously, it is not easy to answer the question of whether the thinkers who undertake such attempts are still genuine Marxists or whether, by virtue of the very fact of revision, they find themselves outside Marxism. We leave the answer to this question to someone else. Let us look at the two examples of revision that once played and still play a rather important role in shaping the ethical consciousness of the Polish intelligentsia. Both examples are results of Christian inspiration. In the first case, the result of the inspiration is a position close to Christianity; in the second, the author goes even further and crosses the borders of Christianity. Marek Fritzhand[110] is the author of the first revision, and Kołakowski, of the second.

Fritzhand is a defender of the idea of humanism within Marxist ethics. This places him close to the adherents of "socialism with a human face," recognized in its time as a "revisionist deviation." Nonetheless, he tries to take a compromise position. Here is a succinct characterization of it.

In my opinion, the initial thesis of socialist morality is the thesis of the human being as the highest value for the human being. Making this thesis concrete within the framework of Communist morality that gives each of its elements its proper meaning, I derived two organically interconnected principles: the principle of self-realization and the principle of socialization. However, they are not sufficient to characterize Communist morality "for today" in the period when the struggle for the introduction of Communism into life is still ongoing. Thus, having in mind the "today" which is at present paramount for us, I added to those principles the principle of class struggle and proletarian revolution because it demonstrates the means of realization of the other principles that in turn lend their moral justification to the added principle. Naturally, this principle is valid as long as the proletarian revolution has not achieved its goals, as long as communism has not become a reality (Fritzhand 1974:74–75).

Thus, a human being is the highest value for another human being, but at the same time he or she requires a realization that is impossible without the "socialization" accomplished by "revolutionary" means.

Some formulations of Fritzhand put him close to the Christian concept.

It is not permitted for one human being to treat another as a means and to abuse that person for the realization of one's own interests. For a human being another human being is only an aim, never a tool or means. Each human being is entitled to the same human dignity and because of that, he or she has the right to corresponding treatment by other persons. This means first, the condemnation of every discrimination developed from racial, cultural or social differences among people; second, the postulate of humanitarianism toward asocial or class–hostile individuals. The necessity of exerting pressure on them must not assume forms that violate their human dignity. Fritzhand's words "equality of people as people, equal right to the respect of their human dignity and to a full share in social benefits" constitute a concise and emphatic formula of the principle of ethical egalitarianism that constitutes an integral element of the Marxist concept of the ethical primacy of the human being (Ślipko 1967: 10–11).

The formulations proposed by Fritzhand, however, did not gain wide recognition either in Marxist circles or in those of Christian thinkers. Marxists considered them close to "revisionism" and accused the author of advancing "abstract humanism." Stanisław Kozyr-Kowalski[111] and Jarosław Ładosz[112] showed particular talent in attacks of this sort. On the Christian side, Rev. Tadeusz Ślipko[113] wrote about Fritzhand with a large measure of sympathy. But there were no reasons for enthusiasm. Fritzhand clearly claimed that at the present stage of building socialism, the principle of class struggle and proletarian revolution is in force. In other words, the lofty ethics of humanism is an ethics of a "different stage," the ethics of the current stage are struggle and revolution. In summary, the thesis was once again confirmed that it is easy for the proletariat to start a revolution but difficult to end one.

The position of Kołakowski is basically different, but it also grows from the atmosphere created by Marxism and its history. Certainly, no

Marxist will agree that Kołakowski's ethical views are the interpretation of Marx's position, but every Marxist will admit that they were formulated in opposition to Marxism. This opposition, however, did not stem from Christian sources. Kołakowski, at least as he was known before he left Poland, quarrelled with Marxism but also with Christianity. Moreover, for some time he insinuated that Marxism too is de facto a religion and under that label should also be rejected. In a critique carried out in this spirit, Kołakowski associated himself with the liberal and lay tradition of French thought. Somewhat like the encyclopedists, but more intelligently and more incisively, he fought on two fronts— with socialization and with Christianity. It is paradoxical, but somehow he could not distinguish one from the other. A complete evaluation of Kołakowski's philosophical activity is still impossible today. He is still en route. One can attempt, however, to evaluate individual stages. Let us deal with one such stage in particular.

In 1959, Kołakowski published a literarily excellent essay entitled "Priest and Jester." The subtitle reads, "Considerations on the Theological Heritage of Contemporary Thinking." The article expresses his defiant stand. The author tries to demonstrate that all the basic problems of contemporary philosophy originate from theology and that their solutions also come from theology. Marxist philosophy also borrows from a theological heritage. Let us take, for example, the matter of freedom and necessity in history. "Marxist literature on this issue presents various themes that usually orbit around solutions close to the decrees of the Council of Trent" (Kołakowski 1959:70). The article was a blow aimed at Marxism. But this was not perhaps the most important thing. The important thing was the point of departure for the critique—a personally understood and personally interpreted ethical sensitivity. The mutiny against Marxism assumed an ethical character. Why such a mutiny? Because Marxism turned out to be a religion. By protesting against Marxism, the author confirms his ethical opposition to Christianity. The figure of the priest is a symbol of Marxism and religion. The figure of the jester is a symbol of Kołakowski's position. "Both the priest and jester alike perform a certain act of violence on the mind; the priest by the dog-collar of catechism and the jester by the needle of irony. In the king's court, there are more priests than jesters, just as in his domain there are more policemen than artists. It seems it can never be otherwise" (Kołakowski 1959:83). The author understands the need for priests because otherwise "the whole thing would be blown to pieces," but this is not "a motive for access to their group." It was astonishing that the censors let the article through. One cannot exclude the possibility that they did so because of the strong antireligious accents contained in its pages.

Kołakowski's aversion toward religion must have been so great that having eyes to see he did not see, having ears to hear he did not hear what was happening then in the country. The church emerged from the Stalinist experiences as a morally pure force. The figure of Poland's Primate was a symbol of that purity. But there would be no Primate as a symbol if behind him there were no clergy and behind the clergy the people. Kołakowski did not perceive that, either in 1953 or in 1959. It is worthwhile to recall what Kołakowski wrote in 1953: "Thomism, its philosophy and sociopolitical doctrine, is today nothing more than a tool in the struggle against the worker's movement and socialist countries. Vatican agitation misses its target. It is not difficult to discern behind the fog of sweet phrases the hypocritical faces of the glorifiers of imperialistic politics, the apologists of human oppression, ignorance and subjugation" (Kołakowski 1953:34). In 1959, his style is already different and the level of argumentation too. Nonetheless, the general tenor is negative: all the evil that menaces us stems only from the priests since they are the "guardians of the absolute and those who sustain the cult of the eschaton and the self-evident realities recognized and contained in tradition." Moreover, "the priesthood then is not only a certain spiritual attitude toward the world but a certain form of the existence of the world itself, specifically the actual persistence of a reality that no longer exists."

Therefore, one must say the following: the ethical opposition to Marxism is only the continuation of opposition to religion in general and Christianity in particular. For Kołakowski, the one and the other live in the same sack.

The positive position is that of the jester.

The philosophy of the jester is precisely the one that in each epoch unmasks as doubtful what has been taken as most unassailable, discloses the contradictions in what appears obvious and indisputable, exposes to ridicule the obviousness of healthy common sense and sees rationality in absurdities—in a word, undertakes the whole daily effort of a jester's profession with the unavoidable risk of ridicule. Depending on place and time, the jester's thoughts may move among all the extremes of thinking, because the sanctities of today were yesterday's paradoxes, and absolutes at the equator are occasionally blasphemies at the poles. The posture of a jester is a constant effort at reflection on the possible rationality in contradictory ideas. Thus, it is dialectical by nature, it is simply the overcoming of that which is just because it is. Indeed, the jester's posture is governed, not by the wish to be argumentative but by a suspicion of the entire stabilized world (Kołakowski 1959:83).

Such a philosophy, however, arises not from intellectual but from moral grounds. At issue is not that this is more true, but that this way is better, more ethical, more courageous. "It is an option for a vision of the world that provides a perspective on the troublesome reconciliation of elements that, in our actions among people, are most difficult to join together: goodness without universal indulgence, daring without fanaticism, intelligence without diffidence, and hope without blind infatuation. All other fruits of philosophical thinking are of little importance" (Kołakowski 1959:84–85).

What then is left to us? Undefined ethical experience.

On the same plane is an essay entitled "Ethics Without a Code." It is an essay-critique of any ethics organized in the form of an exhaustive code. Such an ethics "blinds people in the face of the real properties of the human world and lulls them with an unthinking hope for integral sanctity amid the unholy conditions of their lives; it begets fanaticism, intolerance, irresponsibility." Kołakowski proposes instead "ethics without a code." "We want to counteract the temptation to moral inertia that allows us to believe that any system of values gives safe and perfect shelter for our moral life. We want to stir suspicion of the sanctities and saints. We want to fight the sterile peace and unthinking sense of satisfaction that develop from the belief that our life is provided with perfect road signs" (Kołakowski 1967:185).

There are various kinds of falsification of philosophical texts. Kołakowski's text was subject to falsification in one particular situation. Even before publication, the author read it in Kraków at a meeting of the Kraków section of the Polish Philosophical Society which was chaired by its then-president, Roman Ingarden. The text contained allusions to Ingarden's philosophy of value. Kołakowski unequivocally rejected this philosophy as one of the varieties of "codified ethics." Let us remember that Ingarden, although attacked in Stalinist times by Kołakowski's colleagues, remained unbending and wrote not one word about anything of whose truth he was not convinced. He was dismissed from the university and returned to it only after "October." He was one of the true symbols at that time of an unblemished ethical position in the Jagiellonian University. The reader can certainly imagine how Kołakowski's words sounded in this particular context. "We want to stir suspicion of the objects of veneration." "We want to fight the sterile peace," "the unthinking feeling of satisfaction" of those who proclaim the "ethics of a code." "Suspicion of the objects of veneration." No one made saints of them, especially not they themselves. However, no one could deny, or even had the right to deny, that in those dark times for the nation, these people fulfilled their duty. And this was what mattered then.

Kołakowski failed to free himself from the well-known Marxist principle that so far philosophers only explained the world but that now the real issue is to change it. Even in Kołakowski's world, there was more to change than to learn. But Kołakowski did not notice that degrading human sanctity has its other side: whitewashing the criminal. If the merit is only spurious, likewise spurious is the guilt.

In spite of that, Kołakowski had influence, as a critic of the system. He awakened suspicions of religion and a feeling of bitter disenchantment with Marxism. He educated an entire generation of youth who in 1968 took to the streets to defend, in a hopeless fight, academic and civil liberties. After their defeat and the defeat of their teachers, there came even darker days for the universities. Nevertheless, the March events in Poland had an undeniable effect—they constituted a milestone on the way to the further destruction of the Marxist ethos.

(c) Personality models of the period of socialization

The problem of ethics, however, does not end with what I have said thus far. One must still consider the more "practical" dimensions of the ethical order and the contribution of various proposals for personality models accepted as especially compelling at particular stages of the "construction of socialism." Their source was twofold: ever-important theory and actual practice. The personality models of socialism were the quintessence of the Marxist theory of history and the actual needs of social life. They had to respond to social demands but their answer was to be consistent with theory. They illustrated indirectly the way of deciphering the theory. Considering each model separately, we can grasp what and why at a given time was particularly important for the Marxists, and what was to stay in the shadows as totally invalid or valid for a different place. There were many models of this sort but we shall pause over only two key models, that of the revolutionary and that of the hero of socialist work.

The template of the revolutionary has its origin in Hegel's philosophy, for in it the concept of "revolution" has a deep historical as well as ethical meaning. Marx took this concept from Hegel but at the same time changed it profoundly.

In Hegel, to put it most succinctly, revolution denotes that moment in the history of consciousness in which, because of the conflict between opposites (thesis and antithesis), something decisively new develops, a new "quality"—a synthesis. Hegel emphasizes that the synthesis is not an ordinary composite of related elements, but a creative transcendence beyond and above the past contained in the thesis and antithesis. The synthesis is unpredictable. When the synthesis has taken place, we can discern in it a direct and indirect genealogy, but we cannot anticipate its continuation. This concept is illustrated in Hegel by the master-slave relationship. Between the master and slave, there is a relationship of the "unity of opposites." The master is an opposite of the slave and the slave is an opposite of the master. In spite of this, they are united with each other. There would be no master were there no slave and there would be no slave were there no master.

Between master and slave and slave and master, both an open and a hidden struggle continue. The slave would willingly take the place of the master but the latter cannot allow this to happen. From this comes oppression. One may, however, imagine that the slave has succeeded in revolt and from that moment the master becomes the slave. Does this revolt mean "revolution"? According to Hegel, no. There is no "revolution" at all in this case since everything moves along within one and the same scheme. "Revolution," in the Hegelian sense of the word, is a situation where the slave and the master achieve a "stoic" consciousness, where they become "indifferent," "neutral" and "unaware" of both their slavery and their mastery. "Revolution" is the achievement of a new level of liberation. "Revolution" is a transformation of consciousness that is simultaneously a transformation of reality. Slavery is not outside the human being but within. To "liberate" oneself, one must raise oneself above oneself.

In Marx, the idea of revolution undergoes simplification. Marx sees the human being from one angle only—the angle of one's relationship to the means of production, and thus from an angle that could be called the "possessive instinct." The root from which a human being grows within a human being is the consciousness of possessing. The owner of the means of production realizes a capitalist formula of being human, the one who is deprived of those means realizes a "proletarian" formula. The problem lies in this, however, that neither the one nor the other is capable of renouncing possession. The proletariat fight because they want to have the property of the capitalists. The capitalists fight because they do not want to be stripped of their property. According to Marx, the proletariat win. What does this mean? It means that the proletariat now occupy the place of the capitalists. I am not concerned at this point with the fact that the proletariat now do exactly what the capitalists did before. The issue is more subtle. I am interested that in their heart and soul, the proletariat "declare" themselves as the owners of the means of production. From one big capitalist are born many small ones. To Marx, the process has the form of a wheel. The axle of this wheel is the possessive instinct. The one who was at the bottom is on top; and the one on top is at the bottom. The idea of revolution loses its original sense. It is not a transformation of the human "soul" but a change of label.

In the nineteenth century, the concept of revolutionaries became synonymous with the concept of human beings who have the courage to sacrifice their lives on the altar of radical social change. Revolution was a threat to the established public order, an announcement of something new. Revolutionaries had their courage and their ethics. The principle of their ethics was "the end justifies the means." If there is no other way out, one must use force and coercion to change the social system. Here, I do not want to go into the question of whether and to what extent Marxism is responsible for that revolutionary "ethos." Marxism certainly approves this principle as the rule of action in particularly difficult situations. Certainly, not only Marxism brought forth "revolutionaries." They were born of other ideologies, other philosophies, and, above all, of the social system itself. I want to say something obvious: the revolutionary was at that time a threat to the existing social system, and as such found and still finds favor with the theoreticians of Marxism.

Originally, Marxism emphasized that "revolutionary" is, above all, a trait of the entire proletariat as a class. The proletariat as a social class occupy that place in society which enables them to know best the truth about the capitalist system. They are called upon to take the power from capitalists. It is the proletariat, only the proletariat, that are "revolutionary." When, however, Marx's expectations of an immediate outbreak of a world revolution of the proletariat did not come to pass; when it turned out that the proletariat are unable by themselves to undertake such a deed, it became necessary to organize "revolutionary parties" so that they could indicate what the proletariat should do. The adjective "revolutionary" was taken away from the class and assigned to the Party.

This adjective had yet one more meaning, but in this instance, rather, in the Russian milieu. A "revolutionary" was primarily the kind of person who, although not born to the proletariat, i.e., not a worker, ended up a "revolutionary" through an internal transformation, e.g., by participating in the October Revolution. Participation in the revolution purified a person from the original sin of an improper social origin. On this basis, for example, Feliks Dzierżyński[114] could become a "revolutionary."

After the outbreak of revolution and the stabilization of Soviet rule in Russia, the ideal of the revolution and the revolutionary was totally abandoned in that part of the world. The revolution had already had its day, the revolutionaries too. Now was the time for other heroes. Those heroes were to be the great "champions of work." The ideal of a "champion of work," however, stood in opposition not only to the ideal of a "revolutionary" but also to the ideal of a "comrade in work." The ideal of a "comrade in work" was born from life itself. It depicted the unity among those who worked in the same way, were equally exploited, and who fought in the name of one and the same hope. The basic privilege of a "comrade in work" was the right to solidarity. A comrade cannot betray his comrade. Betrayal is the gravest sin. Against this ideal and against the ideal of the "revolutionary" there arose the "champion of work."

It is very characteristic how the new ideal was to encompass the old, allegedly played out ideals. Nothing better illustrates this process of the transformation of meaning than Stalin's text in which he determines who "truly" is a revolutionary and who "truly" is a comrade in work. Stalin announced at the congress of Stachanovites:[115]

Stachanov's movement is that kind of movement of male and female workers that aims at exceeding current technical norms, projected production potentials, existing production plans and balances. Exceeding—because these very norms have already become outdated for our times, for our new people. This movement overturns the old views on technology, breaks the old technical norms, old projected production potentials, old production plans, and it demands the creation of new, higher technical norms, projected potentials and production plans. The movement is called upon to accomplish a revolution in our industry. Precisely for this reason this movement, Stachanov's movement, is at its foundation deeply revolutionary (Stalin 1949:457).

The revolutionary character of the new ethical ideal lies in the development of technical productive efficiency. The new hero of socialism produces better and more. He or she is an example for the rest of the workers. In this, however, there lies an ember of conflict with these workers. The hero becomes a tool for pressuring the other workers who produce less or worse. The bond of proletarian solidarity breaks down. "The hero of socialist work" stops being an honest and allied "comrade in work." The crumbling of the basic solidarity of working people is a sign of the growing exploitation of work.

Even after Stalin's death, the horizon of efficient, productive work still remained the pathway proposed to the youth for the development of their ethical personality. Although the emphasis was variously placed, the basic direction remained unchanged. This is apparent from the successive leaders of our Party.

As Bolesław Bierut[116] said (1952):

We should diligently and incisively acquire knowledge about the laws of social development, about the life of bygone generations. The task of our generation is to abolish once and for all the division into classes. . . . We should develop a championship of work, constantly increasing the qualifications to contribute to the economic blossoming of the Polish economy. . . . The great and loftiest task of our generation is the fight for science and knowledge to have the freest multifaceted access to the mind . . . in order that, while liberating the working people from exploitation, one also helps them to free themselves from centuries of slavery to superstitions. . . . The task of our generation is to defend peace before a conspiracy of the world's arsonists (Jasińska and Siemieńska 1978:238).

All the basic elements of the Marxist ethos appear in this speech: the struggle against exploitation, the fight against class division, the economic development of the country, access to knowledge, the struggle against imperialists and also against "centuries-old superstitions," i.e., religion. It is interesting that the idea of "struggle" occupies such an important place in the relatively brief text.

Gomułka (1958): "The leading task of a school should be the best preparation of its graduates for productive and socially useful work. . . . For the development of our country we need ever more numerous, highly qualified cadres capable of using modern technology" (Jasińska and Siemieńska 1978:248). The declaration by the Union of Socialist Youth, being created at that time, sketched an ideological picture of youth: "We are that part of the young generation that despite every disenchantment and doubt, carried from past years the deepest, rationally justified conviction that in today's world there is no better perspective than the socialist perspective: socialism free of deviations, of wrongdoing toward the ordinary individual and of wrongdoing toward nations; socialism built under conditions of freedom and democracy for the working people" (Jasińska and Siemieńska 1978:260). Yet, in this text, there are traces of doubt. It speaks, as is true, of doubts being overcome; nonetheless this overthrow is not final. The text lacks battle zeal. We accept socialism because we do not see anything better. It speaks also about the conditions of socialist construction: freedom and democracy. At the same time, attention is drawn to the statement: we want a socialism free of "wrongdoing toward the ordinary person." Why only the "ordinary person"? Did socialism not do wrong to others, e.g., the intellectuals? And further, we want a "democracy for the working people"—but not just simply democracy. And finally, the closing lines of the text refer to the economic ideal: "The struggle for the efficiency and productivity of human efforts, for a high quality of produced goods, for a frugal and rational economy, for harnessing an ever more perfect technology in the service of the working people—this is how we see our role in all the positions of our professional work" (Jasińska and Siemieńska 1978:251).

Edward Gierek[117] (1971):

We want each member of our party and each citizen of our country to become an active participant in this work, to find in it an area for initiative, for involvement . . . because the greatest social value is that way of thinking about the future from which everyone draws practical and constructive conclusions for improving one's work today and putting them into practice without waiting for the miraculous power of decisions from above. . . . Whether we achieve results commensurate with our needs and ambitions will depend on the stance of workers, farmers, economists. . . . Our party organizations will fulfill their task well only if they create those conditions under which social initiative will be fully utilized, and the wisdom and experience of workers, farmers, technicians, engineers, and economists will serve themselves as well as serving the needs of the whole country and our entire economy.

And further: ". . . the leading idea of the socioeconomic program that is presently being realized, the program of a higher stage of socialist construction, is the dynamic development of production forces, a systematic and multisided improvement in living conditions of the working people, the development of socialist social conditions and socialist culture" (Jasińska and Siemieńska 1978:262).

It is worthwhile to give attention to a few aspects of these passages. First of all, the text contains a paradox; there is an appeal for initiative but this initiative is to be triggered, protected and developed by the Party. Thus, it cannot be an initiative against the Party. The participation spoken of here consists of participation in the realization but not in the creation of the concept. The aggressive tone disappears and there is now less talk about struggle. But at the same time, there is no mention, at least when it concerns the "basic tasks," of ethical values. The major object of concern is "production forces." Further on in the text, especially in the resolution adopted, an optimistic conviction appears that youth basically accept socialism and its ideals. This means that the protests against socialization are being ignored. One must continue to imbue the young with the ideology of socialism since under the new conditions "when the major socioeconomic positions of the ownership class have been liquidated, the class struggle runs above all through the minds and hearts of the people" (Jasińska and Siemieńska 1978:264). It is significant that the struggle for control over the means of production passes into a struggle for control over hearts.

The ethical considerations of Marxists strike one as both formalistic and helpless. Marxism's ethical horizon is always the same: the key issue is mastery over the means of production to lead them to their full flowering and also mastery over socioeconomic relationships to adjust them to the level of the means of production. The Marxist revolutionary and Marxist "champion of work" act within the framework of the same horizon; the former acquires the means of production as his own, the latter makes possible their full development. Almost incidental to these activities, both achieve the full flowering of their humanity, which after all is also understood as a "production force" (in Sève's language—an "annex" to socioeconomic relationships). On the exploitation of work, one speaks here only in the context of the struggle with capitalism and its remnants. It should be emphasized that upon closer analysis, it turns out that none of the "ideals" of socialism exceeds this horizon. Even if the word used sounds universal, the content of the word is cut to fit the frontiers of socialization. From this come the formalism and helplessness.

The formalism appeared right at the very beginning. This means that we speak of how to do something but not of what to do. In the life of a Marxist, struggle plays a key role. We read in Sève, for example: "If anyone wishes actually to glimpse what Communist man will be, he should observe and think about the extrapolation of those changes which are brought about before our eyes in the active militants of the modern workers' movement . . . the militant life appears as the bearer of the future of the human personality" (Sève 1978:524). Thus, we have both an example and the essence of the matter. The example for us is the "leading worker activists." But which ones? French, Italian, Soviet? The essence of the matter is a "life of struggle." We are supposed to fight. But against whom and for what? One must know how to find one's enemy. The equivocation of the theory finds its complement in practice; we fight against kulaks, Zionists, clericalists, remnants of capitalism, against the racists in Africa, against American capitalists in defense of the American workers. We create for ourselves a mammoth illusion of struggle, an illusion of bravery, an illusion of victory. What is interesting, however, is that the same "ethics of struggle" calls simultaneously for a "struggle for peace" (i.e., a struggle to abandon the struggle), for respect of the rights of the oppressed, and for tolerance. For all that, we do not pose the essential questions: Who truly is obliged to disarm? Where is the source of the ideology of war? Who should stop the exportation of arms and revolution? Above all, who is obliged to respect the rights of the oppressed? Neither do we ask about the essence and extent of the exploitation of work in socialism, nor about a way to reconcile tolerance with severe censorship. There can be only one result of this method of practicing ethics: it confirms the fact that Marxist reflections on ethical issues are reflections of bad faith.

When one examines the register of the so-called "ideals of socialism," one readily notes that the register is internally contradictory. Some time ago, Kołakowski himself pointed this out as he took a further step forward in the direction of liberation from his own past.

Where are we now? What we lack in our thinking about society in socialist terms is not general values which we want to see materialized, but rather knowledge about how these values can be prevented from clashing with each other when put into practice and more knowledge of the force preventing us from

achieving our ideals. We are *for* equality, but we realize that economic organization cannot be based on equality of wages, that cultural backwardness has
a self-perpetuating mechanism that no institutional changes are likely to destroy
rapidly, that some inequalities are accounted for by genetic factors and too little
is known of their impact on social processes, etc. We are for economic democracy, but we do not know how to harmonize it with the competent running of
production. We have many arguments against bureaucracy and as many arguments for increasing public control over the means of production, i.e., for more
bureaucracy. We bemoan the destructive effects of modern technology and the
only safeguard against them that we know is more technology. We are for more
autonomy for small communities and more planning on the global scale, as if
no contradictions existed between these two slogans. We are for more learning
in the schools and more freedom for pupils, i.e., in practice, less learning. We
are for technical progress and complete security, i.e., immobility. We say that
people should be free in the pursuit of happiness and we pretend to know the
infallible criteria of happiness for everybody. We are against national hatred,
but there is more of it about than ever in human history. We maintain that
people should be considered as material beings, but nothing shocks us as much
as the idea that people have bodies: it means that they are genetically determined, that they are born, they die, they are young or old, men or women, and
that all these factors can play a role in social processes regardless of who owns
the means of production, and thus that some important social forces are not
products of historical conditions and do not depend on class division (Kołakowski
and Hampshire 1974:15–16).

The impression of helplessness appears when one must grasp ethical
problems from the viewpoint of concepts specific for ethics and not from
the viewpoint of economic or political concepts. One of these specifically
ethical concepts is the centuries-old concept of conscience. Significantly,
in the vast majority of dissertations on ethical themes which come from
the pens of Marxists, the concept of conscience generally does not appear. There is no concept of conscience in the works of the classic writers
of Marxism; in any event, it does not play a major role in them; there
is nothing of this concept in the major textbooks of Marxist philosophy
or even in the textbooks of Marxist ethics that are currently in use
in Poland. Therefore, one may call Marxist ethics an "ethics without
conscience."

There is some sign of helplessness in this. Marxists are unable to cross
the threshold of their own conceptual apparatus and to enter into concepts that do not belong to their system. Is this the fault of method or
of experience? Do Marxists lack ethical words or ethical experiences?
From this flows a profound uneasiness: considering the principle of the
unity of theory and practice, could not Marxist "ethics without conscience" also be the fertile soil on which "people without conscience"
could be born? I do not intend to offend anyone, especially those with

whom I am arguing. However, I wish that they, too, would understand the genesis of the questions posed to them and the genesis of the uneasiness that arises when one observes the world they are building. Is it only an accident, an unhappy coincidence, that in point of fact Marxism became the philosophy in our times which has so often served to justify acts of common cruelty? Was it not this philosophy that made possible and even inspired replacing the words "crime" and felony" with the words "error" and "deviation"?

14. Personalism and Marxism

After the war, numerous circles of Catholic intellectuals, already inspired in the interwar period by the works of Maritain, Mounier, and the group of intellectuals gathered around the monthly *Esprit,* were under the influence of French personalism. Maritain's thought had been known in Poland before the war, but only after the war did it bear fruit. His "integral humanism" became the basis of a Catholic dialogue with other currents of thought, among them Marxism. In spite of the fact that they considered themselves Thomists, Maritain and Mounier did not neglect, in contrast to Polish representatives of Thomism, the problem of Marxism, seeing in this philosophy a mighty social movement and an intellectual proposition worthy of attention. At the center of their thought stood the concept of the person and an ideal of the rights of a person. The human being is a self-existing substance composed of spirit and flesh, a responsible creator of history, a person open toward people and God. As a person, the human being possesses unique dignity, the dignity of a person. The personal character of human existence gives a human being particular rights. The rights of a human being are rooted in his person. The fundamental task of personalism is to defend the idea and rights of the person. One must demonstrate the superiority of the human being over the world, over history. Personalism did not intend to avoid a dispute with Marxism; Marxism could not silently bypass personalism. Confrontation appeared unavoidable.

Let us examine at least the most crucial moments of the dispute.

First, a few words on the "prehistory" of the dispute. In 1945–48, a series of articles by the Rev. Jan Piwowarcyzyk[118] appeared in Kraków's Roman Catholic weekly *Tygodnik Powszechny;* these articles were devoted to the current problems of the political system, in particular, the issue of a person's right to private property. The author defended the doctrine of the papal social encyclicals. He believed that this doctrine was still valid. The articles appeared on the eve of the great pressure by the authorities to collectivize agriculture, as well as of increasing totalitarianism. They represent a wise, clearly presented protest against what was happening. Naturally, it was a protest too weak to be effective. Still, it had the value of a witness; it provided evidence of the author's personal courage as well as of the existence of a different way of posing social issues. Both reached out to a searching youth. A great blow was dealt to the espoused doctrine on the person's right to private property by an essay of Józef Keller,[119] entitled "Problems of Property and Natural Law," that appeared in 1954 in the periodical *Zycie i Myśl.* In this essay, Keller demonstrated, in a scholarly manner, that the principle of private property is not based on a law of nature but constitutes a further interpretation of that law, an interpretation connected with the political conditions of modern economic systems. Thus, there is no reason why Catholics should not accept the Marxist solution. This dispute was not carried to a conclusion. Rather, it was resolved in practice. The year 1956 demonstrated the fiasco of compulsory collectivization of agriculture. Since then, the Marxists themselves have begun to tolerate "private initiative" and, within limits, have even promoted it here and there. The issue lost its importance, but was this loss justified?

A frontal attack on personalism occurred in 1953 and was repeated again in 1955. The author of the attack was Kołakowski, who began his philosophical career as a critic of Christian philosophy. His attacks on this philosophy had all the features of the Stalinist way of criticizing idealistic philosophy. Along with more or less substantive arguments appeared political accusations, insinuations, and denunciations. Let us examine some examples.

In 1953, Kołakowski wrote:

This brief and general characteristic . . . allows us to perceive that. . . . Thomistic personalism in particular is a sanctification and justification of the political practices of the Vatican. So understood, the defense of the "rights of the human being" offers what has to be a mystifying justification for, at the very least, the facts that the Vatican was the first to step forward with support for Hitler's butchers when the Nazis took power in Germany, that the Vatican was in favor of Hitler's aggression against the Soviet Union, that some Polish bishops served Hitler's occupation forces with lackey-like subservience, that the Vatican supports and glorifies the bestiality of British and French colonizers toward the heroic nations of Malaya and Tunisia.

And further:

In capitalist countries, Thomistic personalism serves to sanctify the rule of monopolistic capital. Toward the countries where the working class has won political power, the Vatican proponents of neo-Thomism use the phraseology of "personalism" to advance a demagoguery directed against socialist construction, against joint competition in work, and in defense of freedom for the people's enemies, spies, and agents of diversion (Kołakowski 1953:32–33).

The title of the article, "Neo-Thomism in Conflict with Science and Human Rights" ("Neotomizm w walce z nauką i prawami człowieka") published in (note well) the official Party periodical *Nowe drogi,* is significant.

In 1955, the same author wrote "The Rights of the Person against the Rights of the Human Being" ("Prawa osoby przeciwko prawom człowieka"). Here are selected fragments.

One must affirm that the collaboration of the workers' movement with Catholics can, of course, have as its basis a general recognition of human dignity and the rights of the human being in the struggle with the political and cultural degeneration of bourgeois society. However, such a basis cannot be formed by the principles of Christian personalism, which in its authentic version uses those principles in a deceitful and hypocritical manner. Personalism not only deprives those principles of their true sense, but gives them an entirely opposite meaning and subjugates them to the church's program and political tactics. There are various political views among Catholics but there is only one philosophical doctrine of Thomism, particularly where it is a matter of providing a philosophical justification for the actual political actions of the church's hierarchy (Kołakowski 1953:168).

The very definition of the person is the flaw in personalism.

Every consideration betrays the main goal of Catholic personalism: to construct the concept of the human being in such a way that the truly essential components of the "human being" are devoid of any social content. . . . The extrasocial concept of a human person is aimed, at least in Catholic doctrine, not only against the Marxist view of a human being, but also against the entire tradition of bourgeois humanism, against all materialistic, all lay concepts of the human being. The idea of personality is supposed not only to separate the individual from society and vest him with an illusory independence from its laws, but also to separate the individual from other individuals through the proclamation of the principle of the invincible irrationality of personal life, the principle of the incommunicability of the person. Mystical, Catholic monadology has to counterpose the "inexpressibility of existence" to a rationalistic conviction about the universal knowability of the world. . . . It is hard not to notice how easily an inexpressible, mystical content of personal existence can be fitted into the framework of Christian "intellectual humility". The problem of the liberation of the individual would now impose on us a solemn silence instead of a real effort at overcoming inhumane living conditions. Furthermore, the problem can be resolved with extraordinary simplicity by a proclamation that the human personality is a great metaphysical mystery (Kołakowski 1953:171–72).

However, we read further on:

But for all situations of mystery, Catholic doctrine has, as always, unfailing solutions; anything that is impossible for a human being finds an automatic solution in the depth of God's mind. The essence of personality can be neither expressed nor transferred to another because the essence of personality is not at all what constitutes it as autonomous and independent, but is really that which makes it subjugated and subservient—a personal union with the divine person. Autonomy and independence of the person exist only in relation to society. The mere thought about the autonomy of the human being in relation to the supernatural world evokes terror. The Catholic concept of the human being opposes the entire tradition of bourgeois humanism not because that tradition questions the social nature of human beings, but because the Catholic concept itself establishes this nature as ecclesiastical, sacral, sanctified; because it ultimately reduces the essence of a human being to submission to God, whose word the "human person" can hear from the pulpit or read in a papal proclamation (Kołakowski 1953:172–73).

And now the conclusion: "In the hands of the most reactionary social forces of the imperialistic world, Christian personalism is just an additional means that would halt the real liberation of humanity by pushing it into a world of fiction carefully cultivated for this purpose by the church—the major manufacturer of unreal illusions for the needs of a real antihuman world" (Kołakowski 1953:213).

At the time when this critique was being conducted, a close connection between theory and practice was in force. We expected that after those attacks, the Catholic University of Lublin[120] would be closed, that a ban would be issued against the teaching of Thomistic philosophy in the numerous seminaries. The prelude to this could have been the liquidation of the Theological Faculty of Jagiellonian University (1954) and the formation of the Academy of Catholic Theology in Warsaw. This Academy was intended to be the center of priestly education to meet the needs of the whole country, under close control of the state. But the fate of the country flowed in a different direction. The facade of Stalinism cracked. The Polish "October" came. Kołakowski experienced a shock. From then on, he would become an ever sharper critic of the system.

Does this mean that the earlier attacks against the church left no traces? A spirit of suspicion toward the church will persist in the circle of young "revisionists" for a long time. Liberated from one totalitarianism, they are afraid of falling under another. They already know that the accusation of individualism and monadism against the philosophy of personalism is a misunderstanding, but they still carry in their subconsciousness some trace of the old attacks; they still believe that the church wants to embrace them with its mighty arms and force them into obedience.

But then came the year 1956 and the first radical rejection of the process of socialization throughout the nation. This is not the place for a conclusive account of the Polish "October." But let us say what is essential. The Marxist thesis about the parallelism of the base and superstructure did not prove true. The superstructure liberated itself from the oppression of the base and travelled its own pathway. Literary works, films, works of graphic art appeared that had nothing in common with socialism and often violently attacked it. The Party came out with the concept of "errors and deviations." The socialist ideology is correct—only people are clumsy in putting it into life. Religion, too, was recognized as a part of the superstructure—but, somehow, nothing augured its disappearance. Not one of the Marxist theses on religion was confirmed in the history of socialism. Religion came out of the confrontation purified, strengthened, with great moral authority. Only now did it begin to pose a true problem for the Marxists.

In 1959, on the pages of *Studia filozoficzne,* which replaced *Myśl filozoficzna* of unhappy memory, an article appeared that touched on problems of personalism in the context of a discussion of several issues of the monthly *Więź,* a periodical of the Warszawa group of "personalists." The author of the discussion was Kuczyński, whose scholarly career was somewhat similar to that of Kołakowski: from fighting religion to sympathetic interest in it. In this discussion we read: "The significance of the periodical *Więź* extends beyond the sphere of the Catholic problematic. No doubt, the string of personalistic theses leads to social and moral postulates that coincide with those of Marxism. But for many intellectuals, and naturally this includes nonbelievers, personalism is more attractive, more 'Western,' and unblemished by the various sins of the past. Thus, I see for them the possibility of a personalist way to socialist involvement." And further: "Personalism in its present form—in spite of the fact that it is usually a Christian personalism—is a competitor of Marxism, even though the competition has no antagonistic political character. Besides, just such contact with a theoretical formulation of the problems of the person may benefit Marxist philosophy in the end. There is talk everywhere about the necessity for a broad consideration of these problems in Marxist theory; here is a perfect opportunity, even more, a necessity" (Kuczyński 1959:182) A marginal note: the chief editor of *Studia filozoficzne* at that time was—Leszek Kołakowski.

How did the subsequent history of the dispute between Marxism and personalism look?

One cannot give a clear answer to this question because the reality itself was not and is not clear. The dispute seemed to vanish in a fog, to dissolve in a flood of texts on the need, necessity and value of a dialogue between Christianity and Marxism, a dialogue on every topic of interest for a human being. The stage of history changed. After the "October shock" that opened the eyes of Marxists to Marxism, came the shock of Vatican Council II that opened their eyes to—Catholicism. No one is guiltless anymore—one side had the Inquisition while the other side had Stalinism. The difference is, however, that the Inquisition was a long time ago, while Stalinism arose in the twentieth century; and the numbers of corpses are disproportionate. It turned out that Marxism can be a means of oppression of human beings just as religion can be a means of their liberation. Marxists are slowly learning, from reading rather than from looking and listening; but nevertheless, in the end something gets through to them. A struggle with a religion which fills the churches with worshippers no longer makes any sense. Within Christianity there are factions closer to and further from the Marxists. One must now position oneself on the stage, as it were, in such a way that one is able to dance a polonaise[121] with at least some of them. The polonaise is the Polish national dance. It always unified opposing camps in a common step since it was not danced separately but in a procession of the whole assemblage, and the criteria for the selection of partners were not only gender but also height, dress, title, and participation in the struggles for liberation. A dance is obviously not a philosophy, but an invitation to dance may remind one of philosophy, if only because it is a form of dialogue. Thus, a dialogue was born—a strange dialogue in which philosophical words are uttered but in which philosophical questions are lacking.

A dialogue without philosophical questions but with the use of philosophical words, a dialogue of Marxist "shepherds of souls" with Catholic shepherds of souls—a typical dialogue of allusions, curtsies and winking eyes before dancing together—may have great political and even ethical significance (especially if one remembers what had gone on before), but it has not greater philosophical meaning. It should interest us as a phenomenon—a phenomenon that would not have taken place if our world were normal—but not as a proposition of thinking in the medium of truth. This dialogue, even at a distance, smells of political pragmatism. Always at some point, it turns out that the issue is for Catholics to defend the interests of socialization and for Marxists not to interfere with catechization, the construction of churches, religious processions, etc. I repeat, this is not without significance. The building of a space of freedom for dialogue with Christianity is also the

building of a space of freedom for the human being. In this way, however, one creates only the conditions for thinking, but thinking itself is
not yet awakened. Having this in mind, I will try to characterize that
particular phenomenon.

One thing above all strikes us: the representatives of Marxist philosophy devote disproportionately large space to those trends of thought
in Christianity that do not have very great significance in themselves.
French personalism is a phenomenon whose historical role has already
ended. In its time it undoubtedly influenced the direction of the interest
in the contemporary world among Christians; it was a convenient bridge
between the church and the factory, but it did not stamp a deep impression on Christian theology, *sensu stricto*. Jean Lacroix,[122] one of the
leaders of the movement, held that personalism was an inspiration rather
than a philosophy or theology. Today, personalism has played itself out
and other philosophies of the human being are saying more and deeper
things about the human being. Other thinkers today, however, attest
the greatness of Christian thought better than the representatives of its
"official" current. Today, we look at the problems of Christianity with
the eyes of Henri Bergson,[123] Gabriel Marcel,[124] Ricoeur, Max Scheler,[125]
and Heidegger or even St. Augustine and St. Thomas Aquinas,[126] rather
than their commentators. We are living in a time of a return to the
sources, but the Marxists do not sense that. Even if they no longer see
religion through the prism of the concept of "opium," they are still
unable to see it through the prism of extremely fundamental issues and
authors.

I repeat again, what they are doing is not without significance. Despite
this, however, they definitely devote too much effort to examining and
describing the disciples and too little to understanding the masters.
Hence the distortion of the picture of religion, Christianity, theology.
Hence their ridiculous pains and ridiculous satisfactions. From the condition of two shingles on the roof, they manage to draw conclusions
about the condition of the house and even of the entire city.

Another significant trait of the dialogue is the need to emphasize the
role of Marxism in the transformation of Christian thought. In his soul
the Marxist bears the consciousness of an inferiority complex. It so
happens that, somehow, the Marxist can be neither an authentic philosopher, i.e., independent in all respects, nor a consistent political
activist; neither a committed patriot nor a committed cosmopolite. His
love for the Soviet Union can know no bounds, neither can his refusal
to love it. Contrary to appearances, the Marxist can really do very little.
His destiny is compromise, his art is the art of the slalom. The Marxists
in Poland have also had no success with religion. Since they cannot say
that Marxism "abolished" religion, they prefer to say that it led to the

transformation of religion. In this way it appears that they are, after all, worth something. Here is a small example in which it is alleged that Marxism caused an increased interest of the church in the philosophy of work.

The adaptation of the church's interpretation of work to the mentality of the modern human being, the ennobling of work on the basis of church doctrine, belated but with a neophyte's zeal, primarily benefited the interests of the church itself by creating the basis for strengthening bonds between the church and believing workers, and enabling the initiation of a dialogue with nonbelievers. This in turn has its social significance inasmuch as the church and religious doctrine is a significant educational force.

Thorough analysis of the theology of work allows one to notice the borrowings from Marxism. The ideologues of Catholicism are unable to question either the avant garde role of the Marxist philosophy of work or the accuracy of its scientific determinations. They must acknowledge the soundness of the thesis about the role of work in anthropogenesis. They must accept the thesis about its role in the self-creation of the human being's personality. They cannot reasonably question the establishment of associations between the depersonalizing or personalizing character of work in dependence on the social relationships in which the work takes place. They cannot even question the sense of the idea of the liberation of work through a change of social relationships and the realization of conditions of human freedom. The protest against Marxism is more and more reduced to a statement that Marxism, by assigning to work the role of a decisive factor in the self-creation of the human person, impoverishes the personality by negating its transcendent sources (Mysłek 1977:122).

The author of the above text neglects a few rather important details. First, the Christian theology of work has a sense which is generally the opposite of the Marxist philosophy of work. In Christianity, the dignity of human work stems from the dignity of the person, while in Marxism the entire person arises from work. In addition, if the church in contemporary Poland becomes involved in the issues of work, it does so not only to unveil the value of work for a nation of workers (laziness was always considered a capital sin), but also, and even above all, to protest against the socialist exploitation of work. In his analysis, the author neglects major texts on this issue, for instance, the letters of the episcopate. I do not know whether this circumstance will give the author great satisfaction.

The third feature in the dialogue is its, I would say, "pastoral" character. This is a paradox—but the Marxists themselves don pastoral vestments. They address the nation as great, historical "shepherds of souls." They have set out to formulate great, historical projects for the Polish tomorrow. The talent for planning is visible at each step: the world has been explained long enough, one must change it. Planning is a lay form of prophecy that verifies itself—note well—no more often than prophecy does. We know well that the realization of plans and prophecies does not depend on the planners and prophets. Hence, an appeal to all sides to take part in the play becomes necessary. The polonaise is, after all, a social dance. From time to time, the admission of guilt because of a cloudy past is likewise voiced. This, after all, also fits within the "pastoral" convention since a good shepherd beats his own breast.

Here is an example of such a text—perhaps a little bit too long, but this is not my fault.

For the many years of my polemics with Catholicism, I questioned the right of this intellectual system to use the name of humanism. In this I was guided, above all, by a concern for the precision of terms: humanism in the history of Europe, beginning with Protagoras[127] and through the Renaissance and Kant,[128] had a decidedly anthropocentric orientation in its deepest, most precise philosophical works. For that reason I thoroughly rejected Maritain's well-known position, expressed in *Integral Humanism (Humanisme intégral; problèmes temporels et spirituels d'une nouvelle chrétienté)*, which recognized only theocentrism as the rightful heir to humanism. I rejected this position regardless of my esteem for the sociodemocratic tendencies of this work. During the war, this work inspired the heroic struggle of Polish Catholics and wide circles of our youth in general against the occupier. Still in the 1950s I wrote in *Po prostu*, in the course of a discussion of, among other things, the heroic attitude and death of Father Kolbe, that humanistic motivation may appear, to some extent independently, alongside Christian motivation.

Today, I must admit that in this regard I have changed my mind: theoretically and practically, Christianity can be humanism. It can also be recognized as a humanistic current from the viewpoint of Marxist anthropocentrism. I became convinced by three basic facts:

(a) The evolution of Catholic positions during the construction of a humanistic society in Poland. This is a phenomenon that still needs theoretical generalization, especially in the sphere of the daily attitudes of believers, their civic and humanistic involvement.

(b) The basic transformations in Christian doctrine that date from Vatican Council II and the work of John XXIII,[129] and their subsequent development and deepening by Paul VI.[130]

(c) The development of philosophical thought, Catholic and Protestant alike, especially the works of Teilhard de Chardin,[131] the theology of work, liberation, revolution, etc.

Something great, something historic is happening in the Christianity of our days; something great is happening in Polish Catholicism. One should welcome this with the greatest interest and respect. And it is now our common duty to the country to transform this theoretical meeting of the two humanisms, their philosophical world–focused contradictions, into a great, creative sociocultural force. Let each humanism confirm its anthropological and historical theses in a practical, constructive rivalry for the common good of society, for building a truly humanistic society. The process of sociomaterial concretization should become a criterion of credibility for each humanism (Kuczyński 1978:62).

Continuing the thought that "something great is happening in Polish Christianity," the author wrote in connection with the election of Karol Cardinal Wojtyła as pope:

Through the election of a citizen of a socialist country, the experiences of a new social formation, which are both great and at the same time up till now often difficult for the church, become a daily matter in the Vatican. This is, above all, the levelling of the church and its opening to history that, especially since Vatican Council II, has been taking place behind the "Bronze Gate" [formal entrance to Vatican City—translators' note]. Let us say from the start: the College of Cardinals rose (at last) to the task of responding to the contemporary world in a proper way—they acknowledged, in spite of everything and in spite of all their differences—the growing power of the leading social force of our epoch. They also recognized the necessity for the social unification of humanity by noticing the surely decisive role of socialism in this very dramatically complex process of the integration of the societies on the earth, a process that today brings evil as well as the highest hopes (Kuczyński 1979:196)

Once again, I emphasize: all this is not without significance. As Catholics needed the footbridge stretching from the church to the factory that the personalists strove to build, Communists too need gangplanks from the Party office to—well, at least to the sacristy, if not, naturally, directly to the high altar. It is well that people are found to put up these footbridges. I know that this is not easy work and it is even less thankful. Nonetheless, it is not true, as alleged, that Polish Catholic youth fought the occupier even to the slightest degree as a result of the influence of Maritain and his concept of integral humanism. The discovery that Christianity can be a humanism is not really a great discovery for someone who knows how to observe. It is not true that the posture of involvement in the social and economic life of the country that Catholics displayed is thereby an avowal of socialism, and the entire process of socialization. Nor is it true that the election of the pope is an achievement of socialism since the truth is that this election testifies to the defeat of socialization in Poland.

One more thing about the context of the first statement that emphasizes the humanistic elements of religion. Actually, this statement is nothing but the text of a speech at the general convention of an atheistic organization called the Society for the Propagation of Lay Culture, that has as its task the spread of atheist and laicist positions. During this meeting the "improvement of methods" of laicization and atheization was discussed. Kuczyński's statement was also meant to serve this aim. Thus, again, the context determined the merits of the text. The text was like, as sometimes happens, the delight of a gardener in the beauty of—weeds.

Finally, one last characteristic: the political way of assessing religious and philosophical phenomena. Political categories are still the ultimate ones for understanding cultural phenomena; only the principle has changed. In Stalin's time, the primary principle of interpretation was the assumption of the hostility of religion and Christianity toward Marxism. Today, an assumption of agreement, solidarity, and unity is in force. Kołakowski was under the influence of the first principle and for that reason, when writing about personalism, he saw imperialism and a conspiracy of warmongers behind it. Kuczyński is under the influence of the second principle and for that reason, he sees in personalism an interesting and instructive expression of humanism. Another influential author, Tadeusz Jaroszewski,[132] is also under the influence of the second principle; hence he writes: "Mounier's type of Christian personalism creates certain possibilities for dialogue and collaboration of Catholics with Marxists in the struggle against Fascist and neocapitalist tendencies, in the struggle for full democracy, and also in the struggle for the realization of the social, political and economic demands of the revolutionary workers' movement" (Jaroszewski 1970:517). But one is interested in something else: why do the principles of interpretation change? If politics governs the principles of interpretation of cultural phenomena, then what governs politics?

In response to an internal need to develop a philosophy of the human being, several more or less independent works appeared in Poland outside the main current of dialogue. The authors of these works were again Marxists as well as Christians. The Marxists' works are branded by the recent polemic with Schaff's "philosophy of the human individual," as evidenced by their critiques of the concept of alienation, of "abstract bourgeois humanism," of the idea of the incomprehensibility of the intimate sphere of the human being, and by their emphasis on the role of social work in the creation and development of the human being. The works of Christian thinkers do not, of course, have these problems, but in them too, the active aspect of the human person and its multiform rooting in the community will be emphasized. Of the Marxists' works, two stand in the forefront: Jaroszewski's *Personality and Community* (*Osobowość i wspólnota*) and Kuczyński's *Man the Creator* (*Homo creator*). Established in the forefront of the works inspired by Christian personalism are those of Karol Cardinal Wojtyła, *Person and Deed* (*Osoba i czyn*), and Krąpiec's *I—A Human Being* (*Ja—człowiek*). One must admit that the works of the personalists elicit greater interest among Marxists than the works of the Marxists among representatives of Christian philosophy. Cardinal Wojtyła's work has been widely reviewed and Krąpiec's work also evoked rather widespread echoes, whereas the works of Jaroszewski and Kuczyński are generally ignored.

In the circles of Christian philosophers, there is the conviction that after the disputes with Schaff and Kołakowski, nothing interesting is happening in Marxism. Perhaps the pattern of emphasis is slightly different, but the principles remain the same. This conviction is confirmed by the very manner in which Marxists conduct a philosophical analysis. The Marxists lack intellectual curiosity, or a sense for stating the question in issues which they perceive to be simple; they lack conceptual precision—in short, they lack philosophical craftsmanship. One who really wants to philosophize reaches for other texts and other thinkers.

What characterizes the works of the Christian thinkers? Let us linger a moment over the work of Karol Cardinal Wojtyła. This work evolved from a double inspiration—Thomism and phenomenology. From Thomism, the author took the conviction that the human person is a self-existing as well as spiritual being, which means that the human person is basically indestructible. "The force of being" of a person is incomparably greater than "the force of being" of any other thing. Thus, a person cannot be a creation of work, but must be its source and master. But work is not an accidental attribute of a person. Through work—to be more exact, through deeds—persons actualize themselves. A deed is an act of a person. Thanks to deeds, persons acquire confirmation of their internal unity. In addition, the person enters into numerous associations with the world—with other people, with objects, with God. The person "has" the world. But the main problem of a person is not "to have" but "to be."

Although the author wrote a systematic work and touched upon many issues only lightly, without going into detail, this is enough to show the richness of the human being. This work did not develop from the need for dialogue with Marxism. It developed, rather, from a need to witness, witness to the human person as that which is more fully a being than anything else and also the most in need of affirming its own identity. To give testimony does not preclude dialogue, but it is something much more. The book differs from those of the Marxists not only in content but also in its ethical dimension.

Another work developed from similar sources—a particular work that is not mentioned in the context of philosophical writings, but which nonetheless belongs, in my opinion, to the highest achievements of Polish postwar thought about the human being. I have in mind the life's work of Antoni Kępiński[133]—extraordinary psychiatrist, sage and thinker. Kępiński did not consider himself a philosopher and did not participate in the disputes between Marxists and Catholics. Kępiński observed people, treated them. For his medical art, he developed his own vision of the human person, rooted not only in the achievement of the positive sciences but also in philosophy, as well as in something that we may call the "Christian ethos." His human beings are human beings with broad spiritual horizons, human beings as open toward other human beings as they are toward the external world and toward themselves. The essential property of their internal nature is a capacity for "informational metabolism," i.e., the incessant exchange of information with the surrounding world. The basic principle that governs the informational metabolism is the principle of truth. "To be in truth" is the main task of the human being. Disturbances of the informational metabolism express themselves in various forms; one sees their traces in schizophrenia, in neurosis, in psychopathy. The human being of Kępiński calls for truth; the desire for truth is his main hunger. Kępiński assimilates philosophical and ethical concepts into psychiatric thinking about human beings. He speaks of a need for morality, for truth, a need to abandon falsehood and equivocation. He speaks of the right to search freely for the meaning of life, to drop one's mask, to live in a human environment. Kępiński's scientific work contains numerous elements of criticism of the living conditions in our country. In Kępiński's patients, one can read several truths about the sad problems of our daily life. Kępiński's work is also a form of witnessing. On the one hand, it testifies to the tragic lot of a human being among people. The pulpit from which he speaks also has a profoundly ethical character. The author testifies to the human being not only as a physician but also as a sensitive Christian.

Thus, anyone in Poland today who wants to learn the secret of the human being, anyone who wants better to understand himself or herself, reaches for other than Marxist works and for other testimonies. It is always better to drink from pure springs.

15. The Dispute about Principles of Dialectical Materialism

To begin with, I shall recall forgotten matters. A concise exposition of principles of dialectical materialism, first presented by Stalin and then expanded by commentators on his ideas, in our country mainly by Schaff and Władysław Krajewski,[134] asserted that the nucleus of dialectics can be summarized in four theses: (1) nature is a cohesive whole in which things and phenomena are associated with each other, dependent upon each other, and mutually conditioned by each other; (2) nature is in a state of constant motion, development, and transformation; (3) quantitative changes prepare for and pass into a qualitative leap (quantity changes into quality); and (4) internal discrepancies are contained in the objects and phenomena of nature, and the essence of development is to overcome them (the law of the unity and conflict of opposites). The above theses of materialistic dialectics were the framework for views on the character of nature and no discovery of the positive sciences could negate them. On the contrary, it was expected to confirm them.

Rev. Kłósak undertook a critique of the principles of dialectical materialism. He was a disciple of Rev. Michalski and also a graduate of the Catholic University of Louvain. He taught Christian philosophy at the Theological Faculty of Jagiellonian University. During his studies at Louvain, he acquired a stance of broad openness toward the achievements of the contemporary positive sciences. He belonged to that group of Thomists that strove to enter into a deeper dialogue with the achievements of the natural sciences in order to confront, among other things, the results of those sciences with the basic concepts and principles of St. Thomas Aquinas's philosophy. Kłósak was one of the first Christian philosophers in Poland to defend the consistency of evolutionism with Catholic doctrine. He declared himself in favor of the possibility of spontaneous generation, he submitted to criticism the proof of God's existence from motion by claiming, in accordance with modern physics, that motion belongs to the essence of matter (later, he modified his views). His excellent command of the results of the positive sciences evoked universal respect for his works. The very same circumstance made his position particularly close to that of the Marxists who, in those times, also sought support for their theses in the achievements of the positive sciences. The conflict between the positivistic dimension of Rev. Kłósak's thought and that of the Marxists proved unavoidable. Indeed, a conflict erupted in the form of a dispute about the principles of dialectical materialism, i.e., about the principles of the interpretation of natural world phenomena (by strange coincidence, historical materialism found itself beyond the reach of the Catholics' interest).

In 1948, *Dialectical Materialism* (*Materializm dialektyczny*) appeared, in which Kłósak focused on criticism of Schaff's materialism. He though that the theory of materialistic monism is internally contradictory, that the theory of the unity of concept and word is incorrect. In this way, he defended the distinction between spirit and matter. He also dealt with the views of the dialectical materialists on the essence of matter, motion and the theory of evolution. He returned several times to those problems. Thus, on the pages of two consecutives issues of *Przegląd powszechny,* he discusses the dialectical law of the total dependence of things and phenomena. In *Znak,* he writes about a dialectical law of the motion of matter and about the division of philosophical currents in Marxism. Similar topics are to be found also in the pages of *Tygodnik Powszechny.*

We shall not summarize particular critiques here, but shall turn our attention to the method itself. Kłósak tries to demonstrate that the achievements of the positive sciences are generally in disagreement with the views of dialectical materialists or agree only in part. In any case, when the dialectical materialists claim that they are authentic exponents of the spirit of science, they commit a kind of usurpation because the positive sciences are factors that support the religious position to the same extent as the materialist one. The positive sciences do not contradict a religious posture. Here is a conclusion directed against Schaff's interpretation of the theory of evolution, a conclusion that is an example of such a critique: "As the result of our critical considerations, we come to the conclusion that the superiority of the dialectical theory of evolution, as pronounced by Professor Schaff, over the traditional theory of evolution is an illusion. This illusion stems either from insufficient knowledge of the results of the contemporary, relatively newest learning, or from wandering over the path of pseudoscientific understanding about some magical transformations" (Kłósak 1948:117). And another example: "It is not true that the dialectical law of the unity and conflict of opposites is applicable to all objects and to all processes that take place in the sphere of inanimate nature . . . after all, from the fact that the unity of opposites finds confirmation in some physical phenomena, it does not follow at all that such a unity of opposites is present in every physical phenomenon" (Kłósak 1949:163).

The influence of this critique on the contemporary Catholic intelligentsia was enormous. As I have said, this intelligentsia was totally unprepared for an intellectual confrontation with Marxism. Its philosophical consciousness was weak, its ability to operate with scientific arguments was limited. There was no place to draw this knowledge, no source from which to learn. The articles of Rev. Kłósak constituted the only attempt at polemics. Even though not everything in them was clear, the basic result remained: an awareness that one could pursue the positive sciences without thereby being a Marxist, indeed while openly subscribing to Catholicism.

Originally, the Marxists did not reply. When attacked, Schaff remained silent. Only here or there, in new editions of his *Introduction to the Theory of Marxism* (*Wstęp do teorii marksizmu*), did he change the examples illustrating the consistency of science with dialectics. In 1951 and 1954, Kołakowski replied. He wrote "The Methodology of Rev. Kłósak" ("Metodologia Księdza Kłósaka," a review of *Dialectical Materialism* in *Myśl filozoficzna*, 1951) and "Frolics with the Devil" ("Igraszki z diabłem," in *Po Prostu*, 1954). In the first reply, we read among other points: "I wish to draw attention to the amazing manner of argumentation that we find in this work and to the equally amazing lack of knowledge of the theory against which the author (Kłósak) generally intends to enter the lists." Kołakowski criticizes the point of departure of Kłósak's considerations, the so-called "immediate critical realism"; he questions Kłósak's thesis that the very same realism also characterizes Marxist epistemology. This is significant: Kołakowski could not suffer positivism and thus prefers that one not see a positivist epistemology in Marxism. But Kłósak criticized Schaff and the latter held an opinion different from Kołakowski's on this point. The review of Kłósak's work shows that the paths of Schaff and Kołakowski are already different. Further on, Kołakowski writes:

It is known that for the positivists, to whom Father Kłósak's appeals readily (Duhem[135] and particularly LeRoy[136]), it was a matter of so limited a competency in their scientific knowledge as to leave a wide enough field for fantasizing by religious obscurantists. Since scientific methods, naturally, cannot lead us to the knowledge of relationships that take place in the reality of objects, one needs other, extrascientific, in particular mystic paths to comprehension. No wonder then that defenders of the faith readily and often reach for his positivistic argumentation in the belief that citing names of individuals who are often very authoritative in the field of natural sciences has the power to convince the readers that the very poor philosophy of those authorities also has all of modern learning behind it (Kolakowski 1953:247).

On the margin of this and other similar disputes, Father Kłósak wrote:

In connection with the denial of scientific traits to Christian philosophy, I submit, as professor and vice-dean of the Faculty of Christian Philosophy at the Academy of Catholic Theology in Warsaw, a strong protest against the language with which Henryk Holland and particularly Leszek Kołakowski speak of representatives of the aforementioned philosophy or this philosophy itself—against the careless, tactless, abusive, and tumidly disdainful language in which are wrapped expressions like "philosophical castle of darkness", "Catholic obscurantism", "black army of obscurantism and reaction", "openly pietistic philosophy", "Bible-thumping". I protest against the language in which we even find such statements as "Thomism is the *direct* defender of the darkest obscurantism, the *direct* apologist for all mental backwardness and the instrument of a *direct* struggle by the most regressive social forces against the ideology of the revolutionary movement" (Kołakowski), or that the sense of Thomist philosophy rests on "metaphysical arguments that are to incline us to obeisance toward a supernatural society or toward the agency of imperialism that is presented as the *corpus mysticum*" (Kołakowski). One may criticize us substantively, but one may not offend us. It is difficult, after reading Leszek Kołakowski's article "On the So-called Thomist Realism" ("O tak zwanym realizmie tomistycznym") in *Myśl filozoficzna*, 1954, 188–227, not to repeat what Tadeusz Kotarbiński wrote in connection with the article by Holland, "The Legend about Kazimerz Twardowski" ("Legenda o Kazimierzu Twardowskim"). The Editorial Committee of *Myśl filozoficzna* is co-responsible for these extravagancies. How can one permit polemics to be conducted in this manner? Such an article likewise repels the serious reader from what is being argued in it, and in addition, decreases the journal's respectability (Kłósak 1956:89).

Putting our review of those disputes in perspective, one has to say that:

(a) Kłósak's works had a great influence on the Polish intelligentsia of those times, especially those who were associated with the world view of the positive sciences, and made it possible for them to remain truly and emotionally within Catholicism without simultaneously resigning their scientific positions.

(b) The significance of Kłósak's works for Marxism was less, since it turned out that dialectical materialism as a whole is, in Marxism, a secondary and later creation that appeared as a result of the dialogue between Marxism and positivism; that only Stalinism ascribes a larger significance to this part of Marxism; after 1956, the four theses of dialectics had already ceased to be presented as the basic theses of Marxism.

(c) However, the awareness that there is no contradiction between religious theses and the achievements of the positive sciences was fixed in Marxist circles only after the great reception of the thought of Teilhard de Chardin in Poland, a reception that occurred later but for which Kłósak himself, to some extent, prepared the ground by his works on evolutionism and on Teilhard de Chardin.

To complete the picture, I shall once again bring in Kołakowski's view, this time from his latest work, *Main Currents of Marxism* (*Główne kierunki marksizmu*), written after breaking with Marxism. What is his view today of the "dialectics" of those days?

Kołakowski writes:

Among the truisms are such "laws of dialectic" as the statement that everything in the universe is somehow related, or that everything changes. No one denies these propositions, but they are of very little cognitive or scientific value. The former statement has, it is true, a certain philosophical bearing in other contexts, for example, the metaphysics of Leibniz[137] or Spinoza,[138] but in Marxism–Leninism it does not lead to any consequences of cognitive or practical importance. Everyone knows that phenomena are interconnected, but the problem of scientific analysis is not how to take account of the universal interconnection, since this is what we cannot do, but how to determine which connections are important and which can be disregarded. All that Marxism–Leninism can tell us here is that in the chain of phenomena there is always a "main link" to be grasped. This seems to mean only that in practice certain connections are important in view of the end pursued, and others less important or negligible. But this is a commonplace of no cognitive value, as we cannot derive from it any rule for establishing the hierarchy of importance in any particular case. The same is true of the proposition that "everything changes": cognitive value attaches only to empirical descriptions of particular changes, their nature, tempo, etc. Heraclitus's[139] aphorism had a philosophical meaning in his day, but it soon sank into the category of commonsense, everyday wisdom.

The fact that truisms like these are represented as profound discoveries, known from no other source, led the adherents of Marxism–Leninism to proclaim that Marxism was confirmed by "science". Since the empirical and historical sciences are concerned generally with the fact that something changes or that it is connected with something else, it is safe to assume that each new scientific discovery will confirm the truth of "Marxism" as thus understood (Kołakowski 1978:152).

16. The Dialogue of Threefold Involvement

The search for planes common to Christianity and Marxism reached its relatively farthest extent in the ideology of the "socially progressive movement of lay Catholics PAX." The PAX movement, called to life immediately after the war by Bolesław Piasecki,[140] belongs to the particularly controversial and singular phenomena of our social life. It was conceived as a bridge between the new authorities and the church. Its goals were both theoretical and practical. The search for common plans between Marxism and Christianity required, by the nature of the situation, a new reading of the traditions of ideas on both sides. As is known, these traditions were thus far hostile to each other. The aim was to draw them closer for the good of the entire nation. The theoreticians of the PAX movement had to undertake the task of being the "classic thinkers," often exceeding their capabilities in the process; they had to "correct" Marxism for the Marxists and Catholicism for the Catholics. The theoretical activity was primarily a consequence of Marxists and Catholics actually sharing each other's life and work. Whether this shared life and work needed theoretical justification is another matter. The ideologues of the Pax movement believed that such a justification was needed and called it "Christian inspiration in building socialism." However, the movement's practical cooperation with the government and the church turned out to be more important than ideology. The PAX movement defined itself as the "ally of the Party" and this carried with it various practical consequences such as active support for the collectivization of farming in Stalinist times or participation, also in those times, in the action of pitting the clergy against the episcopate. The principles of alliance did not preclude attempts at maneuvering and even some opposition, but these attempts did not play any greater social role. Rather the principle "the enemy of my ally is my enemy" was binding.

There is no space here to describe the entire activity of PAX and its genealogy. The political activity of PAX met with sharp criticism immediately after the famous "October" of 1956. In the political struggle going on at that time, Piasecki, the movement's leader, definitively threw his support behind the so-called "Natolin group" that opposed those who then favored renewal. This evoked a storm of attacks against PAX and its chairman from the supporters of liberalization. One can find those attacks printed in *Życie i myśl* (Nos. 4–5, 1956). In a certain sense, this criticism was continued in the work of Andrzej Micewski,[141] entitled *To Co-Rule or Not to Lie* (*Współrządzić, czy nie kłamać*, Paris: Libella, 1978). Micewski himself had earlier been a member of the ruling body of the PAX association. A general assessment of the movement is contained in the title; PAX, in exchange for its admission to participation in ruling, however minimal, agrees to a lie. Micewski touches on the essential issue for a movement that defines itself as Catholic—the issue of moral image. This issue was earlier poised on a razor's edge, when Piasecki's book entitled *Essential Issues* (*Zagadnienia istotne*) and consisting of articles from 1945–54, was placed on the Index of forbidden books by the Apostolic See. At the very same time, the movement's weekly, *Today and Tomorrow* (*Dziś i jutro*), was also placed on the Index, and because of this the periodical was renamed *Directions* (*Kierunki*).

Independently of these critiques, in the living memory of many clergy and also writers and lay Catholic activitists, there are preserved especially painful incidents from the Stalinist period when the people of PAX, shoulder to shoulder with the secret security forces, joined in forcing Catholics to participate in the Party's propagandistic actions. PAX's alliance with the Party thereupon assumed the character of an alliance between PAX and a police apparatus of oppression. These memories are difficult to erase. For a long time, they cast a shadow upon the later declarations of the PAX association about fidelity to the church.

But PAX's activity did not end with this. PAX is also a huge, living and multifaceted publishing movement. The people of the association put a great effort into cultural publishing activities. Among titles of the Pax Publishing Institute were numerous theological, philosophical, religious, historical books and works in the area of literature without which Polish Christian culture would certainly be much poorer. For a long time, PAX had a publishing monopoly on Catholic literature in Poland. One must admit that PAX utilized this monopoly very well. No one with common sense questions this aspect of the association's activity.

However, we are concerned with philosophy and what is directly associated with it. Let us then pass over, as much as possible, the issues of practice and look at some aspects of the ideology of PAX. PAX's ideology is an example of a dialogue, the plan for which was initiated by the Party and not by Catholics. Anyone who wants to know what the Party understood as a dialogue with Christianity should look at the PAX movement. This does not mean, of course, that the movement did not enjoy some independence in relation to the Party, but this was independence "granted by someone else." The key word in the Party's dialogue plan was the word "ally." The association was to gather Catholics and make of them devoted "allies" of the Party. For that, an ideology was needed. Even though some theses of that ideology could be varied, nonetheless the principle of alliance had to perdure.

Thus, everything hung on the hook of "alliance." This meant that PAX was supposed to be an ally of the Party, but the Party did not have to be an ally of PAX. The PAX association was not included in the so-called "allied groups and parties," as were the Peasant Party and the Democratic Party.[142] The principle of the equality of rights was preempted first by the theory of dictatorship of the proletariat and then by the theory of the "leading role of the Party." The Party defined itself as the spokesman of the most progressive social class, the proletariat. The proletariat exercised its revolutionary dictatorship through the Party. The Party was the key, the center, the principle. The proletariat, as a social class, was important as long as its intentions found approval in the Party. This point of Marxist–Leninist doctrine became the principle of PAX's ideology. When the Party liberalized itself or weakened, PAX liberalized itself; when the Party moved toward the principle of force, PAX had to keep pace.

The principle of alliance brought with it certain consequences. The primary consequence, emerging in times of crisis, was indecisiveness—which side to take, the Party's side or the side of the proletariat in agitation against the Party. The moral and conceptual conflict of the Marxists became a conflict for Catholics due to the principle of alliance. The question emerged: Where then is "political infallibility"? Marx said: "The instinct of the working class is infallible." In December 1970, the proletariat set fire to the buildings of the Party committees. Perhaps under these circumstances the political "instinct of the Party" is infallible instead. The ideology of the "ally of the Party" a priori provided the answer to this type of doubt. The PAX movement, in spite of socialist phraseology, stands in no direct relation to the consciousness of the working class, but sees it through the symptoms observed in the Party. PAX's inspiration is not the Marxist concept of the working class but rather the Leninist concept of the Party.

The doctrinal conflict with the Church has its beginning at this point. The conflict is more fundamental than it appears to be. The church in Poland increasingly realized its responsibility for the basic values of the human person, its freedom, dignity, and autonomy. Thus, the church stood ever more sharply in doctrinal opposition to every dictatorship and hence to the dictatorship of the Communist Party as well. The church in Poland did not declare this opposition directly but indirectly, emphasizing the importance of autonomous human values and the autonomy of the person versus the state. One can seek various forms of understanding and cooperation with a dictatorship in certain areas of life, but one cannot speak of an "alliance," since alliance means acceptance and sometimes submission. For PAX the theoretical situation was not an easy one. The solution was to apply a concept, but without analyzing its meaning.

The ideology of PAX thus swung from two unsteady hooks. Marxists could have accused PAX of betraying the primary doctrine of Marx, while the church could have accused it of failing to understand the spirit of Christian social ethics. But such disputes never occurred within PAX. Merely posing the questions could have turned out to be suicidal.

Let us return to the idea of involvement. The task of the movement was to create conditions for a patriotic, socialistic, and world-conscious involvement of Catholics. Catholics should come from the periphery of social life and take their place among the builders of socialism. What does that "involvement" mean?

Involvement encompassed several things. First of all, one had to submit to proper interpretation the general doctrine of the relation of Catholics to earthly realities. This interpretation was carried out by Piasecki himself. Here are some of his texts.

The Catholic religion proclaims that God is the Master of the world under two aspects, as Creator and as Savior. Christian thought preoccupied itself with the act of salvation while clearly neglecting the act of creation. This unilateralism elicited several far-reaching social consequences. Among them above all is the constant fear of Catholic thinkers that the love of creation might lead to forgetting the Creator. This fear found its expression in their suggestion of very humble and limited temporal aims for people. The origin of the capitulating character of this suggestion is the self-fear that great temporal aims will blind human beings to their ultimate aim (Piasecki 1954:2).

In this respect, the Marxists had no limitations at all. They were able to propose lofty, magnificent goals to the people. However, the kind of minimalism of aims that we observe in the works of some Catholic theologians is contrary to the spirit of Christianity.

Christianity is optimistic. The source of optimism in the Order of Salvation is grace, the source of optimism in the Order of Creation is work. The Savior-God brought grace to earth, thus opening a way for people to achieve their final aim. The Creator-God brought work to earth, placing people between existing reality and a longed-for and possible reality. The act of creation contained a plan for the future perfection of the world that required people to transform the possibilities around them into reality. The means of transforming the world is human work, which under this aspect possesses the dignity of continuing the activity of the Creator-God (Piasecki 1954:2).

The distinction of the twofold deed of God makes it possible for the author to distinguish people who praise God in an "intentional" way from people who praise him "ontologically." We read: "Only those praise God intentionally who believe that God exists and who want to serve him. On the plane of intention, an enemy of God is the *being* who knows that God exists, but does not want to praise him." Subsequently, "ontologically God is praised by those who create things corresponding to his will, regardless of whether they believe that God exists or deny his existence" (Piasecki 1954:3–5). This distinction allows the role of Party members to be emphasized. Party members who strive to rebuild the world "objectively" continue the act of creation. Furthermore, the distinction allows the critique of the traditional positions in Christianity in which God is praised only "intentionally."

Here is how the historical role of the Communist party is defined.

It is extraordinarily important that believers understand that those who deny the existence of God cannot be his intentional adversaries, they cannot intentionally rebel against him. The atmosphere of sympathy connected with negative moral assessment with which Christianity surrounds rebellion against God within its own ranks cannot be applied to people who do not accept the existence of God. One can be the intentional adversary only of a being the truth of whose existence one accepts. Therefore, nonbelievers cannot be supporters or adversaries of God; they can, however, be supporters or adversaries of ideological and social functions that the concept of God fulfills in a given historical epoch (Piasecki 1954:4).

This text puts the atheistic position beyond the reach of religious evaluation, but gives to atheism—especially in its Marxist version—the right to judge every religious position from the point of view of its sociopolitical role. Atheism is beyond good and evil, but religion is always within the framework of politics. One cannot consider atheists as God's enemies, but one can avow at least some Catholic positions to be contradictory with history and progress. The rehabilitation of Marxist atheism goes even one step further. "The atheism of the Party of the working class does not intentionally attack the truths dearest to the faith of Catholics, but intentionally attacks the social function of faith in God as it expresses itself in the relationship of Catholics to the social world and to the world of nature. What is attacked is the result of this function, i.e., the social action of Catholicism and the historical insufficiency of this action" (Piasecki 1954:45).

What then can one say about those who praise God in an "ontological" way?

In this regard the Communist can boast of great successes. The issue is, above all, the construction of a new, very progressive social system. It is vital for Catholics to join in this work. "Regardless of difficulties in world view, the objective allies of the Christian mission toward the world are those forces that struggle in each historical epoch with social backwardness, against people's intellectual and material handicaps. . . . Thanks to socialism, all people of good will, thus believers as well, cease to be inconsequential simpletons in the sphere of their understanding of the capacity for directing social processes. For this reason, with a feeling of the dignity of Christian universalism, but at the same time with a feeling of healthy criticism of the social function of Catholicism in modern times, one should state that socialism helped and objectively supports the regenerating revision of the social function of Catholicism." From this flow more concrete recommendations. Thus, one has to "break the bonds imposed by collaboration with the classes of proprietors, bonds with the capitalist system and remnants of feudalism . . . and participate consistently in the work of transforming the world by socialism. One must understand one's presence in the socialist camp as a return to the place that one should never have left" (Piasecki 1954:9).

There could be only one basic aim for these analyses: to provide the ruling Party with additional importance—the importance of a particular tool of Divine Providence in the work of rebuilding the world.

One consequence of the revision of then current theological doctrines was the introduction of some elements of Marxism–Leninism–Stalinism into Catholic teaching. This was done either by Piasecki himself or by other ideologues of the movement. According to the principle "the earth for socialism and heaven for Catholicism," publicists of the movement accepted the major doctrinal principles of Marxist socialism: the principle of abolishing private property, of dictatorship of the proletariat in the transitional stage between capitalism and socialism, of class division of society and class struggle, etc. Also accepted as consistent with the spirit of Catholicism were administrative actions by the state toward the church that limited its free activity. "Objective" worshippers of God had to have greater rights than "intentional" worshippers.

The polemic of a PAX journalist against a series of articles by Father Jan Piwowarczyk, who used the pages of *Tygodnik Powszechny* to attempt a debate with the assumptions of Marxism, can serve as a small illustration of the situation. This polemic shows how far the revision of Catholic doctrines went in practice. Thus, we read:

The most striking characteristic of these articles is a lack of knowledge of Marxism; this includes the texts of the classic authors as well as the more important monographs. The second feature is a particular lack of knowledge of economics, not only Marxist economics but bourgeois economics as well. The basic starting point for the assessment of and polemic with Marxists is a work published in 1922 by Father Antonin-Golbert Sertillanges, O.P.,[143] *Socialism and Christianity* (*Socialisme et christianisme*). Bebel[144] and Kautsky[145] are defined in the articles as "all conscientious and objective Marxists"; we find references to Bukharin[146] and Niedziałkowski,[147] but only once is there an allusion to the person of Josif Stalin, and Lenin's contribution to the theory and practice of the proletarian revolution is totally omitted. The polemic in the sphere of basic assumptions about a world view could not convince anybody, since this series of articles was disputing with a mechanistic materialism. The polemic in the area of social and economic changes is naive in that, without taking account of the concrete circumstances surrounding the effective realization of those changes, it demands remuneration for the owner from whom property has been expropriated in cities and villages (Kolendo 1955:76).

Significant here is (a) the treatment of Stalin as a classic author of social science, (b) the protest against the postulate of remuneration for those affected by expropriation, (c) the defense of Marxist philosophy on the pages of, after all, a Catholic periodical. Was there still any difference on these points between the Party and the PAX association?

There is another example of the intrusion of Marxist doctrine into the heart of Catholic ethics. In 1950, the PAX press supported the removal of the charitable organization "Caritas" from the church and its transfer to state control. This support was justified by the principles of Marxism–Leninism. Here is a fragment: "Is it possible in the era of planning, generally the modern era, for this huge apparatus not to be in any formal relationship to the state? All else aside, there is a by no means small problem—in what spirit is the activity there carried out? Incidentally, does not that dangerous atmosphere of political hostility, about which we spoke a moment ago, become connected with the Catholic spirit?" (Kolendo 1955:74). The question is particularly embarrassing since "Caritas" at that time was involved with such activities as care of the elderly in nursing homes, of children in kindergartens, of the poor, and the like.

In the summary then, this new interpretation of Catholic social ethics, carried on during the Stalinist period by PAX journalists, denoted something more than the undertaking of work, planned by the socialist government, by Catholics in the name of the inspiration of a Catholic world view. It was simply an attempt to imbue Catholic social and ethical doctrine with elements of Marxism–Leninism–Stalinism. The party, an "ally" for PAX, acquired a particular significance for the movement's ideologues. It was not only the source of historical force but also the source and rationale of the truth. Are all the theses of this kind found in the publications of Piasecki and PAX to be explained by the pressure of Stalinist terror?

The further history of the PAX movement, that is, its history after October 1956, and after Piasecki's work was placed on the Index, remains closely correlated with the history of Poland's socialization and of the relationship between the state and the church. This is a history of internal fractions and splits, and a courting of respect in the eyes of the public both at home and abroad. Since in 1956 the entire country had changed to some extent, the PAX association itself had also changed. There were no more attempts to split the clergy community, there were no attacks against particular members of the hierarchy. The ideology of the association became vague and no one was eager to make it more precise. Although Piasecki did not recant his concepts, he no longer referred to them. It seemed that the issue withered on its own. Great personal esteem for Piasecki, who died in 1979, still lives on in the association, but it is not linked with acceptance of his outmoded ideas. The association has entered a period of renewed search for its identity.

All the ideological reflections of the PAX movement revolve around the idea of "threefold involvement"—socialist, Catholic in world view, and patriotic. Depending on the circumstances, one or another aspect of the idea is accentuated. What does this involvement ultimately mean and to what does it oblige one? Which of the three is the most basic? There is no unequivocal answer to these questions.

Socialist involvement (1980): "Our determination in favor of socialist involvement, a consistent line for an ideological ally of the Party, is the result of the orientation that, in a real situation, one must serve the interests of the human being and the nation through socialism and by striving for the development of socialism" (Reiff 1979). The bonds with the Party are indicated by the following words: "Three factors define the PAX situation. First, a point of view that is consistent with the policies of the Party. The Party displays an open attitude toward the new trade unions [written in September 1980—translators' note] and in this way testifies to its ability to stand up not only to the exigencies of the crisis, but also to the demands of development in the spheres of theory as well as practice . . ." (Reiff 1980:3–4). However, critical postulates are occasionally addressed to the Party. "One should define precisely what the leading role of the Party must consist of in every sphere of life: public, state, economic, social, cultural and so forth; simply to know where an abuse of this role eventuates" (Reiff 1980:3–4). That this postulate was formulated at the time of another "renewal," after the waves of strikes in 1980, is not at all surprising. It simply attests the existence of the question: the ally of the Party, but what kind of

Party? In the meantime, it seems that for a movement defining itself as "socialist" this question and this dilemma are not the essential ones. The real dilemma lies in the way in which the Party's relationship toward the proletariat, toward the working class, will define itself; in the role and significance that will be granted to this class in the development of social life. It was precisely this dilemma that confronted the Party and all sympathizers of socialism in a particularly glaring way in 1980. The issue was not a choice between one Party and another, between a dictatorial Party and a liberal one, but a choice between the self-awareness of the working class and the self-knowledge of the Party. The principle of "conceptual alliance with the Party" does not even permit the formulation of the problem.

From involvement according to the Catholic world view comes the defense of "the pluralism of world view and political pluralism in Poland." The PAX association, one must admit, from the very beginning defended the thesis that materialism and atheism are not integral components of socialism, and in this way it modified the views of the classic authors of Marxism. Socialism, in the opinion of the association's ideologues, is by its very essence a pluralistic ideology. From this comes the postulate that believers are to join in the construction of a new world and thereby be able to gain recognition of their rights from its builders. At this juncture it is worthwhile to record a certain change of view. Piasecki included Catholics in the socialist construction without demanding guarantees for believers. He wrote: "There is neither doctrinal necessity for nor the possibility of formal historical guarantees for Catholicism. One need only be aware that regardless of the complex appearance of matters, each objective advance is a partial realization of Christianity" (Piasecki 1954:9). Ryszard Reiff,[148] Piasecki's successor, goes one step further, since the circumstances also changed. He writes that the issue is "appreciation of the religious needs of believers not only as permanent, but also as noncontradictory with the patriotic and socialistic involvement of citizens who even outside of their private lives are Catholic."

This demand, however, is bilateral, since the issue is also that of "acceptance by the church of the socialist system of work as equally dear to it as are other systems traditionally considered by the church as natural stages of historical development" (Reiff 1979:26). Hence again "acceptance." The trouble here is that it is not very clear what is to be the object of this "acceptance." Who among us knows what in fact the "socialist system of work" is? What is hidden behind the words "appreciation of the needs of believers . . . who even outside of their private lives are Catholics"? Operating with such generalities, it appears that something has been said, but in reality nothing has been said. Again, it seems that the real problem lies on a totally different plane. The crisis of socialist ideology, as we are witnessing especially in Poland, has its main roots in a highly equivocal philosophy of the human being, a philosophy inherited and assumed by the ideology. At issue here are not details, but a radical revision of nineteenth-century anthropology that is like a leg iron for "socialism." If socialism means that the human being is only "a basic production force," then one must defend the human being against socialism. Alternatively, if one defends socialism one must undertake the intellectual effort to demonstrate that behind the word socialism there is hidden some other worthwhile vision of the human being. But, does a conceptual alliance with the Party permit the possibility of such a far-reaching revision?

The question of the nation is associated with national–patriotic involvement. The idea of nation seems to be shallow. For PAX, the truly national elements are those of historical tradition and currently developing culture that are consistent with the so-called *raison d'état,* and thus with the categories of current politics. We read among other things:

> We serve a nation in whose identity are written particularly deep moral and cultural bonds with Christianity and the church; we serve a nation that history is leading along the road toward socialism. We contributed to eliminating the false dilemma of Polish consciences: faith or participation in the socioeconomic and political development of socialist Poland. We formulated the principle of a Catholic, world-encompassing inspiration in terms of public, common action. We created a school of thought in the categories of realism and national responsibility, but we were also able to provide our service with a powerful charge of emotion (Reiff 1979).

Each sentence of this text evokes a critical response. In general terms, the issue of the nation is understood "realistically" but nonetheless "emotionally." Thus we have a formula: "emotional realism." Realism means that only those national values have a raison d'être that are consistent with the ideals of socialism: the socialization of the means of production, the leading role of the Party, alliance with the Soviet Union and other socialist countries. Emotionalism means that the PAX movement has an emotional relationship to *those* values. The conclusion is simple: we look at the nation through the prism of the *raison d'état* and not at the *raison d'état* through the prism of national interest. We value a nose because of the snuffbox and not vice versa. Absurd? Inconsistencies? Quite simply, I think that this is a *style of thinking,* a style in which the axiom of "alliance" is compulsory.

To summarize: the concept of dialogue between Marxism and Christianity proposed as a movement for socially progressive Catholics was born out of political need. In the plan for the dialogue proposed in a general outline by the Party, the primacy of politics over ethics, or more precisely, the acceptance of the political postulate as the highest ethical demand, prevailed. In this context, the socially progressive movement of Catholics was to be "a conceptual ally of the Party." The consequence of this state of affairs was the dependence of the fate of the dialogue, conceived in this way, on the fate of its proper creator and ally—the Party. A certain influence was exercised by the church, the proletariat, and the entire nation on the fate of the Party—especially in times of social tensions—but the socially progressive movement of Catholics had no influence. It did not represent a sufficiently large social or intellectual force. The Party, in talking to this movement, in reality talked to itself. This, of course, does not preclude an indirect influence on the Party and Marxism through the publication of books and articles that in a general way contributed to elevating the level of religious and cultural life in the country.

The a priori principle of the primacy of politics imposed limits on all theoretical reflections on the issue of collaboration between Christians and Communists. First, this restricted theological reflection. An attempt to reinterpret the idea of the creation of the world by God and the continuation of the work of creation by the working person, proposed by Piasecki, ended in catastrophe. It set up a psychological barrier to a deeper, more independent reflection on the theology of earthly realities. It also limited possible reflection on the achievements of socialist thought. After the rejection of materialism and atheism, no one undertook a deeper, independent attempt to connect the socialist idea with more contemporary concepts of the human person. It is even stranger that in various nonprogrammatic PAX publications one could find a relative wealth of informative material concerning these concepts. There was a lack here of bold, truly attractive thought. No wonder, then, that with the passage of time, PAX became an institution that did more "arranging" and less "inspiring."

17. Aspects of Leszek Kołakowski's Thought

In the imposing work, *Main Currents of Marxism,* Kołakowski recalls the times of criticism of the so-called "bourgeois philosophy" in Poland of the 1950s.

Another target was Thomism, which had a lively tradition centered in the Catholic University of Lublin. (This university—a fact unparalleled in the history of socialist states—was never suppressed and functions to this day, despite various measures of pressure and interference.) Many Marxists of the older and younger generation—Adam Schaff, Bronisław Baczko, Tadeusz Kroński, Helena Eilstein,[149] Władysław Krajewski—took part in these battles; so did the present author, who does not regard the fact as a source of pride. Another subject of study was the Marxist contribution to Polish culture in past decades. A significant majority of those who in those times participated in these activities on the side of Marxism later broke with Marxism (Kołakowski 1978:173).

There is something incredible in the picture of Marxist philosophy painted for us by Kołakowski in his three volumes on the history of Marxism. This is not an ordinary history. Behind each of its chapters it is as if one could trace yet another withered human hope, the hope of the human being who sought in Marxism a tool for liberation, but at the end did not find liberation. Kołakowski himself was one such human being. The author through his work repaid some kind of debt. We know that before the war Polish philosophers, with very few exceptions, did not prepare the Polish intelligentsia for a confrontation with Marxism. Only now does Kołakowski do this, but for him Marxism was a part of his own life. In settling accounts with Marxism, the philosopher is also settling accounts with himself. Something of the atmosphere of a cemetery emanates from this unusual book. Among the graves of the Marxists stands the grave of the young Kołakowski as well. "Let the dead bury their dead." Kołakowski also buries himself, his past history, his youth, his tragedy. He closes the door in order to open a door. But what door will he open?

The medium of Kołakowski's thought was hermeneutics. Hermeneutics is a method of cognition in the humanistic sciences, although recently it has been made into a basic method for the interpretation of meanings, senses that belong to what is objective as well as to what is subjective. What was the real sense of your behavior yesterday? What meanings do you ascribe to your words? What meaning do these words truly have? I know that in doing this or that you act in good faith, but in whose interest is your action? Recently, hermeneutical thinking has become the basic method of philosophy, tied to the German "philosophy of life," to Friedrich Nietzsche,[150] to psychoanalysis, to Heidegger, and also to Marx, who himself is acknowledged as one of the classic authors of the method. Kołakowski's thought also belongs to this general current. A significant trait of Marx's method, and later of Kołakowski's, was the study of the various meanings associated with social life, cultural phenomena in particular, in order to discover what is most essential for their origin and development; what decides their contents. For Marxist hermeneutics, the decisive factor was always to be "class interest." Kołakowski asked: In whose interest, in the final analysis, is one or the other philosophical view? In whose interest is a given religious faith, a given trend in art, etc.? By asking in this way, a hermeneut wished to unmask, to disperse some illusion, to reveal the truth hidden to the naked eye. Ricoeur called the classic authors of contemporary hermeneutical thinking the "masters of suspicion." Kołakowski entered our postwar culture as one of them.

The hermeneutical method is based on certain assumptions. First of all, the method assumes that there is a basis for an unmasking process, some untouchable evidence that functions as the basis of the entire process. This assumption is not always clearly formulated and does not always appear as the same factor of interpretation in the texts of one and the same author. Marx avowed that essentially each facet of culture must be "in someone's interest." In Kołakowski, the principle of unmasking is partially variable, but essentially it always serves some ethical ideal.

Every hermeneutics, but particularly that of Kołakowski, is open to the accusation of arbitrariness. Perhaps the things that a hermeneut does are interesting, but are they true? How can one verify one interpretation and falsify another? It is sufficient merely to alter a principle so that what was right yesterday will have to be accepted as an error today. Each issue looks this way from one side and that way from another. Which point of view is correct? Hence Kołakowski's opponents say: During the Stalinist period, Kołakowski was "interested" in Marxism; hence, he declared himself in favor of it. Subsequently, he changed his place of residence, discovered his "interest" in something else and became the enemy of Marxism. His present fight with Marxism is worth just as much as his previous fight with Thomism. They also say: Kołakowski oscillates, is unable to be faithful to himself, he performs stylistic legerdemain; he would rather change the world than learn about it. Are these accusations correct? Does Kołakowski's hermeneutics not unveil any truths about Marxism? And also, in spite of everything, is not Kołakowski faithful to himself and does he not, in the name of this fidelity, undertake the bitter task of "burying his dead"? Looking at the development of Kołakowski's thought, I have in my mind one question: What is unconditionally important in this thinking? I ask about the ground of his critiques and the ground of his affirmations. I ask about convictions so basic that they were as present when Kołakowski was an enthusiast of Marxism as they are now when he is its critic. In other words, where in Kołakowski's thinking does interpretation end and the persuasive force of absolute experience begin? The answer to this question is not easy, not least because sometime ago Kołakowski compared himself to a jester whose motto is vigilance against accepting "any absolute whatsoever." But the answer is necessary, since one must realize that Kołakowski is not only a writer who simply describes something, but is above all a thinker who testifies to something. But, to what?

I have before me a collection of his critical articles on Christian philosophy entitled *Sketches from Catholic Philosophy* (*Szkice z filozofii katolickiej*), about which the author stated "they do not bring me honor." Let us, however, consider the issue coldly and from a distance. These articles are simultaneously a critique and the protest of a rebellious spirit. A protest in the name of what? In the name of what value? In other words, what is the hermeneutical principle of his unmasking efforts? The principle is clear; it is not at all one or another dogmatically accepted Marxist thesis, but the natural *sensitivity* of the author to any degradation of human dignity. Kołakowski's writing differed from the writings of other Marxists of that epoch in that it was deeper and more authentically permeated by the element of human rights. If I am returning to those texts today, I do so not only to reproach the author with them but also to discover the origins of something that later bore fruit as *Main Currents of Marxism.*

Once again, I leaf through the pages of the book. I read the titles: "Neo-Thomism in the Struggle with Science and Human Rights," in another place, "The Rights of the Person against the Rights of the Human Being." Fragments of the second article indeed sound threatening:

One could say that the church in the service of a regressive capitalist world wreaks the vengeance of a medieval theocracy on the antichurch tradition of the bourgeoisie; the blasphemous principle that proclaims that the human being is an end in himself suffers ruthless condemnation as a perverse overturning of the entire moral order "since the main goal of the human being is to serve God and thus to reach eternal life" [citation from a textbook of moral theology by Victor Cathrein.[151] J.T.]. The idea of Augustine and Thomas Aquinas that everything actually in the world is grace finds expression in the saying that, in a broad sense, all duties of the human being are duties toward God and that "the dignity of the person" finds its realization in obeying divine commands [ref. to St. Thomas Aquinas]. As Maritain says, "Theocentric, i.e., truly Christian, humanism accepts that God is the core of the human being" and "the human being is accepted as a being of sin and incarnation that has God as his core and not himself" [ref. to J. Maritain] (Kołakowski 1953:173).

Kołakowski does not invent the quotations. I admit that the writings of Cathrein and Maritain were not unequivocal and were readily exposed to a critique such as Kołakowski's. The manner of presenting the critique is unacceptable but the fact of the critique and the questions posed are justified. One may only protest against the fact that Kołakowski accepts the formulations cited as a finished expression of Christian thought, that he does not try to get into the spirit of the texts but remains at their letter, and above all that he accuses the authors of "objectively supporting imperialism." The natural way of seeing things is mixed with schemata taken from Marxism. The contents of the natural view are human rights.

For the hermeneutical way of thinking, a key issue is the ability to separate what one sees and feels from what is accepted as understood. The understood world cannot eclipse the experienced world. In Kołakowski's case this was not so. Kołakowski was learning about the church from the texts instead of looking at what was happening with this church outside his windows. Kołakowski seemed to believe more in words read than in his own ears and eyes. For these reasons, most likely, he did not grasp the difference between the obedience that a Christian owes to God and that which one human being owes to another human being. But not only this. Although Kołakowski was sensitive to human dignity, he was not sensitive to what was happening with this dignity in the Poland of those times. He did not see the concrete reality, the reality of popular faith. He had no share in the experiences of the simple peasants or workers who knelt on Sunday before the altar and in this posture nevertheless felt themselves in no way less human or less dignified. To see and to feel all this, one did not at all need to be a believer oneself. It was enough to live in touch with Poland. Kołakowski resided in Poland, but he viewed it from above, from afar.

I think that the entire period of Kołakowski's activity, until the emergence of the first ideas that gave birth to *Main Currents,* is a period of fundamental disagreement between the data of understanding and the data of experience—experience became overshadowed by categories of understanding, more precisely, by a pre-understanding of surrounding reality. Thus, good intentions in effect produced works from which he later had to distance himself.

Marx said: "Philosophers so far have only explained the world, the issue, however, is to change it." Kołakowski decided to be a thinker for whom the issue was to change the world, to change it by unmasking it. The first object of unmasking was religion; later it was Marxism. Was the manner of unmasking the same? I think it was totally different. Kołakowski stood outside of religion and had only indirect insight into its contents. In contrast, he had insight into Marxism from the inside. Kołakowski truly wanted to be a Marxist, with all his heart and soul. And probably he really was—if I am free to make some judgment about this. When he came to unmask Marxism, he had to unmask himself. The hermeneutics that he applied for the critique of religion was based on second-hand data beyond the reach of his primary experience. The hermeneutics applied to exposing Marxism, on the other hand, grew from the elements of original experience.

Let us then look more closely at his effort to settle accounts with Marxism. Kołakowski places Marxism before a dual tribunal—a tribunal of conscience and a tribunal of reason. What is the result of this trial? Marxism stands accused on ethical grounds for becoming a philosophical-ideological form of justification for crimes. When he reviewed the history of Marxism's practical incarnation, Kołakowski registered a process of increasing numbers of corpses. The longer the experiments last, the more victims are swallowed up. Simultaneously, the needs and demands also increase to justify somehow the necessity for these victims, to justify their need, their inevitability. Marxism must provide these justifications. In it there is no principle that could become a permanent principle of protest. To start a revolution is easy, but to end it is difficult. First one must pay the costs of preparation, later come the costs of maintenance. Under these circumstances, Kolakowski concludes, one cannot correct Marxism, but instead ought to reject it. Kołakowski says this primarily to himself.

The second, intellectual, defeat of Marxism is seen on several levels when the author takes into consideration the many different spokesmen of the movement. Let us stay with the example of Stalinism. We read among other things:

Marxism as the ideology of the Soviet state very soon ceased to be an independent factor in the determination of policy. Of necessity, its content had to be so vague and general as to justify any particular move in home or foreign affairs: NEP[152] or collectivization, friendship with Hitler[153] or war with Hitler, any toughening or relaxation of the internal regime, and so on. And indeed, since the theory states that "on the one hand" the superstructure is a creation and instrument of the base, but "on the other" it also affects the base, it can be shown that any imaginable government policy for the regulation of the economy, or for controlling culture in a greater or lesser degree, is in accordance with Marxism. If "on the one hand" individuals do not make history, but "on the other" exceptional individuals who understand historical necessity do play an important part (and both points of view can be supported by quotations from Marx and Engels), then it is equally in accordance with Marxism to pay divine honors to the socialist despot or to condemn this practice as a "deviation". If "on the one hand" all nations are entitled to self-determination, but "on the other hand" the cause of world socialist revolution is paramount, then any policy, whether mild or severe, with the object of discouraging the national aspirations of the non-Russian inhabitants of the empire, will be indubitably Marxist. Such in fact was the ambivalent basis of Stalin's Marxism, and its vague and contradictory tenets were alike put down to the "dialectic". From this point of view both the function and the content of official Soviet Marxism have remained the same since Stalin's death. Marxism has become simply a rhetorical dressing for the Realpolitik of the Soviet empire.

And the key issue: "The rationale of this change was very simple: since the Soviet Union is by definition the bastion of human progress, whatever serves Soviet interests is progressive and whatever does not is reactionary" (Kołakowski 1978:104–05).

A philosophy that is able to justify everything that is actually beneficial for the authorities is no longer philosophy. For this reason, "At present Marxism neither interprets the world nor changes it: it is merely a repertoire of slogans serving to organize various interests, most of them completely remote from those with which Marxism originally identified itself" (Kołakowski 1978:530).

What does the moral defeat of Marxism look like? Again, let us stay with the chapter on Stalinism, even though the issue threads through the entire book.

Every step of the way, Kołakowski emphasizes the ethical repercussions of Marx's thought; this philosophy was born out of the protest against oppression and out of the hope of overcoming it. It was supposed to be a tool for abolishing the exploitation of work. To eliminate exploitation, it justified social revolution and the state that developed as its result. In the "socialist state" exploitation did not disappear in the least, but was "justified" by the need for a further struggle for socialism, especially in other countries. To abolish exploitation, one must build socialism in the whole world. For that one needs a strong state. In this way Marxism itself postulates the introduction of totalitarian authority

into a state in the name of realizing proposed Marxist aims. One totalitarianism is replaced by the other.

In connection with his dealing with Stalinism, Kołakowski writes:

> It may be said that the great purges were a macabre irrelevance, in the sense
> that the purpose they served could quite well have been attained by other means.
> Yet they were, so to speak, part of the natural logic of the system. It was a
> question not only of destroying any actual or potential rivals but of wiping out
> the sole organism in which there were still any remnants, however faint and
> impotent, of loyalty to any cause other than the state and its leader—in partic-
> ular, remnants of a belief in Communist ideology as a frame of reference and
> an object of worship, independent of the leader and the party's current direc-
> tives. The object of a totalitarian system is to destroy all forms of communal
> life that are not imposed by the state and closely controlled by it, so that
> individuals are isolated from one another and become mere instruments in the
> hands of the state. The citizen belongs to the state and must have no other
> loyalty, not even to the state ideology (Kołakowski 1978:85).

Exactly. The tragedy was that this sort of state was supposed to be a
"state of the working people of the cities and villages."

Kołakowski exposes more broadly the functioning mechanism of Stalin's terror. In order for terror totally to disarm human beings, it must
disarm them spiritually, it must create a guilty conscience everywhere.

> The paralysis of the individual was complete; and, at the same time, it could
> not be denied that the Party was acting in accordance with the principles that
> had obtained since the beginning. All its members had taken part in mass acts
> of violence against the public, and when they themselves became victims of
> lawlessness there was nothing to which they could appeal. None of them had
> objected to fake trials and executions as long as the sufferers were not Party
> members; all of them accepted, actively or passively, that "in principle" there
> was nothing wrong in judicial murder. They all agreed, too, that at any given
> moment it was for the Party leaders to decide who was a class enemy, a friend
> of the kulaks, or an imperialist agent. The rules of the game, which they had
> accepted, were being brought to bear against them, and they had no moral
> principles that might have fostered a spirit of resistance (Kołakowski
> 1978:86–87).

The system had something demonic in it. The "demonic" is evil endowed
with intelligence. The aim of the operation of this intelligence was to
let all participate in the organization of oppression; "as in all magical
thinking, an object connected in any way with the evil spirit was con-
taminated forever and must be cast out and blotted from memory. Soviet
citizens were allowed to remember the existence of a few traitors mentioned in the *Short Course*[154] so as to include them in ritual condem-

nations, but the rest of the satanic crew were supposed to be forgotten and no one dared to speak their names." And further: "In private conversations, citizens were obliged to repeat in ritual fashion grotesque falsehoods about themselves, the world, and the Soviet Union, and at the same time to keep silent about things they knew very well, not only because they were terrorized but because the incessant repetition of falsehoods which they knew to be such made them accomplices in the campaign of lies inculcated by the Party and state" (Kołakowski 1978:95 and 96).

Stalinism, one might say, was only an episode in the history of Marxism. Can one judge the whole on the basis of Stalinism? Kołakowski maintains that Stalinism was not an episode but the coronation of the contents immanent in Marxism. Because of this, not only can one judge, but one should. One should judge because Marxism provided Stalinism with a coherent justification. One should judge because the situation of Stalinism was repeated in other countries and still repeats itself. One should judge because intellectual opposition against Stalinism had to reach out to other, extra-Marxist, sources. Thus, the sense of the second charge against Marxism is summarized in one thing: Marxism became a philosophy and ideology that justified the cruelty of one human being toward another.

I cannot touch here upon the other aspects of Kołakowski's critique of Marxism. There are so many and they are so different that one would need a separate book to treat them. One thing, however, appears to me particularly important—a question: what will be left in our culture from the whole adventure with Marxism? Kołakowski maintains—nothing. Everything runs like sand through the fingers. He writes: "To say that Marxism is a fantasy does not mean that it is nothing else. Marxism as an interpretation of past history must be distinguished from Marxism as a political ideology. No reasonable person would deny that the doctrine of historical materialism has been a valuable addition to our intellectual equipment and has enriched our understanding of the past. True, it has been argued that in a strict form the doctrine is nonsense and in a loose form it is a commonplace; but, if it has become a commonplace, this is largely thanks to Marx's originality" (Kołakowski 1978:523). Indeed, this is not at all an impressive inheritance. To the statement that a human being lives not by bread alone, Marx replies that in the final reckoning it is by bread alone. But practice indicates that the truth is on both sides; there are those who live by bread alone and there are those who live not by bread alone. This was already known before Marx. So what good is Marxism?

Let us try to draw a few conclusions.

Kołakowski's significance for the history of the dialogue with Marxism is enormous. In the end he did something that Christian thinkers should have done—he produced a radical criticism of Marxism. But their voice would not be as valuable as Kołakowski's voice, because it was not only the voice of an expert, but also the voice of a witness. A witness has spoken from within the system. Kołakowski is both moralist and rationalist. As a moralist he also speaks in the name of values that are Christian values. As a rationalist he speaks on behalf of values that are the foundation of wisdom that creates science.

Kołakowski, who in some sense began a dialogue in our country between Marxism and Christianity, now marks its ending. Leaving Christianity in this case meant some sort of return to it—not a return to its dogmas but to its ethos, the ethos incarnated in the sacrifice of Jesus of Nazareth. While still in Poland, Kołakowski wrote: "Jesus Christ . . . taught how, without resorting to violence, one can face oneself and the world. He was, therefore, a model of that radical authenticity in which each human individual can truly give life to one's own values" (Kołakowski 1965:6–7).

Later things went still further. Interest in Christian mystics, the election of a Polish pope, the pope's visit to Poland, all these instigated in Kołakowski's spirit a series of further reflections that evidence a rapprochement with Christianity.

The issue of the relationship of Kołakowski's later philosophy to Christianity presents a distinct topic. Perhaps it is still premature to take up this topic. However, one thing can be said: the rapprochement with Christianity went along the same road as did the original protest against it. The core of the issue was the dignity and rights of the human being. It seems that Kołakowski shows in a crystalline form what many others of his generation lived through.

18. Attempts at Testimony

Could one find no one in past years who would pose the issue of a dialogue with Christians from the side of the most broadly defined "intellectual Left," in a more honest and fruitful manner? According to popular opinion, Jan Strzelecki[155] and Adam Michnik[156] could be the advocates of an authentic dialogue, undertaken with all the risks connected with such a dialogue. Strzelecki today is a learned sociologist, the author of beautiful reflections on ethical themes in which the difficult problems of choosing a stance, by the generation that initially organized the resistance movement against the German occupiers and later, in extremely complicated circumstances, built postwar Poland, came to expression. Michnik interests us above all as the author of a book entitled *The Church, the Left, Dialogue* (*Kościół—lewica—dialog*), published abroad and written from the position of so-called "democratic socialism." Both authors are on the fringes of official Marxism. When they speak on general matters, they do so exclusively in their own name. Nonetheless, in their formulations, ideas that flow through the consciousness of many people shine through. They occasionally enunciate such bold opinions that it is difficult to say whether they are still Marxists. In spite of deep differences between them, they essentially declare themselves on the side of socialism and define socialism in such a way that its socioethical contents move into the foreground. Socialism for them is above all a particular ethos, an ethos determined by a rebellion against exploitation, injustice, enslavement. Strzelecki's proclamations are relatively old; they were formulated during the war at the time of resistance. Michnik's declarations are of a more recent date and were shaped by the social reality of the People's Poland. This is the source of their different standpoints. Strzelecki holds himself aloof from the political stage, a disenchanted socialist, carrying out primarily scientific activity. Michnik is at once a thinker and activist, hotheaded and involved, full of faith in his "democratic socialism," always ready to protest against various abuses by the authorities.

I hesitated for a long time as to whether to include these two positions in my book. It seemed to me that Kołakowski closes the history of the dialogue in a sufficiently eloquent way. Of course, in this history, new names may appear, but will new ideas also appear? Is it not rather the case that all theoretical possibilities are already exhausted? It was called to my attention, however, that in this case the entire thought of the Left will be impoverished. It was also said that democratic socialism represents the future of the country and that one must deal with the future and not with something that has gone by and was compromised. I accepted this criticism, but I did not do so gladly. The character of the declarations by Strzelecki and Michnik does not supply sufficient motivation for a general discussion on the theme that interests us here. It is difficult to require that a text say something more than it intended to convey. Strzelecki gives a socialist's testimony of his attachment to Christianity and his bonds with patriotism. Michnik wants to unveil for his friends on the Left the true face of the church that acts as an advocate of human rights in a people's democratic socialism. These friends, amazingly, know nothing of this, despite the fact that they live in Poland. The authors themselves, through the way they formulate the theme, give a determined sense to their declarations. Can one see in them an announcement of a new quality of Polish dialogue? The answer is not entirely clear. Some minimalize and others magnify their importance. Nevertheless, one should examine them more closely. (Strzelecki's reflections played a significant role in shaping the ethos of "self-defense" youth groups in 1975–1980.)

Let us consider Strzelecki's sayings. Strzelecki carries out a sort of internal dialogue with himself from which comes a testimony, "Attempts at Testimony" as he titled one of the main texts on this theme. Strzelecki belongs to the generation of Marxist–socialists for whom the war and Nazi occupation had a key significance. Strzelecki had become a socialist earlier, even before Marxism came to be the official ideology of the people's state. He remained a socialist in the Stalinist period and did not renounce his basic views in the post October period or later. Strzelecki's position in Polish theoretical–philosophical thought never equalled that of either Schaff or Kołakowski; nor did he ever become the target of truly sharp attacks and suspicions from "dogmatists," even though many of his ideas had a provocative character. Despite this, Strzelecki used to fascinate and still does. This may be accounted for primarily by the deeply ethical repercussions of his thinking. Strzelecki shows the ethical background of his and his friends' decision that led to a more or less consistent support of the "people's democracy." Perhaps Strzelecki is, as some believe, a master of compromise. He was above all, however, a witness of *Polish rooting* inasmuch as he shows, through his writing, the circle of values without which certain generations of Poles cannot conclusively understand themselves.

For people like Strzelecki, the war brought the discovery of two values that subsequently left a deep mark on the way that Marxism was emotionally perceived, values like that of nation, patriotism and the value of interpersonal brotherhood. Patriotism for them became one of the forms of brotherhood. A common brotherhood with the oppressed did not preclude patriotism. Through the prism of these values the idea of proletarian internationalism must have looked different. Internationalism could not be in conflict with patriotic ideals and the postulate of class struggle could not undermine the principle of a common brotherhood of the oppressed. We read, "The war removed [the concept of nation] from the category of festive, intellectual images to the category of direct, daily, unquestionable feelings that constituted the lifeblood of our actions. None of us tried to explain that those who fell at Westerplatte[157] perished for superstition" (Strzelecki 1974:76). We also read: "We knew what brotherhood is. Brotherhood means to identify oneself with another, to refrain from separating another's fate from one's own, even more, to see another's danger more sharply than one's own, to feel that the other's death is more difficult to experience than one's own" (Strzelecki 1974:13).

The discovery of the values of patriotism and of brotherhood constituted a direct heritage of the war. With this experience people entered the world of the "people's democracy," then being built, and gave it their rather far-reaching support. Soon it turned out that they gave support to—Stalinism. They wanted a Poland of equality and justice, but they received a Poland of "intensifying class struggle." Stalinism questioned both their values. It did this in its own brutal way. Many companions of Strzelecki perished because of "opportunism." Many of them denounced patriotism and common brotherhood. Still others backed out of their original faith in socialism. Strzelecki essentially stayed with his faith. With this ragged faith in his soul, he remained a witness to tragedy.

He was rooted in Christianity. It could not be otherwise. If anyone in this country claims that he or she is not rooted in Christianity, they do not know themselves. While still under the occupation, Strzelecki finished a translation of fragments of Mounier's works for the benefit of his friends of the Left. He is fascinated by the style of thinking of Maritain; the work and achievement of the life of Dietrich Bonhoeffer[158] are dear to him. But not only they. He has a more direct access to the world of religious faith through the patriotism of Polish Catholicism. This Catholicism is not at all an "opium for the masses," but rather an inexhaustible source of inspiration for the struggle for human dignity and the nation's independence. From this arise the questions and critiques addressed to Marxism. It is worthwhile to examine some of them.

As it seems, materialism is an essential component of Marx's views. How does Strzelecki assess materialism? For him, materialism is synonymous with the domination of the flesh over the spirit. But especially "they"—the younger generation fighting for freedom—were concerned with something opposite, i.e., the domination of the spirit over the flesh. He writes: "We lived for several years at the edge of the circle of the ultimate test. Deep in our hearts we carried an unceasing question aimed at ourselves, aimed with all the merciless need for truth about ourselves as human matter. The question asked: Would I withstand, would I not turn out to be only flesh? The flesh was the term that denoted in us everything that would be disposed to accept torture as a sufficient motive for behavior, as the bridge to a world of determinism, a rough and indifferent world. This is a world that is indifferent to the existence or privation of identity, deaf to this very concept, a world that accepts any solution." And a bit further: "The human person, faithful to values despite the cries of tired flesh—this was our problem, our task, which we have to confront constantly in the days and nights of the long five years of our second education. This was one of the border situations of our existence, a possibility—thick and tangible. And it was just this human person that imposed on us the theme of the relationship of the body and the person, a question about the sources of our identity when the flesh becomes an obstacle" (Strzelecki 1974:27).

After this came other questions. Strzelecki and others like him could not agree with the view that the human being is only the material from which socioeconomic conditions carve either a genius or a criminal. In the human being, there must be some nature that puts a limit to the force of conditions. One ought to recognize this nature; one ought to respect it. One should not identify human beings with the places assigned to them in the social division of work. A human being totally adapted to the tasks assigned to him "appeared to us a half-human being. In this was contained a judgment about what is valuable in human nature; prominent here was a refusal to accept history as the main point of reference, a separation of hope from the idea of the limitless plasticity of human nature from which the train of events forms ever more beautiful shapes. The roles were switched. The frontiers of nature became a call of the Left. The mentors of the SS-men[159] proclaimed the crossing of these frontiers" (Strzelecki 1974:44).

Their main idea and concern was ethics. But what ethics? Strzelecki at one point alluded to Austrian social democracy from before World War I. Indeed, in this text he gives evidence of the idea of "ethical socialism." Marx's economics and his historical utopia stand beyond the pale and the fundamental ethos of socialism that was akin to Christianity moves to the forefront. There was no mention in Strzelecki's work of the class character of morality. All of us are bound by the same basic values. "These few truths—the first of which proclaimed respect for life; the second, recognition of humanity in everyone and not only in the members of our own tribe; the third, love and not mastery over one's neighbor—belonged in those times to the truths against which mass ridicule was directed." But precisely because of that, "the experience of the fragility of these truths coexisted with the experience of their deepest rooting in human beings" (Strzelecki 1974:39–40).

Thus, they remained consistent and rejected the theory of "a double morality," different for those who rule and for those who are ruled. Politics cannot be taken as the chief area of life. The political militancy of "our side" is not the sign of the highest value of a human being. The attitude of the authorities toward the citizens cannot be the attitude of "a carpenter toward an unhewn plank" (Strzelecki 1974:81). Indeed, they were for the use of force; the slogan "dictatorships in defense of democracy" was not just a phrase for them, but "there is a considerable difference between the use of force which flows from the necessity to act in defense of values and the use of force which flows from the inclination of those who act in defense of simplifications. We must see this difference. Moreover, we must see it constantly and without respite, and above all, in our own action" (Strzelecki 1974:44).

Reading these confessions, we face the key question: why socialism in spite of everything? Why the involvement in building a new system in spite of all this? What explains this far-reaching blindness to all that time had brought? We have neither the basis nor the right to question good will. But question we must. At issue is not an individual matter. In the fate of the individual, general truths are reflected.

Here is an attempt to justify the choice. In 1948, clearly conscious of growing Stalinism and simultaneously defending himself against the attacks of Schaff, who in those days was the advocate and ideologue of Stalinism, Strzelecki tried to answer the question, What is Marxism? He wrote:

Marxism, from a sociological point of view, is not a collection of theses, nor is it just a scholarly theory. It is the form and content of a social movement, it is not a logical but a social phenomenon. For this reason, its development and significance do not have so great a connection with the question of the logical rectitude of thought as might appear from a superficial, rationalistic point of view. On the other hand, it has a profound connection with what one may call, technically speaking, the mentality of the working class, a mentality based on historically formed social attitudes and expectations. If one looks at the theory of Marxism from this sociological rather than the ideological side, it is evident that the same parts of this great totality were not necessarily assimilated with equal vigor in different years and different countries, and even in different strata within the working class. It is seen that assimilation followed not so much from logical as from sociopsychological causes.

Professor Schaff looks at Marxism from a "typically ideological point of view". In the meantime, the doctrine, precisely as a living doctrine, is too strongly connected with the emotional attitudes of the worker militants, Party activists and rank and file participants in the movement. But then, the psychology of the thinking of these people is somewhat different from that of the intellectuals (Strzelecki 1974:119).

This fragment is both accurate and still valid. Not only that, it implicitly takes away the monopoly over "proper Marxism" from the various more or less self-proclaimed "specialists," Schaff and Stalin included. In it, Strzelecki continues Marx's old idea that Marxism is primarily an expression of the social self-consciousness of the working class. Where Marxism did not include the contents of this self-consciousness, one could not speak of a living Marxism even if, we might add, whole ranks of professors of Marxist philosophy and their faithful disciples appeared at the universities. Hence, Strzelecki has in his eyes "his own" Marxism, different from the official one. But did such a Marxism exist outside of Strzelecki's mind? Was it not simply one of the dreams of a socialist?

Strzelecki and the others like him treated the concrete doctrine of Marx and his successors selectively. We read:

Joint analysis of individual and common fate, and that of the extent of the relationships of production, met with a basic agreement, as did the declaration that no forms of human existence, not even the loftiest calling, is exempt from responsibility for the element of unevenly distributed duress existing in those relationships. This element is present in every human fate. Assigned in those years to roles burdened with a double duress, and choosing free roles in the sphere of revolt against both kinds of duress, we were opened, as to the kind of truth that would be an image of our own fate, to everything in Marxism that depicts the existence and interaction of various forms of exploitation and oppression, and that summons one to participate in the common struggle (Strzelecki 1974:60).

Yes, this is understood. In the concrete case, this meant that the new Poland could not be a repetition of prewar Poland. They plunged into the new with the momentum of escaping the old. Hence: "We realized that . . . no system will guarantee brotherhood. But we wanted a system whose basic institutions would be more consistent with brotherhood. Because of that we stood directly in the mainstream of the socialist movement" (Strzelecki 1974:76).

Thus, the "socialist movement." What does this mean? Above all, it means building a classless society.

At the bottom, under the rubble of the state that was crushed and destroyed the existing social structures by its fall, under the pressure of an oppression whose size and organization equalled and even surpassed the dark legends of history, interpersonal bonds grew. These bonds were based on the principle of the communion of the oppressed, the communion of a tribe condemned by its conquerors to suffer the elimination of all the features of its existence which raise the tribe above its condition of servitude. All this became a system of stimuli which caused us to accept the call for a "classless society" as our own call—the symbol of the future life of our nation in the world after the deluge (Strzelecki 1974:66–67).

Socialism also means the synthesis of "the best traditions of European social thought about the further possibility of the development of social democracy and the kind of life based on respect for the human being. For this reason, the nation was not an absolute goal for us but the nearest sphere of responsibility in a struggle of more general import. The best traditions of socialist internationalism became dear to us" (Strzelecki 1974:76–77).

In summary then—why? Let us briefly take stock: the spell of the socialist ethos, of the same morality for everyone, of the struggle for social justice, of a classless society in the Poland of tomorrow; the spell of a proletarian internationalism without the elimination of the principle of brotherhood, the spell of the dignity of the working person, and so on. All this, in spite of basic doctrinal reservations in regard to such ideas as the materialistic concept of the human being, the concept of class morality, of human existence deprived of a permanent nature, of the determinism of the base over the superstructure; all this in spite of the peculiarity of the views on the nation, patriotism, religion. To this general theory the author assigns the name "socialism." We understand the author's intentions. We do not blame him for anything. For people who went through the experiences of the war, who wanted the rebuilt Poland to be better than it was before the war, who were deeply convinced that the word "socialism" summarizes the noblest traditions of European culture—for those people there was no other choice. They did not and could not see another way. No option was left them but to give fundamental moral support to the emerging system. I repeat, "fundamental moral support" because they could argue about details.

They were close to Christianity. They were fascinated by personalism, they were under the spell of the writings of Simone Weil.[160] They spoke about Catholicism and the church in different tones than their "principled comrades." They searched together with believers for common bridges and pathways of understanding. Their standpoint became the beginning of many friendships over the barriers. Their tragedy was that they constantly had to register reservations about the system and its methods; and with the passing of time their voice counted less and less rather than more. They wanted to be faithful to the idea, even when the idea, by revealing its utopian form, began to betray them.

We know that Stalinism treated many of them cruelly. They came to pay a great price for their doubts about the correctness of the principle of proletarian internationalism, about the class character of ethical principles, about the theory of the dictatorship of the proletariat, about the policy toward culture and religion. Some did not survive Stalinism. Others went for a compromise; in essence they agreed that they were dealing with dreamt-out socialism, but they demanded adjustments in its realization. Occupying more or less important positions in society, they tried to realize their ideals as much as possible. Whatever one would like to say, many of them permanently entered the records of Polish heroism of the most recent past.

Let us turn from the personae and consider the content of their thought. Two things appear to be essential.

Strzelecki's text gives expression not to Marxism and socialism as definite sociopolitical doctrines as much as to the ethos of socialist and Marxist thinking that is at their source. Socialism and Marxism were born as the expressions of the rebellion by a thinking conscience against the situation in which human work and working human beings found themselves in modern society. At the beginning was the ethos; doctrines came later. Were the doctrines always faithful to the original intention? No, not always. But, according to Strzelecki, living socialism consists exactly in the fact that in order to express better the germinal ideal, one can always subject a definite doctrinal concept to revision. Strzelecki adds: at the level of ethos there is no abyss between socialism and Christianity. Indeed, there is not. The Christian may say: at the roots of socialism there lies Christian inspiration. In reality, we all are growing from a single, basic trunk.

All this is true, but at the same time it awakens some uneasiness. There are various ways to carry out ethical reflections. The way presented by Strzelecki is fascinating but it is rather easily exposed to criticism. Strzelecki, in making some sort of an a priori definition of ideals, says that socialism contains in itself the noblest values that humanity over the centuries has considered as its most sublime aims. What is socialism? It is what is most sublime. What is most sublime? Socialism. One who carries out an ethical reflection in this way commits the common error of *petitio principii*. Strzelecki is an outstanding sociologist but one who at the level of critical, ethical reflection does not go beyond the level of naiveté. Perhaps he does not want to go beyond it. Strzelecki gives testimony, he writes what he felt, what he thought, how the facts looked to him. It may be that particular external circumstances cause some people to look upon this testimony as a critical textbook of ethics. Perhaps, then, we should not make of the text something that it is not? Let what I am saying not be held against the text, but against the ethical consciousness of those about whom the text speaks and to whom it gives testimony. In summary, it is a testimony about the lack of a moral alternative. One who defined the ideal this way did not have another option but to "basically accept the system" and argue only about its realization. Later, from this basic acceptance, came all the disquietude and guilty conscience of the generation we are talking about.

Let us draw a little contrast. Another way of pursuing ethics is to attempt to define real criteria for a choice in a real situation, criteria that here and now permit us to make a right choice. We do not define ideals, we do not look for general, common values. Nothing is simpler than to define an ideal and determine a value. It is difficult to decipher the sense of greater and lesser events properly. But we aim at exactly this—we practice ethics as a reflection on the practical conscience. Conscience is like the sense of art, it sees itself as it is. It is watching on election day, on the day of a strike, on the day of testimony for or against the truth. It builds ethics by starting from the bottom, it accepts not words but concrete decisions. It makes the theory of conscience a skeleton of ethical doctrine. This conception is what I find a bit lacking in Strzelecki.

Did all the socialists of the past three decades have sharpened consciences? Certainly they all lived by lofty ideals, but conscience is not an ideal, it is an internal reality of human beings that governs and rules them. Did it rule our socialists at every moment of their involvement?

It is not my business to give the answer to this question.

One more marginal remark, but still in connection with the ethics of socialism.

Ethos: "attempts at testimony," as it seems to me, is the ethos that characterizes many positions of Communists and Socialists about whom it was said in common parlance that they are "true Communists," or "prewar Communists," or simply "idealists," in contrast to those who became Communists only for the sake of a career. The people who were spoken of in this way distinguished themselves not only by conceptual authenticity but also by a relatively good knowledge of history and Marxism. Despite this, most often they did not fill very high posts in the power apparatus. They were useful, rather, where no important economic, political, or social decisions were made. Because of that, in popular opinion, they could pass for people with "clean hands." Many of them found positions in education, scientific institutions, news media, or generally in culture. They distinguished themselves by a relatively great civil courage that expressed itself mostly in words. In practice, they followed the silently accepted rule of the "lesser evil." Despite this, they were able, even in the darkest times, to do a great deal of good in individual matters. Obviously, they were not preventing the emergence of Stalinism. Generally, they also did not strike with the strikers, did not demonstrate with the demonstrators. One could call them "knights errant of socialist construction."

Some perished during Stalinist times. Many survived. After the period of Stalinism, it seemed that their idealism and their criticism might be useful for the power apparatus. Thus they were dispatched to an incited and disgruntled people in order to talk to them on a semiofficial level. They were allowed a relatively extensive criticism of party policy since it was criticism based on the axiom of ideal socialism. After all, the critique always confirmed the ideal. Only the great ideal allows one to see so sharply the prosaic aspect of our life—thus, "long live the ideal." This was reasoning within the framework of an initial *petitio principii*.

Despite this, they were not liked by the power apparatus, not because they criticized too sharply, but because they transferred to others the burden of "dirtying their hands." One does not make a revolution with clean hands. The knights errant of socialism clipped the coupons from the achievements of those comrades who dirtied their hands. They themselves were clean. But even this was forgiven them.

Recently, one hears about the collapse of morality among the young, about the growth of consumerist and petty bourgeois attitudes. Most likely, the issue is that the figure of the "true Communist" is disappearing from the stage. But does this disappearance mean the decline of morality? Did the disappearance of the figure of the knight errant, that was characteristic for a certain period of European history, also mean that all piety and virtue were dying in the nation?

19. On Behalf of the Lay Left

Who is Michnik, the author of *The Church, the Left, Dialogue,* which was published in Paris by the Literary Institute? Stefan Kisielewski,[161] the noted journalist of *Tygodnik Powszechny,* answers the question in his introduction to the book.

Adam Michnik, born in 1946 in Warsaw, is one of the main figures of the famous Polish March of 1968 and also, preceding that March, of the contesting ferment among Warsaw's academic youth. For his participation in this youthful "contestation" Michnik paid by being dismissed from the university, tried, and sentenced to one and one-half years in prison. After release from prison, he worked for a while as a blue collar worker in one of the big Warsaw factories and then received permission to continue his studies of history by correspondence at Poznań University. He graduated in 1975 with an M.A. degree, awarded for the thesis *Selected Problems from the History of Polish Political Thought during the Emigration of 1864–1870.* He specializes in the modern history of Poland. He is also the author of numerous articles devoted to this topic, articles both analytic and purely historical that are published under pen names in Polish Catholic periodicals and abroad.

Michnik uses pen names because he lives the life of a second-class citizen in Poland. His name cannot be printed in the press and he has repeatedly fallen victim to various repressive actions. In spite of this, he lives an energetic life, inspires various acts of opposition and protest. He is very popular and esteemed among Warsaw youth, as well as in so-called intellectual circles. He likes to push a stick into an ant hill and has done a great deal in this respect, and promises still more (Michnik 1977:7).

Michnik's book is a historical sketch, although it contains certain political and even philosophical ideas. Michnik analyzes the history of relationships between the church and state as well as between the so-called "Lay Left" and Catholicism, Catholics and religion. He rests his analyses on numerous sources such as the pastoral letters of the Polish episcopate and the primate, commentaries and articles from the press, and various legislative acts of the Polish People's Republic. He arrives at conclusions, not long ago unacceptable to the Left, that the church and Christian religion, Catholics and Catholicism in general played a creative, "progressive" role in Poland and became the authentic defenders of human rights, the defense of which was also the aim of this Left. From this comes a political postulate: the Lay Left should recognize the role of religion, enter into dialogue with the church, better understand the nature of Christianity and Catholicism, and together fight the common enemy of the human person, the totalitarianism of political authority. In Michnik's book we run into a new tone in writing about religion. Michnik tries to talk about religion without prejudice, to understand from it more than others, to seek planes of agreement with Polish Catholics. He does not thereby want to make religion a tool for coming to power and strengthening authority; he is concerned with finding a formula for living together in the pluralistic society of tomorrow. The book is something more than the expression of the author's personal views. Michnik participates in the uneasiness of many like him and expresses their hope; he is a sign of a current which, to some extent, pervades the soul of not a few Poles. The book proved to be a true "sign of the times."

From what positions does Michnik come? What theory does he feel to be behind him, for what ideals does he want to fight?

He defines himself as a representative of the "Lay Left." What does this mean? He writes:

What is the Left presently in 1976? I cannot give this question an uncomplicated answer. In recent years, as a result of the defeat of the official Communist ideology, nationalistic feelings became intensified and widespread. This is clearly visible in the circles of authority as well as within the opposition milieu. Both the authorities and the opposition are divided. I am more interested in the divisions within the opposition. To use the formulation of one of my friends, I will say that the opposition consists of those who oppose because they are convinced of the superiority of the capitalist system over any other system, and those whose program is the idea of democratic socialism. I am aware how much I am simplifying, but holding to this simplification I will say further that I identify the Left with the second group. The Left thus understood proclaims ideas of liberty and tolerance, ideas of the sovereignty of the human person and the liberation of work, of a just division of national income and an equal start for all; but it fights chauvinism, national oppression, obscurantism and xenophobia, lawlessness, and social wrong. The program of the Left is a program of anti-totalitarian socialism (Michnik 1977:15–16).

Coming from these positions, Michnik discovers Polish Catholicism and the Polish church. It is primarily the discovery of a historian, but a historian who deals expertly with political categories. After examining relevant documents, Michnik concludes:

Citing the above facts, referring extensively to documents from those times, I wished to inform my friends from the Lay Left, who generally did not know the cited texts and facts, what the real situation of the church and the position of the Catholic bishops was during the Stalinist period. If they confront the demands of the episcopate with what they read about them then and thereafter in the official press, then they will perhaps see the entire magnitude of their ignorance. If they compare these demands with the practices of the state authorities at the time, then my question will become more understandable to them: Where in those times was the chief enemy of progress and goodness? In the Catholic churches or in the Party committees and secret police?

Some statements in the pastoral letters may disturb, others may seem anachronistic. However, the basic questions are: Did the church, in the Stalinist period, defend human rights? Did it defend human freedom and dignity? I answer these questions affirmatively. I fully share the opinion of Czesław Miłosz, who wrote that in the Stalinist period the church building was the only place where the official lie did not penetrate and the church Latin permitted us to keep faith in human speech, otherwise degraded and bent to the worst tasks (Michnik 1977:45).

The church's positive role, however, does not end with the Stalinist period. Michnik continues his search and concentrates above all on the year 1968, which was special to him, a year in which the so-called "revisionists" made their claim for democratic freedoms in the country. Michnik sees this unequivocally. Indirectly, the church also took those "revisionists" under its protection, despite the fact that these were often people known for their antireligious activity. It took them under its protection in the sense that it called for the rule of law, democracy and tolerance. On this point, Michnik's voice is particularly loud.

We read:

Atheism and anticlericalism were constant components of the ideology of Polish revisionism. Even the sharpest critiques of Stalinism by the revisionists did not denounce the persecutions of religion and the church at all or they saw in them only erroneous tactics that, by pushing the church to the verge of the catacombs, reinforced "religious superstitions". I would risk the view that many revisionists considered the significant limitation of the influences of Catholicism and the church as one of the few virtues of this period of errors and deviations. The fact that the revisionists, in their criticism of the Party and Party orthodoxy, often had recourse to an analogy with the Catholic church, was of no small importance. One might say that for them the Party grew more repugnant the more it reminded them of the church. Exposing in their periodicals the irrationalism and fideism of the fuzzy construction of Stalinist dialectical materialism, the revisionists were heirs to the ideas of the rationalistic philosophers. To the "fanatic faith" of the Stalinists, they juxtaposed "wisdom" and "tolerance".

And a bit further:

One can imagine that from the point of view of a bishop, who only yesterday was persecuted, the "rabid" revisionists represented a particularly appalling coterie. Only yesterday attacking religion and bishops, only yesterday activists of the Party's ideological front, extollers of the regime when it was particularly cruel—and today, still not accepting their own personal guilt, shifting the responsibility to objective conditions and other people, beating someone else's breast and at the same time, again dressed in the cloak of the moralists, condemning intolerance in others, who only yesterday were persecuted. The opposition of the revisionists to the new leadership of the Party must also look highly suspicious to the persecuted Catholics (Michnik 1977:46–47).

Michnik demands that the discovery of Christianity be carried as close as possible to its conclusion. One should revise the assessments of religion that were carried out until now by the "Lay Left." It is difficult to resist the temptation to quote yet one more fragment.

Our intellectual revision must reach deeper. It must touch the very roots of that arrogant conviction that after all, in reality, we know the true road of progress and wisdom, because, in reality, we do not know such a road; neither we nor anybody in the world knows the roads along which history will roll. We in particular, more than anyone else, should understand that such pseudo-knowledge about the secrets of the *Weltgeist* occasionally has criminal consequences. That is, it grants the right, on the basis of a knowledge of the imaginary laws of history, to direct to the road of "wisdom and progress" thousands of people who are totally unaware of the necessity and inevitability of the New Order. The realization of the projects of the New Order, however, this kingdom of Progress, Wisdom and Liberty, leads unavoidably to contempt for people, to the use of coercion, and to moral self-destruction.

I think that the arrogant conviction about the nonexistence of a supernatural order carries with it an equally threatening consequence. I say "arrogant" since we may have total certainty only of the fact that death will not pass us by. Everything else is a blunder, a burden of existence, a tedious passage to the truth. While on this passage full of searching, stumbling and soaring, let us respect those who believe that a superhuman order was revealed to them. Let us judge them by their deeds and not by their words, twisted and deformed by others. Only under this condition shall we be able, with heads held high, to demand from the people of the church an analogous attitude toward us (Michnik 1977:93).

I would not like to prolong this characterization of Michnik's views. Therefore, I regretfully omit some extremely interesting fragments in which the author tells by which roads he came upon his discovery of Christianity. I omit also his assessments of various "dialogue" movements inspired or supported by the state—thus, his evaluation of the PAX movement, of the ODiSS movement of Janusz Zabłocki[162] or the so-called "pseudo"-Znak. I want to concentrate further upon the very idea of dialogue.

Michnik puts into practice a certain idea of dialogue until now foreign to Marxists or to leftist elaborations in general on the problem of Marxism-socialism-Christianity. Whatever one would say about the deficiencies of his book, after Michnik it will no longer be possible to carry on a dialogue as was done before him. That is, of course, if one wants to say something sensible on the question or from the position of dialogue. On what does this idea rest?

A conversation between people is not yet a dialogue. Rather, the word dialogue denotes only those conversations in which the testimony of another person is accepted as an indispensable source of knowledge about the object of the conversation. Dialogue is, above all, a certain method of cognition. Naturally, it is not a universal method, one suited to every science or every manner of acquiring knowledge. For example, in mathematics cognition does not have the character of dialogue, but is a monologue. To recognize that a given mathematical solution is true, I do not have to call upon the testimony of others; it is sufficient simply to compare the conclusions with the assumptions. Dialogue is a method of cognition in the humanities, social sciences, history, and is also an intergral component of religious cognition. Authentic social life cannot get by without dialogue. In order to know who I am, I must look at myself not only with my own eyes, but also with the eyes of others, as from the outside. Similarly, others, if they want to know the truth about themselves, must call upon our, my testimony about them.

Michnik's book was not written to develop an abstract theory of dialogical cognition. In our circumstances, however, the book brings more to this theory than many other books devoted explicitly to it. Simply, it brings to reality the fundamental conditions of the idea of dialogue. It does this under difficult political circumstances, when merely publishing the work in an emigré house may be considered an illegal act and bring unpleasant consequences upon the author. This fact has an enormous moral meaning.

Let us try, however, to formulate certain questions in the spirit proposed by Michnik. These questions will not concern the strictly factual aspects of the book, since this would lead us too far away from the main line of our considerations. We shall concentrate on a specifically ethical note of the considerations, that is, a direct expression of the idea of "democratic socialism." Not much is written about this idea although it is a rather basic issue since the book, in our social context, acquired a broader political significance. As it turns out, the aim was not only to "set the Lay Left straight," but also to dispel the biases of Christians and the church toward this Left. That the church has no confidence in the Left is understandable. Now, however, one will be able to say: "We have revised our assessments, now you revise yours." What judgment can be made about this stratum of the book's significance?

It should be emphasized that Michnik's proposition has been welcomed with great sympathy in wide circles of Catholic intellectuals in Poland. No one questions the basic intention of the author. No one rejects the fundamental theoretical propositions. Generally, all underscore the great courage of Michnik's thinking. Still, some uneasiness is evoked by the generality and equivocality of the principles that define Michnik's own position. "Democratic socialism," "Lay Left"—what do they mean?

"Democratic socialism," as we remember, proclaims "ideas of freedom and tolerance, ideas of the sovereignty of the human person and liberation of work, ideas of a just division of national wealth and equal opportunities for all"; and opposes "chauvinism and national oppression, obscurantism and xenophobia, lawlessness and social wrongdoing." All this is lofty, worthy of respect, beautiful. But is it fully thought out? First, the idea of democracy contains in itself the thought that the ultimate subject of authority is the entire nation—people regardless of social class. On the other hand, the idea of socialism contains the thought that this subject is above all the "leading class of the nation," the industrial proletariat. Thus, the concept of democratic socialism, from a purely theoretical point of view, is like the concept of a square circle. Second, again from the point of view of pure theory, such a definition of socialist ideals is a circular argument since it first establishes a certain ideal, then a priori defines exactly this sort of ideal as socialist, and finally leaves no place for any ethical alternative. Third, from a practical point of view, the whole thing smells like some sort of "moral demagoguery," for what is left to me if I do not support the ideals of the Lay Left? Nothing but "chauvinism, national oppression, obscurantism, lawlessness" and similar atrocities. In the past, during Stalinism, we had no choice because the "iron rules of history" did not permit one. Today also we have no option because the lofty—I would even say too lofty—ethics of "democratic socialism" do not allow an option. We did change the level of considerations but somehow their framework remained the same.

Michnik says "socialism." This concept also functions in the official language of those with whom Michnik is in conflict, in the language of the Party, the propaganda apparatus, in the language of ideologues. A question arises: To what extent does this concept convey the same meaning to both sides? Could the word perhaps be the same but its contents diametrically opposite? Or is there perhaps a common denominator? These are not only theoretical questions; the issue is whether Michnik's thought, in spite of everything, bestows approval upon what came to exist in Poland after World War II, or whether he considers everything to have been in error. Does Michnik believe that at least the beginnings were good? Does he thus, in spite of his whole criticism and opposition, grant a moral sanction to the groundwork of the current system? I think he does. There is no indication to the contrary. This is an issue of great weight. Regrettably, it has not been developed further. Equivocation in this matter awakens various speculations, and speculations in turn easily become transformed into suspicions, for which not only the reader is responsible.

There remains one more detail, which is characteristic, I think, of the entire "leftist mentality."

I do not know whether there is any social theory other than the Marxist that would so much blunt the natural human sense of reality. It is amazing that the people of the "Lay Left" have lived in the midst of our country, have had eyes and ears, and did not realize what was and is the role of the church in this country. It took Michnik's book to change their opinion. But, is the book going to convince them? Will the old fears and suspicions disappear? Besides, are there not to be found in Michnik's own text some traces of that "overcome" mentality? The way of looking at society presented in Michnik's book is characteristic. Michnik turns primary attention to dialogue at the *level of authority,* thus at the level of: episcopate—government, bishop—prime minister, church—Party apparatus. All the while this level of dialogue was secondary. The essential dialogue and basic choice were made at the level of the nation. The nation, the so-called "ordinary people," filling the churches and pilgrimage sites, were fighting against the processes of socialization. The voice of a bishop was most often only an exponent of what was happening within the heart and soul of the nation. I am not saying that such a voice was without significance. I am only saying that the main source of its significance was beyond it. Michnik appeared not to see this, he appeared to look through the prism of a "leftist" fascination with "authority."

Michnik says "Lay Left." Does he realize how these words sound today to the ears of ordinary people who have problems with bringing up children, with the "lay" school, with more or less official atheistic indoctrination? Maybe there is still some vital content to those words, but certainly they are not as important today as they were between the wars. Besides, one must look reality in the eye; laicism and the Left belong to the vocabulary of concepts that have been totally compromised by our reality. I cannot imagine anyone who, standing at some time as a candidate in a free election under the banner of the "Lay Left," would win a deputy's seat in this country, after all that this country has experienced. This does not mean that people are for intolerance and discrimination; it means that people simply have had enough of all this. If Michnik thinks that those words after all contain something valuable for the nation's life, let him define this content more precisely instead of reaching for words played out and lost.

And finally, a last question.

Originally, I did not intend to include Michnik, nor Strzelecki, in this study of Christian–Marxist dialogue, since even if these authors appeal to socialism, hardly anything connects them with Marxism. Now, after presenting the details, my doubts increase still more. I am not sure at all that their theses point to an evolution within the theoretical thought of socialism. They come rather as a voice from outside the theory. It is an important voice, a strong, convincing voice, but nonetheless, a voice from outside. This voice does not incorporate religion into the world of socialism as, for example, Christian negative theology incorporated atheism into the world of religion. The bond between religion and socialism is a bond of alliance. The latter is above all a political matter. Although such an alliance, from the ethical point of view, may be something desirable and valuable, in the final analysis for left-thinking, it has political repercussions. I do not think, and I do not see evidence, that we have finally freed ourselves from the primacy of politics over ethics.

A synthesis of politics with ethics is an old myth, the myth of utopian socialism—the myth that, according to the testimony of orthodox Marxists, Marx and Engels elevated to the dignity of a science. In the case of Strzelecki and Michnik, we are outside Marxism, and hence as if at its beginnings. Do we, after the many years of the stormy development of Marxism, need to return to its beginnings? Could it be that these are not the beginnings, but rather the final accords? Could it be that one of the last of the "knights errant of socialism" discovered that the church, in the past the object of his and his comrades' attacks, is not at all the "forerunner of imperialism" but just an ordinary windmill that grinds flour for those who live not by bread alone? Whatever one would say, the end of fighting with windmills has its positive meaning too.

IV.
Final Reflections

During this work, time after time, the following thought has recurred: The essential level of the dialogue between Christianity and Marxist theory and practice in Poland was an ethical one; to be exact, the level of an integrally understood ethos as a way of existing according to the hope cherished by the human being. Thus, on the one side, we have had an earth-centered hope, the essential component of which was the promise of abolishing the exploitation of one human being by another. On the other side, there was the more universal hope in which the essential value proved to be the dignity of the human being. This kind of dialogue itself had the result that practically the entire nation participated in the dialogue. There was no person in the country who, at one time or another, did not have to declare himself or herself more or less firmly for the one or the other side. The course of events engaged everybody. At one time, the problem was the baptism of a child, at another the participation of a child in religious instructions, at still another time participation in processions, religious celebrations, the welcoming of John Paul II to his fatherland. There were various ways of getting involved. There was also a place for appropriate forms of philosophy. Although the social role of the dialogue conducted at this level was not too great, nevertheless such a dialogue was interesting because it brought to expression in a pure form the opinions which permeated the social consciousness.

What are the results of the dialogue?

Above all, one of the important effects of the dialogue—effects conditioned by multiple factors—is the space of freedom that exists in our country. We know that this space is greater than in other countries similar to ours. No one has any illusion that the achievement of such a space of freedom is to be credited to the Christian spirit of resistance, the pastoral work of the church, and also the postconciliar theology of the church's presence in temporal life. With the achieved scope of freedom, a risky event like the pilgrimage of John Paul II to Poland became possible. Let us recall that in the times of Pius XII[163] and Bierut, this was unthinkable; in the times of Paul VI and Gomułka, the matter was, to be sure, thinkable, but proved to be unrealizable. In spite of the exertions of the episcopate and the desires of Paul VI, the pope was not invited for the millennium celebrations in Częstochowa;[164] the subsequent turn of events surprised everybody. Obviously, it is difficult to balance all the factors suitably, but certainly somewhere in the distant background of the conditions of possibility for the recent papal pilgrimage was the fact that the Marxists' anticlericalism, atheism, and "militant godlessness" burnt themselves out. Something similar also happened on the Catholic side, especially after the Council, when the church entered the period of dialogue with the contemporary world and also with the governments of Eastern Europe. Thus, we have our space of freedom. We know that this space is not very large, but in the past it was much smaller. The visit of John Paul II enlarged and strengthened this space and also added to the spirit of those who work for its expansion.

The visit closes a certain important period of the dialogue. It was something on the order of a national plebiscite. The nation—let us not be afraid of this word since we have no word like it to designate what we are thinking about—essentially the entire nation stood on the side of those hopes that are symbolized by the Polish pope. What is the core of these hopes? It seems to me that it is a particular concept of the dignity of the human person. All the homilies of John Paul II in Poland elaborated this concept. Within this concept other values found a place: the dignity of the Pole as an heir of the heroic history of the nation, the dignity of the working person (which was a concern of Socialists), the significance of freedom, traditional tolerance, fidelity to the truth, courage in sacrifice. The intellectual space of the papal homilies was so broad that every person of good will could find a place in it. Suddenly, the relationship changed. No longer did Socialists and Communists invite Catholics to dialogue and collaboration, but Catholics invited all others. This collaboration extends deeper than the struggle for peace and social discipline. The issue is the reconstruction and continuation of the deepest values of the national spirit, the values symbolized by such figures as St. Stanisław, Blessed Queen Jadwiga, Paweł Włodkowic, Mikołaj Kopernik, Fr. Maksymilian Kolbe—figures that were at the center of John Paul II's attention. In awakening the feeling of dignity, the pope was awakening a hope commensurate with this feeling. Simultaneously, he strengthened the feeling of responsibility. The events of the pilgrimage became an integral part of Polish national self-knowledge. As in the past the partitions[165]—examples of national disaster—were the content of national self-knowledge, so presently the pilgrimage—a symbol of undefeated spirit—became the content of that self-knowledge.

In this, whose is the success and whose the defeat? Is this a success of Christianity and the church, and a defeat of Marxist-socialist indoctrination? Yes. But someone who says so does not look deeply enough.

It is, above all, a success of the nation. The nation made the choice, the nation unveiled its face, the nation remained itself. On this occasion, all those who erased the concept of nation from their vocabulary and replaced it with a concept of society or class could directly see, feel, and hear what the nation is. It was the nation, not this or that class, that turned out to be the leading force of history. I think that each of us Poles somehow believes in Poland. But at that time one could abandon faith for actual experience, at that time each of us experienced Poland. Poland is not a symbol, a metaphor, it is a living, thinking, feeling, choosing nation.

Only through this choice may we speak about the success of Christianity. This success rests in the fact that the nation chose Christianity and not earth-centered proposals. Some are afraid of such statements because they anticipate in them the danger of religious triumphalism. I think these are two different things: triumph and triumphalism. The triumph of Christianity is a fact, but it does not have to lead to triumphalism at all. "There is no imperialism of the church, there is only service," said John Paul II in Kraków's Błonia.[166] Triumph has primarily an ethical character. It does not leave corpses behind it. It rests on the fact that Christianity per se provided people with a relatively uniform language, a language both concrete and universally understood, with the help of which it was possible to demonstrate and define the various forms of exploitation of one human being by another that was characteristic of the so-called "period of socialist construction." By defining exploitation, Christianity and the church thereby took under protection the wronged human being. This protection had not only a declarative character but it translated into the practical defense of life, of truth, of the right to work and freedom. Due to the universal understandability of this language, the protests of people against the absurdities of Marxist "terraism" were reinforced by the entire might of human conscience.

Can one say that the church protested against the details but essentially accepted the socialist system? I think not. The church still is not finally convinced of this system. The "knights errant of socialism" seem to forget this. Never in the letters and documents of the episcopate has the word "socialism" appeared, even in a descriptive sense. Nor was this word in the papal homilies. John Paul II spoke generally about the "system of work" (homily in Nowa Huta).[167] This, obviously, does not mean that the church accepts capitalism. This word is also absent from the language of the contemporary church in Poland. The church remains reserved. It is an institution that escapes the vicious circle, described earlier, of definitions used by some "ethicians" of the socialist idea.

Catholic thinkers participated in the success of Christianity. One must emphasize once again, however, that the essential criticism of Marxist philosophy in Poland did not come from their pens but from the pens of Marxist themselves. External critique from the Christian side concerned either marginal issues or, overestimating the intellectual values of Marxist propositions, bowed to banalities. One must agree with many Marxists that knowledge of Marxism in Catholic intellectual circles was not very great. Thus, Catholic thinkers neither transplanted onto Polish soil the Western critique of Marxism nor came forward with their own critique.

One should also emphasize that the church emerged from the confrontation with Marxism to some degree purified and strengthened. An increase in church authority also came from Vatican Council II. The Council reforms in Poland had a specific course and decidedly contributed to the strengthening and deepening of religious life in the country. The church, it seems, understood somehow better that its main social strength comes from the faith of the people, from the strength of the nation, from presenting and representing its ethical traditions. It also understood that the strength of the faith of ordinary people would be blind were it not for the reflection of intellectuals, writers and creators of national culture. From this comes the church's deep bond with the community of people who create science and culture, a bond that did not exist on such a scale before the war. The church also tore itself away from an attachment to private property; it freed itself from an obsession with ownership. Private property ceased to be an idol, a dogma of daily life, a center of daily worry, as may be noticed, unfortunately, here and there in the West. From this comes a feeling of independence and spiritual freedom. The church learned to speak with a more evangelical language about the dignity of human beings, their freedom, and the essence of the nation. The church appeared to be different from its earlier images. It did not correspond with the images of its critics and even surpassed the images of its panegyrists. The church never directly fought the political system in which it found itself, nor the alliances in which this system enmeshed our country. But, it did not accept them a priori either. It was alert to the concrete events that time was bringing. The church was poised more for "propositions" to than for opposition against the authorities. It built and created those values that are above coercion; it protected the national hope. When John Paul II kissed the soil of his forefathers, everybody felt emotion, for here was a visit to the country by someone who had become a symbol of an independent and sovereign Poland. He was not only a Person, he was also a Thought. He demonstrated how one can survive socialism, preserving a clean conscience. Never before in the history of the nation was so much content focused in a single human being.

For over thirty years the Polish church lived and coexisted with the processes of "socialist construction." It was submerged in socialization like a fish in water. Time and again, it was forced to protest. Does not the reality of such a coexistence cause it to take something of its adversary upon itself?

Perhaps one could aptly say that at a certain moment the church managed to "wrest the ethical initiative" from the hands of its adversaries. As a result, it will be the church that will call for the realization of basic social ideals that until now constituted the basic ethical horizon of Marxism. The church and Christianity discovered, as it were, the false bottom of Marxist thought. They found therein, slightly dusty, slightly deformed, their own social ideals. There is nothing surprising in this. Marxism was a sort of neopaganism that was born after the defeat of the Christianization of Europe. Christians in Poland seemed to discover their own Christianity after the defeat of the processes of "socialist construction" in Poland. In a sense, therefore, they are "neo-Christians," that is, those who turn back to Christianity as the result of a confrontation with the enemies of religion. Thus, "neo-Christianity" would be a return to the sources, the common sources of European thought, religious as well as atheistic. It also is an attempt to recapture the initiative—not political, but ethical—from the Marxists, the initiative of improving the world of human work. This is an enormously important moment. Retaking the initiative from an adversary causes the adversary to cease being needed in the world.

An important consequence of the confrontation, it seems to me, is a better understanding by Catholics of the sense and value of atheism. One may say that an atheist does not need religion in order to be an atheist, while for the faithful, atheism is necessary as a factor in purifying his or her faith in God. On this seem to depend the results of numerous reflections on atheism that are so abundant in Christian thought of recent times. Atheism was integrated in a certain way into Christianity as a particular form of negative theology. This does not mean that the church accepts atheism as an ultimate expression of human thought. It only means that the church treats atheism as a matter of dialogue. It seems that without taking into account what the atheist thinks of the church, the church cannot gain the full truth about itself. This deeply changes the spirit of Catholicism; it makes it open, tolerant, and, in the full sense of the term, dialogic.

And against this background, what happened with Marxism? What became of Marxism in Poland after the visit of John Paul II?

Some time ago, Marx wrote that religion will disappear when it proves to be no longer needed. Thus, according to Marx, it would disappear not as a result of polemics, advances in knowledge, or the pressure of force, but somehow in a more ordinary way, just as the spinning wheel disappeared in the era of textile industry. The history of socialism in a way has not verified this theory. It seems, however, that, by paradoxical coincidence, Marx's theories found confirmation in the history of Marxism itself. One should not exaggerate when it comes to the importance of theoretical disputes with Marxism. Marxism may last in the political system called socialism even after we no longer have even one convinced Marxist in the country. More important than theoretical disputes is the uneasiness about the entire ethos of this philosophy. Marxism in Poland ceased to be a thought that unmasks the exploitation of work and inspires social changes leading to the abolition of exploitation. Instead, it became a thought aimed at a single goal—the justification of the existing system and its flaws as objective necessities. From this come the uneasiness that is ethical in character and embraces all people rather than just the specialists in ideology. Presently, there is a growing awareness of another question: For what and for whom is Marxism still needed? This question does not deal with this or that thesis, but concerns the ethical sources of the entire process of ideologizing and the entirety of Marxist thought. For what is Marxism needed? Who needs Marxism?

These two questions seem to summarize the current state of our dialogue; they seem ultimately to define its Polish, contemporary shape.

V.
Explanatory Notes

1. COMMUNIST SEIZURE OF POWER   Following the secret protocol signed by Ribbentrop and Molotov on August 23, 1939, the Soviet Army crossed the eastern borders of Poland (September 17, 1939) and occupied almost half of the Polish territory. The design of Soviet policy at that time was to annex and incorporate into the Soviet Union the Baltic states of Estonia, Latvia and Lithuania, as well as the eastern part of Poland.

After the fall of Poland in October 1939, leaders of the Polish government and of the political parties, as well as military commanders, formed the Government–in–Exile led by President Raczkiewicz. This government, in which all the major prewar political parties (see note 142) were represented, was recognized by all the democratic countries as the sole legitimate representative of Poland. It exercised authority over patriotic civilian and military groups abroad and inside occupied Poland. In the latter case, the delegate of the government and its emissaries constituted a link between the authorities abroad and the resistance forces inside the country. These forces, organized with the authority of the commander–in–chief of the Polish Army and considered an integral part of Polish Armed Forces, were consecutively—Polish Victory Service (SZP) in 1939, Union of Armed Struggle (ZWZ) in 1940, and Home Army (AK) in 1942. As the result of political negotiations, AK was joined by several other groups such as Peasant Battalions (BCh), National Military Organization (NOW), and National Armed Forces (NSZ).

After being attacked by its former ally Nazi Germany in June 1939, the Soviet Union recognized the Government–in–Exile and signed an agreement to cease all hostilities, to free all those Polish citizens who were arrested and deported in 1939, and to form Polish military forces in the Soviet Union. Diplomatic relations were broken by the Soviets in 1943 in response to the request of the Government–in–Exile for an investigation into the murder of Polish officers whose bodies were discovered by the Nazis in the Katyń forest near the city of Smolensk. However, even earlier, the Soviets had fostered a small group of Polish Communists who emigrated to the Soviet Union, or to the territories occupied by the Soviets in 1939 (Nowotko, Finder, Zambrowski, Lampe, Jaszczuk, Berman, Minc, Grosz, Ochab, Krasicki, Gomułka, see note 57). Included in this group were leftist officers and intellectuals (Berling, Zawadzki, Świerczewski, Borejsza, Wasilewska, Bierut, see note 116). These Communists and self-appointed "leaders" in 1942 in Saratov formed the Union of Polish Patriots (ZPP) as a front to be used by the Soviets in pursuing their aims. In occupied Poland, Communists sent from Moscow (Nowotko, Fornalska, Finder, Gomułka) organized a Communist Party (PPR) as the Soviet proxy that controlled a small resistance force initially called the People's Guard (GL) (a name usurped from a group that had earlier joined the democratic resistance) and later the People's Army (AL), and led by the leftist General Michał Żymierski, who before the war had been dishonorably discharged and sentenced to five years in prison for financial fraud. Polish Communists, under Soviet auspices, organized the Central Bureau of Polish Communists in the Soviet Union (CBKP) that was to exert control over the Communist Party inside Poland. The latter formed the National Homeland Council (KRN) under the chairmanship of Bolesław Bierut (see note 116) that opposed the Council of National Unity (RJN) organized by the broad spectrum of political parties involved in the resistance movement. Subsequently, KRN was recognized by the Soviets as the basis for the future Communist-dominated government of Poland.

In June 1944, the Delegature of KRN for the Liberated Territories was formed in Moscow with representation from both the ZPP and the Communist underground in Poland. Within a few days (July 20, 1944), the name was changed to the Polish Committee of National Liberation (PKWN, known also as the Lublin Committee). On July 22, 1944, this committee issued a manifesto (see note 85) prepared, printed and proclaimed in Moscow and formulated in the form of a decree that authorized several social, political and military actions. The manifesto was signed by Bierut, but its contents were neither known to nor approved by leaders of the Communist underground in Poland. The place of the release was given as Chełm, although members of the PKWN arrived in that city on July 27, 1944. They arrived in the city of Lublin only on July 28, 1944 from Moscow, and later, July 31, 1944, from Warsaw. One of the very first acts of PKWN was relinquishing to the Soviets executive power within the territory of Poland; this agreement was in force until May 1945. This delivery of control of postwar Poland to the Moscow regime recalls that of Targowica in the eighteenth century that signaled the second and third partitions of Poland (see note 165).

The legitimate Polish Government–in–Exile tried to convince the Western Allies to withhold their recognition from any Soviet-sponsored authorities as being nonrepresentative of the wishes and desires of the

Polish people. Unfortunately, both the United States and Great Britain not only declined to support the position of the Government–in–Exile, but actually exerted a not so subtle pressure on it to come to an agreement with the Soviets. Faced with this pressure and even overt threats, the Prime Minister of Poland, Stanisław Mikołajczyk, agreed to talks with the Soviets. The subject of these negotiations was, incredibly, the removal of the president, commander–in–chief, and two cabinet ministers of the legal government, as well as the formal relinquishing of the eastern territories of Poland which had been occupied by the Soviets since September 1939. The talks were broken off by the Soviets through an ultimatum delivered on June 23, 1944 that requested nothing less than the disbanding of the Government–in–Exile. This ultimatum was encouraged by President Franklin D. Roosevelt who, on June 17, 1944, gave the Soviets a free hand in dealing with the Poles, to whom he denied political support in contradiction of earlier promises given to Prime Minister Mikołajczyk.

Mikołajczyk carried out negotiations with the Soviets and essentially agreed to all their demands with respect to territorial concessions. The agreement negotiated by Mikołajczyk was not ratified by the Government–in–Exile and as a result Mikołajczyk resigned and was replaced by Tomasz Arciszewski. The government has never recognized the authority of the PKWN.

The PKWN was unilaterally recognized by the Soviets as the Provisional Government of the Polish Republic (RTRP) in January 1945, in total disregard of the Government–in–Exile. The RTRP immediately signed a formal treaty with the Soviet Union, ceding the eastern territories to the Soviets and committing Poland to an alliance with the Soviets. The latter arrested civilian and military leaders of the patriotic resistance, accused them of collaboration with the Nazis and sentenced them to prison in the Soviet Union or secretly executed them. In 1944 alone, there were 100,000 political prisoners in Poland, and the number reached half a million by 1956. All these actions preempted the decisions of the Yalta Conference (February 1945) and the Conference of the United Nations in San Francisco (April/June 1945). On June 28, 1945, the RTRP was transformed into the Provisional Government of National Unity (TRJN), reflecting the Yalta Declaration that called for the union of "all democratic and anti-Nazi elements in Poland." The TRJN was formed as the result of negotiations between the head of the RTRP, Bierut, and the then former Prime Minister of the Government–in–Exile, Mikołajczyk. The TRJN was promptly recognized by the Western powers which at the same time (July 5, 1945) withdrew their recognition of the Government–in–Exile—the only legal representation of Poland and, for all the war years, the most loyal ally of the democratic forces.

According to the decisions of the Potsdam Conference (July/August 1945), the TRJN was to govern until free elections were held as soon as possible. Instead of elections, the TRJN called for a national referendum on June 30, 1946 in which the Communist position on the structure of a future government was defeated. The postponed election was finally held in January 1947 and by that time Communists, supported by secret security forces of the Soviet Union (NKVD) and their Polish subordinates (UB), had consolidated their grip on power to such an extent that the elections could be rigged with impunity. Although Mikołajczyk, who opposed the Communists, retained his position, he was under threat to his life and ultimately had to leave the country in October 1947. Thus began the Soviet domination of Poland through their Polish servants that lasts even to this day.

2. PAPAL VISITS   There have been three visits of John Paul II to Poland. The first, on June 2–10, 1979, took the Pope to Warszawa, Gniezno, Częstochowa (see note 164), Kraków, Wadowice (his birth place), Oświęcim (see note 88), Nowy Targ, and Mogiła. The principal theme of the visit was the dignity of the human being and the value of faith, love and tradition. It inspired hope and resolution in the Polish people and some claim that it gave a spiritual birth to the Solidarity movement (see note 4). The second visit (June 16–23, 1982) took John Paul II to Warszawa, Niepokalanów (see note 87), Częstochowa, Poznań, Katowice, Wrocław, Góra Świętej Anny, and Kraków. It ended with the Pope going for a short retreat in the Tatra mountains. This visit brought a ray of hope to the Polish people dispirited after the tragic events of martial law (see note 4). The Pope confirmed his support for the struggle for human dignity and freedom, made attempts at a dialogue with Wojciech Jaruzelski, leader of the military junta, and significantly, received in private audience Lech Wałęsa—the chairman of the outlawed trade union *Solidarność*. During the third trip (June 8–14, 1987), John Paul II visited Warszawa, Lublin, Tarnów, Częstochowa, and Lodz. In his homilies, he defended human rights and the ideals of Solidarity. Most memorably, he declared to workers in Gdansk that he was speaking not only to them, but also for them.

3. JOHN PAUL II   Karol Wojtyła (1920–   ) was a student of philology, literature and theater. During the Nazi occupation, he worked as a laborer in a quarry and participated in resistance activities. Beginning in 1943, he hid in the palace of the Archbishop of Kraków, Stefan Cardinal Sapieha, and studied to become a priest. Ordained in 1946, he was consecrated bishop in 1958, appointed Archbishop of Kraków in 1964, and named Cardinal in 1967. Besides his ecclesiastical work,

he pursued a scholarly career as lecturer and chairman of the Department of Ethics at the Catholic University of Lublin (see note 120), and also produced literary works under the pen name Andrzej Jawień. In 1976 he was asked to give a Lenten retreat for Pope Paul VI (see note 130). Elected Pope in 1978 he assumed the name John Paul II in honor of his predecessors. He is the most traveled pope in the history of the papacy, having made, thus far, thirty-six trips to all corners of the globe. Phenomenology forms the philosophical background for his conservative theological view. Nonetheless, he is beloved by millions of Catholics and non-Catholics for his charismatic personality, and his honest and genuine love and concern for those who suffer. For Poles, he is a spiritual leader and the symbol of their highest hopes for freedom. His major works include: *Miłość i odpowiedzialność* (*Love and Responsibility*) (1960), *Przed sklepem jubilera* (*The Jeweler's Shop*) (1966), *Osoba i czyn* (*Person and Deed*) (1969), *Segno di Contradizione* (*Sign of Contradiction*) (1977) and the encyclicals *Redemptor Hominis* (1979), *Laborem Exercens* (1981), and *Slavorum Apostoli* (1985).

4. AUGUST 1980   After the strikes of 1976, there was a small movement of the Free Trade Unions (WZZ) organized in response to the brutal repression of the workers' protest. As the economic situation in Poland steadily worsened, local protests erupted with increasing force until, on August 14, 1980 a strike was proclaimed in the Lenin shipyard in Gdańsk. The striking workers, led by several leaders, among whom Lech Wałęsa was the most prominent, organized the Interenterprise Strike Committee (MZKS), refused an otherwise favorable settlement and demanded a nationwide agreement and guarantees for all factories. The settlement between workers and the deputy prime minister was signed in Gdańsk on August 31, 1980 and was followed by a similar agreement in Jastrzębie. The agreement consisted of clauses that gave the workers the right to strike and to organize independent, free unions. The new trade unions were registered formally on October 24, 1980 under the name *Solidarność* (Independent Self-governing Trade Union Solidarity) and soon attracted a membership of close to 10,000,000 blue- and white-collar workers. Solidarność, in spite of its efforts not to do so, was forced to challenge the primacy of the Communist Party in Poland. Solidarność undertook the monumental task of reforming society, but it was constantly harassed and provoked by the Communist authorities. Ultimately, on December 13, 1981 the Communists, under pressure from and support by the Soviets, carried out a *coup d'état* under the leadership of General Jaruzelski. Jaruzelski proclaimed martial law, suspended all authorities and introduced repressive measures. During the time of martial law, Solidarność was first suspended and then de-

legalized, and the oppressive measures of martial law were codified into the normal law, giving the Communist authorities virtually unlimited power even after martial law was lifted (1982).

5. SOCRATES   Greek philosopher (469–393 B.C.) at Athens. Originally a sculptor and soldier, he ventured into philosophy in search of right conduct that would lead to the intellectual and moral development of citizens. He developed the dialectical method of approaching knowledge and ethics, i.e., examining statements through their implications, with the assumption that if a statement is true it cannot lead to a false conclusion. In his philosophical system, virtue and knowledge are identical and it follows that virtue can be taught and that no person does wrong knowingly. Being an outspoken teacher of virtue, justice and piety, Socrates made many enemies who accused him of corrupting youth and of religious heresy. Tried and sentenced to death, he refused to escape from prison and thus violate his own principle that the law, even a bad law, must be obeyed or changed, but never broken. His writings have been lost and his views were reported by his disciples, Plato and Xenophon, and by other ancient scholars.

6. CHRISTIANITY IN POLAND   Christianity was probably first introduced to Southern Poland by one of the Apostles of the Slavs, St. Methodius (died 884), who during his mission to the Great Moravian Empire reached the banks of the Wisła River. However, it was the baptism of the Polish prince Mieszko I in 966, just before his marriage to the Czech princess Doubrava, that marked the actual introduction of Christianity to Poland. The act of baptism, which resulted in establishing a missionary bishopric in Poznań, was dictated by the political consideration of stopping the German (Saxon) expansion under the guise of spreading Christianity, but it led to lasting ties between the Polish people and the Catholic faith. Over the centuries the history of Poland was connected with that of the church and the papacy in more ways than one. Although conflicts between the church hierarchy and the secular powers occasionally occurred (see note 89), by and large the two coexisted peacefully to the benefit of the state and the nation. Christianity and the church had an immense impact on the foreign policy of Poland as it assumed the role of the bulwark of Christendom (see note 53) against non-Christian powers such as the Tartars and Turks. In the realm of internal policy, the Polish state and the church exercised an exemplary tolerance, so that in 1772 Roman Catholics constituted only 43% of the population, while Uniates (33%), Russian Orthodox (10%), Jews (9%), and Protestants (4%) made up the rest. Notably, in Poland neither the Reformation nor the Counter–Reformation resulted in religious wars as it did in the rest of Europe.

7. STEFAN WYSZYŃSKI (1901–1981)   Primate of Poland and statesman. Ordained in 1924, he received his doctorate in sociology and canon
law from the Catholic University of Lublin (see note 120). Before World
War II, he was a professor at the seminary in Włocławek (1931) and a
member of the Social Council for the Primate of Poland (1937). During
World War II, he participated in the resistance as chaplain to the Home
Army (see note 1). He was consecrated Bishop of Lublin in 1946, appointed Archbishop of Gniezno and Warszawa, and hence Primate of
Poland, in 1948, and was named Cardinal in 1953. Although he arranged
an agreement between the church and the Communist authorities in
Poland, he brought upon himself the wrath of the Communists for his
defiant stance in defense of the church and human rights during the
Stalinist era. Removed from his office and imprisoned (1953–1956), he
was restored to his position by the post-October regime (see note 73).
Unbending in his stance, he was repeatedly harassed by the authorities,
but still his influence was sought during the social crises in Poland. He
was respected by the hierarchy, the faithful and his opponents alike, as
an outstanding person. In the words of John Paul II (see note 3), Cardinal Wyszyński was "a keystone of the whole Church in Poland" and
for most Poles he represented an immense moral authority. He worked
very hard for the moral and spiritual renewal of Polish society. In the
last years of his life, he threw his support and authority behind the
Solidarity movement. Major works: Doctoral thesis "Rights of Family,
Church and the State to School" (1925) and *Zapiski więzienne* (*Freedom
from Within*) (1982), written while in prison.

8. VATICAN COUNCIL II AND THE POSTCONCILIAR CHURCH   The
Council was opened by Pope John XXIII (see note 129) on October 11,
1962 and closed on December 8, 1965 by Pope Paul VI (see note 130).
The Council was attended by over 2300 bishops, as well as by superiors
of religious orders, representatives of religious congregations, lay observers, and non-Catholic observers. The Council, following the guide-
lines of Pope John XXIII, was pastoral rather than dogmatic. It
addressed fundamental issues of the church in the twentieth century,
opening a new era in its history. It led to new structures of ministry,
authority, worship, and practice within the church, as well as to efforts
to relate to currents of thought and belief in the world at large.

9. BRATKOWSKI, STEFAN (1934–   )   Journalist. He studied jour-
nalism at the Jagiellonian University and wrote articles and essays for
the periodicals *Po prostu* (1956–57), *Kulisy* (1967–70), and *Życie i no-
woczesność* (1970–73). Member and activist of the Communist youth
organizations (1949–57), he became a member of the Communist Party
(1954). In recognition of his journalistic honesty he was elected president

of the Polish Journalist Association during the Solidarity era. After the imposition of martial law he resigned from the Party and was released from his post as president of the Association, which was soon suspended. At present, he writes only for unofficial, i.e., uncensored publishers, and prepares an audionewspaper (taped commentaries). Major works: *Księga wróżb prawdziwych* (*Book of True Predictions*) (1969), *Oddalający się kontynent* (*Continent Drifting Away*) (1978), *Nie tak stromo pod tę górę* (*Not so Steep a Mountain*) (1980), *Nowy Marsyliusz czyli społeczeństwo inteligentne* (*New Marsylius or Intelligent Society*) (1981).

10. SIX-YEAR PLAN   This was an economic plan spanning the years 1950–55, and aimed at the industrialization of Poland and the forced collectivization of agriculture. During this period, the Lenin Steelworks at Nowa Huta (see note 167) and the city of Nowa Huta were constructed and there was a large increase in the number of collective farms (up to 29,000). The latter threatened the existence of individual farmers who were the most efficient segment of Polish agriculture.

11. INGARDEN, ROMAN (1983–1970)   Philosopher, esthetician, and prime exponent of phenomenology in Poland. He studied in Lwów (see note 92), Goettingen, Vienna, and Freiburg. He taught at the University of Lwów (1933–41) and the Jagiellonian University (1945–70, see note 91); during the Stalinist era, however, he was temporarily dismissed from his position and returned to the university only after October 1956 (see note 73). He was a member of the Polish Academy of Sciences (after 1957). N.B: The author of this book was a disciple of Ingarden. Unlike his master, Husserl (see note 24), Ingarden opposed transcendental idealism and rejected the concept of reality being a product of consciousness. While working on the theory of cognition, he became interested in works of art as intentional objects and creations of consciousness. Major works: *Das literarische Kunstwerk* (1931), *Spór o istniene Świata* (*The Controversy about the Existence of the World*) (1947–48), *Szkice z filozofii literatury* (*Sketches on Philosophy of Literature*) (1947), *Studia z estetyki* (*Studies on Esthetics*) (1957–58 and 1979), *Z badań nad filozofią współczesną* (*From the Studies on Contemporary Philosophy*) (1963).

12. TWARDOWSKI, KAZIMIERZ (1866–1939)   One of the greatest Polish scholars of his period—philosopher and pedagogue. He studied with Brentano in Vienna and was professor and chairman of the Department of Philosophy at the University of Jan Kazimierz in Lwów. Major works: *Zur Lehre von Inhalt und Gegenstand der Vorstellungen*

(*The Theory of Content and Subject of Concepts*) (1984), *Wyobrażenia i pojęcia* (*Images and Concepts*) (1898), *O istocie pojęć* (*On the Essence of Concepts*) (1924), *Philosophical Dissertations and Articles* (1927).

13. AJDUKIEWICZ, KAZIMIERZ (1890–1963)   Logician and philosopher. He studied in Lwów as a disciple of Twardowski (see note 12) and Goettingen. He taught at Warszawa University (1926–28 and 1955–61), the University of Lwów (1928–39) and the University of Poznań (1945–55). He was a member of the Polish Academy of Sciences (PAN), as well as founder and first director of the Department of Logic at its Institute of Philosophy and Sociology. He was an editor of *Studia Logica*. His interest was in formal logic as a tool to solve classic problems of epistemology, but primarily he worked on the semantic theory of language and developed radical conventionalism. Major works: *Główne zasady metodologii nauk i logiki formalnej* (*Main Principles of the Methodology of Sciences and Formal Logic*) (1928), *Logiczne podstawy nauczania* (*Logical Basis of Teaching*) (1938), *Zagadnienia i kierunki filozofii* (*Problems and Currents in Philosophy*) (1949), *Język a poznanie* (*Language and Cognition*) (1960).

14. CZEZOWSKI, TADEUSZ HIPOLIT (1889–1981)   Logician and philosopher, disciple of Twardowski (see note 12). He taught at Wilno University (1923–39, see note 98) and the University of Toruń (1945–61). He was editor of the periodical *Ruch filozoficzny* (1938–39, 1946–49 and after 1958). His scholarly interest was in formal logic, history of logic and methodology of sciences. Major works: *Klasyczna nauka o sądzie i wniosku w świetle logiki* (*Classic Science on Judgment and Conclusion in the Light of Logic*) (1931), *Główne zasady nauk filozoficznych* (*Basic Principles of Philosophical Sciences*) (1946), *Logika (Logic)* (1949), *Odczyty filozoficzne (Philosophical Seminars)* (1958).

15. ŁUKASIEWICZ, JAN (1878–1956)   Logician and philosopher, cofounder of the Warszawa-Lwów school of philosophy. He studied and taught logic and mathematics at the University of Jan Kazimierz in Lwów (see note 93) (1906–15) and the University of J. Piłsudski in Warszawa (1915–39). He also was Rector of this university (1922–23, 1931–32), and a member of the Polish Academy of Learning (PAU). He received a degree of *Doctor honoris causa* from the Irish Royal Academy of Sciences, Dublin, Ireland (1945). He was the inventor of the "Polish notation" used in calculators and computers. Major works: *O zasadzie sprzeczności u Arystotelesa* (*On the Principle of Contradiction in Aristotle*) (1910), *Elementy logiki matematycznej* (*Elements of Mathematical Logic*) (1929), *Aristotle's Syllogistics from the Standpoint of Modern Formal Logic* (1951).

16. DAMBSKA, IZYDORA (1904–83)   Polish philosopher. She studied in Lwów under Twardowski (see note 12) and at the Jagiellonian University (see note 91). Originally she taught at high school, but later became professor and chairman (1957) at the Jagiellonian University. After 1964 she was an independent member of the Institute of Philosophy and Sociology of the Polish Academy of Sciences. She closely collaborated with the Catholic University in Lublin (see note 120). During World War II she participated in underground educational activities and was a member of the Home Army (see note 1). She was the first woman to be elected to L'Institut International de Philosophie. She was the editor of *Ruch filozoficzny* (1938–50) and collaborator of *Archives Internationales d'Histoire des Idées* and *Bibliographie de la Philosophie*. Major Works: *Zarys historii filozofii greckiej* (*Sketch of the History of Greek Philosophy*) (1935), *O konwencji i konwencjonalizmie* (*On Convention and Conventionalism*) (1975), *Znaki i myśli* (*Signs and Thoughts*) (1975).

17. LEŚNIEWSKI, STANISŁAW (1886–1939)   Logician, philosopher and mathematician. He studied in Leipzig, Zurich, Heidelberg and Lwów and was a disciple of Twardowski (see note 12). He was professor of philosophy and mathematics at the University of J.Piłsudski in Warszawa. Major works: *Podstawy ogólnej teorii mnogości* (*Fundamentals of the General Theory of Multiplicity*) (1916), *O podstawach matematyki* (*On the Fundamentals of Mathematics*) (1931), *Über die Grundlagen der Ontologie* (*On the Fundamentals of Ontology*) (1932).

18. TARSKI, ALFRED (1901–83)   Logician, philosopher and mathematician. He taught at Warsaw University (1925–39) and the University of California, Berkeley (after 1942). He was primarily interested in mathematical logic, metalogic and semantics. He contributed to the development of the standard formalization theory and then popularized it. He created the semantic definition of truth. His works strongly influenced neopositivism. Major works: *Pojęcie prawdy w językach nauk dedukcyjnych* (*The Concept of Truth in the Languages of Deductive Sciences*) (1933), *Logic, Semantics, Mathematics* (1956).

19. ŚLESZYŃSKI, JAN (1854–1931)   Mathematician and logician. He lectured at the University of Odessa in Russia and after World War I, he was professor of mathematics and logic at the Jagiellonian University (see note 91). Major work: *Teoria dowodu* (*Theory of Proof*) (1926–29).

20. CHWISTEK, LEON (1884–1944)   Logician, mathematician, philosopher, painter, and art theoretician. He studied painting in Paris and

with Mehoffer and was a member of the formists' school of painting. He also was professor of logic at the University of Jan Kazimierz in Lwów (1930–40). Major works: *Wielość rzeczywistości w sztuce* (*Multiplicity of Reality in Art*) (1918), *Antynomie logiki formalnej* (*Antinomies of Formal Logic*) (1921), *Teoria typów twórczych* (*The Theory of Creative Types*) (1923), *Zagadnienia kultury duchowej w Polsce* (*Problems of Spiritual Culture in Poland*) (1933), *Granice nauki* (*Frontiers of Science*) (1935), *Zagadnienia wiedzy o malarstwie* (*Problems of Knowledge about Painting*) (1936).

21. KOTARBIŃSKI, TADEUSZ (1886–1981)   Leading Polish philosopher, logician and praxeologist. He studied under Twardowski (see note 12) in Lwów (1907–12). He taught logic at Warszawa University (1912–61) and the University of Łódź (1945–49). During the Nazi occupation he worked in a secret underground university. He was a member of the Polish Philosophical Society since 1927 and a member and the president (1957–62) of the Polish Academy of Sciences (PAN), as well as member of several foreign academies and member and president of L'Institut International de Philosophie. He formulated his own philosophical system of ontology that he called reism, pansomatism or concretism, and proposed the general theory of effective action (praxeology). He also proposed a program of ay ethics. Major works: *Szkice praktyczne* (*Practical Sketches*) (1913), *Elementy teorii poznania, logiki formalnej i metodologii nauk* (*Elements of the Theory of Cognition, Formal Logic and Methodology of Sciences*) (1929), *Z zagadnień ogólnej teorii walki* (*Some Problems of the General Theory of Struggle*) (1938), *Idea wolności* (*Idea of Liberty*) (1936), *Traktat o dobrej robocie* (*Treatise on Good Work*) (1955), *Sprawność i błąd* (*Capability and Error*) (1956), *La logique en Pologne* (*Logic in Poland*) (1959).

22. TATARKIEWICZ, WŁADYSŁAW (1886–1980)   Historian of philosophy, art and esthetics. He studied in Warszawa, Zurich, Paris, Berlin and Marburg. He taught at Warszawa University (1915–19 and 1923–61), Wilno University (1919–21, see note 98) and Poznań University (1921–23). He was editor of *Przegląd filozoficzny* (1923–48) and a member of the editorial board of *Revue International de Philosophie* (after 1938) as well as a member of the Comité International de l'Histoire de l'Art and the Polish Academy of Sciences (PAN). Major works: *O bezwzględności dobra* (*On the Unconditionality of Goodness*) (1919), *Historia filozofii* (*History of Philosophy*) (1931–50), *O szczęściu* (*On Happiness*) (1947), *Historia estetyki* (*History of Esthetics*) (1960).

23. POINCARÉ, RAYMOND (1860–1934)   French statesman and politician. He was member of parliament (1887–93 and 1920–22), minister

(1893–1906), prime minister (1912, 1922–24 and 1926–29), and president of France (1913–20). As a politician he tried to increase the military strength of France and after World War I called for the stiff punishment of Germany; with this in mind he ordered the French occupation of the Ruhr (1923). Even after retirement in 1929, he voiced his opinion, calling for increased security for France. Major works: *How France Is Governed* (trans. 1919) and *Memoirs* (trans. 1926).

24. HUSSERL, EDMUND (1859–1938)   German philosopher and founder of phenomenology. He studied at Olmutz, Leipzig, Berlin, and Vienna and lectured at Halle (1886–1901), Goettingen (1901–16), and Freiburg (1916–28). His main preoccupation was the study of consciousness, which led to the conclusion that consciousness has no life of its own outside of the object it considers. In later stages he claimed that objects cannot exist outside of consciousness. His influence was principally through his teaching, in which he allowed a large measure of freedom to his students. This accounts to a large degree for the variety of ways in which his teaching has been interpreted and developed by his followers. Ingarden (see note 11) was one of them. Major works: *Logical Investigations* (1900–01), *Idea: For a Pure Phenomenology* (trans. 1952).

25. TYMIENIECKA, ANNA TERESA (1923–   )   Polish phenomenologist and a disciple of Ingarden (see note 11) in 1945–46. She received her doctorate (1952) from the University of Fribourg, Switzerland. She taught philosophy at the University of California at Berkeley, Oregon State University, Bryn Mawr College, and Duquesne University. She brought Ingarden's philosophy into the West, but also opposed the classical phenomenology by her own system of the "phenomenology of life and of the human condition." She founded the International Husserl and Phenomenological Research Society and the World Institute for Advanced Phenomenological Research and Learning. She is editor of *Analecta Husserliana, Yearbook of Phenomenological Research,* and *Phenomenological Inquiry*. Major works: *Essence et existence. Etude à propos de la philosophie de Roman Ingarden et Nicolai Hartmann* (*Essence and Existence. Study on the Philosophy of Roman Ingarden and Nicolai Hartmann*) (1955), *Phenomenology and Science in Contemporary European Thought* (1964), *Leibniz's Cosmological Synthesis* (1964), *Eros et Logos: Introduction à la phenomenologie de l'expérience créatrice* (1972).

26. GIERULANKA, DANUTA (1914–   )   Disciple of Ingarden since 1945. Presently Docent in the Department of Philosophy at the Jagiel-

lonian University, Kraków, Poland. She was the translator of the works of Husserl (see note 24) as well as the editor and translator of the works of Ingarden (see note 11).

27. PÓŁTAWSKI, ANDRZEJ (1923–)   Disciple of Ingarden since 1945. Presently teaching at the Academy of Catholic Theology, Warszawa, Poland. He translated into Polish Husserl's book *Introduction to Phenomenology*.

28. GOŁASZEWSKA, MARIA (1926–)   Disciple of Ingarden. Presently Docent in the Department of Philosophy at the Jagiellonian University, Kraków, Poland. She teaches and studies esthetics.

29. WĘGRZECKI, ADAM (1937–)   Disciple of Ingarden (1957). Professor and chairman of the Department of Philosophy, School of Economics, Kraków, Poland. He translated into Polish the works of Scheler (see note 125) and Ingarden (see note 11).

30. CICHOŃ, WŁADYSŁAW (1926–)   Disciple of Ingarden and Dąmbska (see note 16). He is Docent at the Jagiellonian University and in the Institute of Social Sciences at the Polytechnic School of Kraków. His work focuses on philosophy and pedagogy and their interrelationship.

31. SZEWCZYK, JAN (1930–75)   Marxist philosopher. He studied and later taught at the Jagiellonian University (1969) and the Higher School of Mining. Subsequently, he worked at the Center for Studies of East–West Relations. He became a member of the Communist Party in 1957 and was primarily interested in the Marxist philosophy of labor. Major works: *Filozofia pracy* (*Philosophy of Work*) (1971), *Krytyka teorii przyczynowości Dawida Hume'a* (*Critique of David Hume's theory of Cause*) (1980).

32. STRÓŻEWSKI, WŁADYSŁAW (1933–)   Disciple of Ingarden at the Jagiellonian University. He has taught philosophy at the Jagiellonian University since 1957 and also at the Catholic University of Lublin (1958–78), Music Academies in Kraków, Gdańsk, Warszawa and Katowice, and the Theatrical School in Kraków. He is chairman of the Department of Philosophy at the Jagiellonian University and the dean of the Faculty of Philosophy and History. He was a member of the editorial board of the periodical *Znak*. He is a member of several learned societies (Polish Philosophical Society, Société Internationale pour l'Etude de la Philosophie Médiévale, International Academy of Philos-

ophy) and a vice-chairman of the Philosophical Committee of the Polish Academy of Sciences. Major works: *Historia filozofii średniowiecznej* (*History of Medieval Philosophy*) (1979), *Istnienie i wartość* (*Existence and Value*) (1981).

33. STĘPIEŃ, ANTONI (1931–   )   A member of the Faculty of Christian Philosophy at the Catholic University of Lublin (see note 120), where he was chairman of the Department of Ethics. He teaches epistemology. He represents the so-called existential Thomism of the Lublin school. Major works: *Wstęp do filozofii* (*Introduction to Philosophy*) (1976), *Elementy filozofii* (*Elements of Philosophy*) (1980).

34. SIEMIANOWSKI, ANDRZEJ (1936–   )   A member of the Faculty of Christian Philosophy at the Academy of Catholic Theology in Warszawa and also professor at the Seminary in Gniezno. He teaches methodology. He collaborates with the monthly *W drodze*.

35. MICHALSKI, REV. KONSTANTYN (1879–1947)   Neo-Thomistic philosopher and Catholic theologian. He was professor (since 1918) and rector (1931) of the Jagiellonian University (see note 91) and a member of the Polish Academy of Learning (PAU) (since 1927). During the Nazi occupation he was arrested with several other professors and sent to the concentration camp at Sachsenhausen (1939–40). His main interest was in medieval philosophy and he organized the edition of *Corpus Philosophorum Medii Aevi*. Major works: *Tomizm w Polsce na przełomie XV i XVI wieku* (*Thomism in Poland between the 15th and 16th Centuries*) (1911), *Prądy filozoficzne w Oxfordzie i w Paryżu w XIV wieku* (*Philosophical Currents in Oxford and Paris in the 14th Century*) (1920), *Odrodzenie nominalizmu w XIV wieku* (*Renaissance of Nominalism in the 14th Century*) (1926).

36. ST. AUGUSTINE (354–430)   Christian philosopher and theologian. As son of St. Monica, he was brought up in the Christian faith, but abandoned it for Manicheism (dualistic religion of Persian origin) while studying in Carthage. He travelled to Rome (376) and Milan (384). Under the influence of the bishop of Milan, St. Ambrose, he reconverted to Christianity (387). After returning to his native Tagaste in North Africa, he led a monastic life until being forced to become presbyter (391) and then bishop (395) of Hippo. He is considered the founder of Christian theology and is recognized as a Father and Doctor of the church. St. Augustine considered history as the reflection of divine providence that prepares two mystical cities—city of God and city of the devil—to which man is led. In his writings he systematized Christian

doctrine and arrived at the concept of church authority through the apostolic succession. He engaged in polemics with various heresies such as Donatism and Pelagianism but, ironically, misinterpretation of his teaching was used to justify schismatic theologies of Calvinism and Jansenism. Major works: *Confessions* (400) and *City of God* (412).

37. ST. PAUL (APOSTLE)   Hellenized Jew born in Tarsus in Asia Minor. He studied in Jerusalem under the Jewish sage Gamaliel and became a follower of Pharisaism and zealous opponent of the Christian "way." In about A.D. 33, he was converted and baptized in Damascus. Afterward he studied Christianity while living in the Arabian desert, Antioch, and Tarsus, and occasionally visiting Jerusalem. Starting in A.D. 47, he set out on his missionary trips that took him all over the Mediterranean basin. During his journeys he preached, organized small communities of converts (churches), and wrote epistles to the faithful. These fourteen epistles became part of the New Testament, although Pauline authorship of some of them is questioned by modern biblical studies. Most importantly, he attended the so-called Council of Jerusalem (ca. A.D. 51), during which his missionary efforts among the Gentiles were affirmed. Arrested by Jewish authorities (in A.D. 57 or 59) on charges of inciting riots, he claimed his rights as a Roman citizen and was sent to Rome (A.D. 60). While in prison he carried on his ministry until, during the period of Neronian persecutions (A.D. 64–67), he was beheaded, most likely south of Rome near the Via Ostia. His writings are occasional pieces in response to community problems and questions rather than works of systematic theology, but they provide an inexhaustible source of inspiration for Christian and Catholic doctrines. St. Paul formulated the concept of the Church as the mystical body of Christ, and provided incisive analyses of law, grace, justification, Christian life, and death.

38. PAROUSIA   Greek word for the arrival of the ruler on an official visit, applied in the New Testament to the second coming of Christ as the ruler and judge of the world. It also means the completion of the divine plan of salvation that started its definitive stage at the first coming, i.e., birth of Jesus (Messiah). From the eschatological point of view, at the parousia the faithful enter eternal union with Christ in the Father.

39. ODRA AND NYSA RIVERS   Two rivers that form the western border of modern Poland and separate it from East Germany. The two rivers were designated as the western borders of Poland as early as December 1941, in talks between the Soviets and the Polish Government–in–Exile (see note 1) represented by Stalin (see note 69) and

Sikorski (see note 101), respectively. The decision was confirmed at the Potsdam Conference, which also authorized the expulsion of close to 5,000,000 Germans from the so-called Recovered Territories, consisting of Silesia, Pomerania and East Prussia. The expulsion was executed in accordance with an agreement between Polish and British representatives since the expellees were to settle in the British occupation zone.

40. LAND OF THE PIASTS   This term refers to the ethnic Polish territories of about 130,000 square miles that comprised the domain ruled by the first Polish royal dynasty of Piasts (966–1382). The territory is circumscribed on the west by the Odra River (see note 39), on the north by the Baltic Sea, on the east by the Wisła, Wkra and Bug Rivers, and on the south by the Tatra Mountains. Some of these territories— Pomorze (Pomerania) and Śląsk (Silesia)—fell under German domination through dynastic marriages and through conquests. They were given to Poland after World War II and are referred to as the Recovered Territories (see notes 1 and 39).

41. MARITAIN, JACQUES (1882–1973)   French neo-Thomistic philosopher. He studied in Paris and Heidelberg and was strongly influenced by Bergson (see note 123). He taught in France and the United States and for a while (1945–48) was French ambassador to the Vatican. He opposed the tendency to underestimate the significance of reason and considered philosophy—especially the study of being—as the highest type of intellectual activity. His views on the involvement of Christians in secular affairs influenced conclusions of Vatican Council II (see note 8). Major works: *Art and Scholasticism* (1920), *The Degree of Knowledge* (1932), *A Preface to Metaphysics* (1934), *Integral Humanism* (1936), *Education at the Crossroads* (1943), *Existence and the Existent* (1947), *Man and the State* (1951), *On the Use of Philosophy* (1961).

42. WORONIECKI, O.P., JACEK (1879–1949)   Dominican theologian and Thomistic philosopher. He was professor of ethics at the Catholic University of Lublin (KUL) (see note 120) and professor of moral theology and pedagogics at the Angelicum University, Rome. Major work: *Katolicka etyka wychowawcza* (*Catholic Pedagogic Ethics*) (1948).

43. CHOJNACKI, REV. PIOTR (1897–1969)   Thomistic philosopher. He studied philosophy at the seminary in Kielce (1913–17) and in Fribourg (1917–21) and psychology in Louvain and at the Collège de France (1923–25). During World War II he was one of the organizers of the secret underground university. He was professor of philosophy at the University of Warszawa and of logic at the Academy of Catholic The-

ology in Warszawa. Major works: *Wolność woli na tle badań empiry-cznych* (*Freedom of Will in the Empirical Studies*) (1930), *Postulaty i logika budowy i nadbudowy filozofii tomistycznej* (*Postulates and Logic of the Structure and Superstructure of Thomistic Philosophy*) (1932), *Filozofia tomistyczna i neotomistyczna* (*Thomistic and neo-Thomistic Philosophy*) (1947), *Teoria poznania* (*Theory of Cognition*) (1969).

44. STEPA, REV. JAN (1892–1953)   Thomistic philosopher. He studied in Lwów (1915–18) and Louvain (1922–25), and taught at the University of Lwów. He was named bishop ordinary of Tarnów in 1946. Majors works: *Neokantowskie próby realizmu a neotomizm* (*Neo-Kantian Attempts at Realism vis-à-vis Neo-Thomism*) (1927), *Poznawalność świata rzeczywistego w oświetleniu Św. Tomasza* (*Cognition of Real World in the Light of St. Thomas Teachings*) (1930), *U źródeł niemieckiego totalizmu* (*At the Sources of German Totalitarianism*) (1938), *Bóg–świat–człowiek* (*God–World–Man*) (1947).

45. SAWICKI, REV. FRANCISZEK (1877–1952)   Thomistic philosopher. He was ordained in 1900 and in 1903 became professor at the seminary in Pelplin. His views were strongly influenced by St. Augustine (see note 36). He published most of his works in German. Major works: *Wert und Wuerde der Personlichkeit im Christentum* (*Value and Dignity of Personality in Christian Doctrine*) (1906), *Der Sinn des Lebens* (*The Sense of Life*) (1913), *Lebensanschauungen alter und neuer Denker* (*Views on Life in New and Old Philosophies*) (1923), *Filozofia ducha w walce z filozofią życia* (*Philosophy of Spirit in the Struggle with Philosophy of Life*) (1938), *Philosophie der Liebe* (*Philosophy of Love*) (1930), *Filozofią życia* (*Philosophy of Life*) (1936), *Die Philosophie der Gegenwart* (*The Contemporary Philosophy*) (1952).

46. KRĄPIEC, O.P., MIECZYSŁAW ALBERT (1921–)   Thomistic philospher. He was professor of the Catholic University of Lublin (since 1957, see note 120), and for many years its rector and a member of the Papal Academy of Theology in Kraków. He is a recipient of the Order of L'Académie Française (1985). Major works: *Realizm ludzegofjj poznania* (*Realism and Human Cognition*) (1959), *Metaphisics* (1966), *Ja—człowiek* (*I—a Man*) (1974), *Człowiek—kultura—uniwersytet* (*Man—Culture—University*) (1982).

47. KŁÓSAK, REV. KAZIMIERZ (1911–82)   Polish Thomistic philosopher. He studied initially at the Jagiellonian University (see note 91) and later in Italy and Belgium (Louvain University). He taught at the Jagiellonian University, the Catholic University of Lublin (see note 120),

and the Academy of Catholic Theology in Warszawa. He was a member of the Commission of Philosophical Sciences in the Polish Academy of Sciences and the editor of the periodical *Studia Philosophiae Christianae*. His major interest was in the philosophy of nature. Major work: *W poszukiwaniu pierwszej przyczyny* (*In Search of the Primary Cause*) (1955/57).

48. ZDYBICKA, O.S.U., ZOFIA (1928–)   Ursuline sister and a member of the Faculty of Christian Philosophy, chairman of the Department of Philosophy of Religion and dean at the Catholic University of Lublin (see note 120). She teaches philosophy of religion and represents existential Thomism. Major works: *Partycypacja bytu* (*Participation of Being*) (1972), *Człowiek i religia* (*Human Being and Religion*) (1977).

49. JAWORSKI, REV. MARIAN (1926–)   Thomistic philosopher. He studied in the seminary in Lwów. He teaches at and is rector of the Papal Academy of Theology in Kraków. He also serves as secretary of the Scientific Council of the Polish Episcopate (1973). Consecrated as bishop ordinary of Lubaczów in 1984. Major works: *Arystotelesowska i tomistyczna teoria przyczyny sprawczej na tle pojęcia bytu* (*Aristotelian and Thomistic Theories of the Causative Reason in the Light of Concept of Being*) (1958), *Byt* (*Being*) (1961).

50. ŚWIEZAWSKI, STEFAN (1907–)   Catholic Thomistic philosopher with a particular interest in the history of medieval philosophy. He has been since 1946 a professor at the Catholic University of Lublin (see note 120) and collaborator of the Institute of Philosophy and Sociology of the Polish Academy of Sciences. He served as an auditor during Vatican Council II (see note 8). Major works: *Byt. Zagadnienie metafizyki tomistycznej* (*Being: A Problem of Thomistic Metaphysics*) (1948), *Zagadnienie historii filozofii* (*Problem of the History of Philosophy*) (1966), *Historia filozofii średniowiecznej* (*History of Medieval Philosophy*) (1979).

51. KONWICKI, TADEUSZ (1926–)   Novelist, screen writer and film director. During World War II he fought in the ranks of the Home Army (AK, see note 1), but then joined the Communist-controlled establishment; his books became required reading for high school students. However, with the passing of time, he became disenchanted with the Communist regime and fell from its favor. Major works: novels: *Przy budowie* (*At the Construction Site*) (1950), *Władza* (*Authority*) (1954), *Godzina smutku* (*An Hour of Sorrow*) (1954), *Z oblężonego*

miasta (*From the Besieged City*) (1956), *Kalendarz i klepsydra* (*Diary and Hourglass*) (1976); screen plays: *Zimowy zmierzch* (*Winter Dusk*) (1956), *Zaduszki* (*All Souls Day*) (1962); motion pictures: *Ostatni dzień lata* (*Last Day of Summer*) (1960), *Dolina Issy* (*The Issa Valley*) (1981).

52. FOREST OF WILNO   Wilno (Vilnius) has been the capital of Lithuania since its founding on the banks of the Wilja River in 1323 by the Grand Duke Gedyminas. It remained the capital of the Grand Duchy of Lithuania after the union with Poland (Krewo 1385) that lasted until the third partition of Poland in 1795 (see note 165). After the partition, it came under Russian control and became a provincial capital. The Russians suppressed all Polish institutions and prevented the development of Lithuanian ones. In 1918, when Lithuania regained independence, it claimed Vilnius as its capital despite the fact that the city and its vicinity were inhabited mostly (94%) by Poles. Russians, at that time, attacked Poland, took Vilnius and turned it over to the Lithuanians, but the city and its vicinity were soon retaken by the Polish Army in routing the Soviets in 1920. Originally, semiautonomous Middle Lithuania was formed under the auspices of Poland from Wilno and its surroundings, but in 1922 after a plebiscite (the validity of which is in some dispute), Wilno was incorporated into Poland. Lithuanians were forced by political pressure to abandon their claims to Wilno in 1938. The city was occupied by the Soviets in 1939 and again transferred to Lithuania, only to be annexed as part of the Lithuanian Soviet Republic. In 1941 it was occupied by Germans, heavily damaged, and its large Jewish population was almost totally exterminated. During that German occupation, a strong resistance was organized by the Polish Home Army (AK) in Wilno and its vicinity. In fact, the city was liberated by a short uprising led by the Home Army. The leaders of the Home Army made contact with entering Soviet forces, but were arrested and deported to the Soviet Union, where many of them perished. Field commander of AK, colonel Alcksander Krzyżanowski, was extradited to Poland in 1947, and died in Polish prison in 1951. Thus, the hopes of retaining Wilno as a Polish city were dimmed. Presently, Vilnius is the capital of the Lithuanian Soviet Socialist Republic, with about 372,000 inhabitants.

53. CHRIST OF THE NATIONS   This expression by the Polish poet of the romantic era, Adam Mickiewicz (1798–1855), reflects the sentiment that since its baptism in 966 Poland has been a bulwark of Christianity (see note 6) and has suffered from the hands of those whom she defended. Indeed, more than once Polish troops, often single-handedly, defended the rest of Europe from the invasions of Islam. At Legnica (1241) the Silesian prince Henryk Pobożny (Pious) was defeated by the

invading Tartars but the tide of the invasion was reversed. The Polish king Władysław III led Polish and Hungarian forces in opposition to the advancing Turks at Varna (1444), even though Genoans and Venetians reneged on their obligations to help. The Polish king Jan III Sobieski commanded a joint Polish and Austrian force that lifted the siege of Vienna by the Turks (1683). In spite of these deeds, Russia, Austria and Prussia annihilatcd Poland in three partitions (1772, 1793, 1795) (see note 165).

54. MARX, KARL (1818–83)   German social philosopher and foun-der of communism. Marx studied law and philosophy and under the influence of Feuerbach and Hess, rejected the idealism of Hegel (see note 59) and turned to materialism. He proposed the existence of laws of history which through class struggle assure the ultimate triumph of the working class. He believed that the consciousness of the working class should be stimulated by revolutionary parties. Banned from most countries, he settled in London (1849), where with financial help from Engels (see note 58) he devoted himself to study and writing. He or-ganized the First International (1864) and became its president, but after the clash with Bukharin (see note 146) he destroyed this organi-zation to avoid losing control over it. Marx is considered a great theo-retician of economics and the founder of the sociology of economics and sociology of history. His views were authoritarian and he advocated iron-fist policies for revolutionary parties. His views, often erroneous and contradictory, were further perverted by overzealous and unscru-pulous followers (Lenin and Stalin, see notes 80 and 69, respectively). Major works: *Communist Manifesto* (1848), *Das Kapital,* vol. I (1867), vols. II and III (1885–94), edited by Engels (see note 58), vol. IV (1891) edited by Kautsky (see note 145), *Gotha Program* (1891).

55. MOUNIER, EMMANUEL (1905–50)   Catholic philosopher, pub-licist and literary critic. He founded the monthly *Esprit.* As philosopher he was a phenomenologist, existentialist and personalist who was influ-enced by Bergson (see note 123) and Maritain (see note 41), as well as by Marx (see note 54). He formulated a concept of the personalism of social involvement in which he considered the person not merely as a being, but as a "presence" directed toward the social world. He con-sidered social revolution as spiritual change and believed that the full realization of Christian ideals will occur at the building of a just social system. During World War II he was a member of the French resistance. Major works: *A Personalist Manifesto* (1938), *Personalism* (1952), *Be Not Afraid: Studies in Personalist Sociology* (1954), and numerous essays collected in a book, *What is Personalism?* (1950).

56. Miłosz, Czesław (1911–   )   Polish poet born in Lithuania and educated in Wilno (see note 98). After World War II he accepted the position of cultural attaché in the Polish legation in Paris. Disenchanted with the policies of the Polish Communists, he went into self-exile (1951) and came to the United States (1961), where he became professor of Slavic languages and literatures at the University of California, Berkeley. In 1980, he was awarded the Nobel Prize in literature, thus becoming the third Polish writer (others were Henryk Sienkiewicz in 1905, and Władysław Reymont in 1924) to receive this coveted distinction. In the same year he visited Poland, where he was welcomed by workers and intellectuals alike. A moving passage from his poem "Poet remembers" has been inscribed at the base of the monument erected in memory of those killed in December 1970 (see note 102). Major works: *Captive Mind* (1953), *The Issa Valley* (1955), *Native Realm* (1959), and numerous volumes of poetry. Miłosz also translated books of the Bible from the original languages.

57. Gomułka, Władysław (1905–82)   Communist activist and member of Communist Party of Poland (KPP) (1926). Delegated for indoctrination to the Soviet Union (1934–36), he returned to Poland to work as a Communist agitator. In 1942, he returned to Nazi-occupied Poland from the Soviet Union, joined the newly formed Polish Communist Party (PPR), and soon became the Secretary of its Central Committee. In 1945, he became Minister and Deputy Prime Minister in the Provisional Government (see note 1). Elected Secretary General of the Party (1945–48), he was later accused of rightist-nationalistic deviations, removed from this post, and arrested (1951). As a result of events in October 1956 (see note 73), Gomułka, by that time released from prison, was made a member of the Central Committee, of the Politburo, and was the First Secretary of the Communist Party. Originally welcomed by society, he soon introduced oppressive measures and followed a strictly pro-Soviet line. In the wake of the December 1970 massacre of workers (see note 102), Gomułka was removed from his post and replaced by Gierek (see note 117).

58. Engels, Friedrich (1820–95)   German socialist and founder of communism. Son of a wealthy industrialist, Engels embraced the views of Karl Marx (see note 54) in 1844 and from then on actively organized revolutionary movements in Germany, France and Belgium. He co-authored *The Communist Manifesto* (1848), but after 1850 he lived in England as a well-to-do businessman. Still, he financially supported various literary endeavors of Marx and in fact strongly influenced Marx's theories. Engels was a key figure in the First International (1864)

as well as in the Second International (1889). He edited and published the second and third volumes of *Das Kapital.* Major works: *The Conditions of the Working Class in England in 1844* (1845), *Anti-Duhring* (1878), *The Origin of the Family, Private Property and the State* (1884).

59. HEGEL, GEORG WILHELM FRIEDRICH (1770–1831)   A German idealist philosopher. He studied classics, philosophy and theology at Tübingen. He began his career as a private tutor in Bern, Switzerland (1793) and moved consecutively to Frankfurt on Main (1796–1801), Jena (1801–08), Nuremberg (1808–16), Heidelberg (1816–18) and Berlin (1818–31). Hegel had an historical outlook and proposed idealism as an absolute system of knowledge, considering all reality as a self-unfolding of the absolute. Hegel's method of exposition is dialectical; he believed that thinking always proceeds according to the pattern in which a positive thesis is negated by its antithesis, but after further thought a synthesis results. This process continues on indefinitely in a circular fashion to a synthesis identical with its starting point (thesis), with all that was implicit now being explicit. His system provided no principle of deduction because its suppositions were without content. This dialectic of contradictions gave no new insights. He was concerned with what the mind can comprehend and not with being as such. His system was an attempt to unify opposites—a synthesis of the philosophies of his predecessors: idealism and realism. His philosophy provided a theoretical basis for absolute and totalitarian governments as well as the basic ethical concept of revolution. Major works: *The Phenomenology of Mind* (1807), *Science of Logic* (1812–16), *Encyclopedia of the Philosophical Sciences in Outline* (1817), *The Philosophy of Right* (1821).

60. SCHAFF, ADAM (1913–)   Leading Marxist philosopher in Poland, whose major interest was in the theory of cognition, semantics and the philosophy of man. He taught at the University of Łódź (1945–48) and Warszawa University (beginning in 1948). A member of the Polish Academy of Sciences (since 1952) and director of its Institute of Philosophy and Sociology (since 1957), he was editor of *Myśl filozoficzna* (1951–56), a member of the executive board of the Fédération Internationale des Sociétés de Philosophie (1956), and director of the European Center for Social Sciences UNESCO (1963). A staunch supporter and apologist of Marxism–Leninism, he became a member of the Communist Party in 1932 and a member of the Central Committee in 1959. His books, in which he defended and propagated Marxism–Leninism, were standard and required texts for all university examinations in philosophy. However, in 1968 (see note 67) he was removed from the Central Committee and was expelled from the Party in 1984,

in both cases for his criticism (revisionism) of Party policies. Major works: *Pojęcie i słowo* (*Concept and Word*) (1946), *Wstęp do teorii marksizmu* (*Introduction to the Theory of Marxism*) (1947), *Obiektywny charakter praw historii* (*Objective Nature of the Laws of History*) (1955), *Marksizm a jednostka ludzka* (*Marxism and the Human Individual*) (1965).

61. BACZKO, BRONISŁAW (1924–   )   Marxist philosopher. He was professor of modern philosophy at the University of Warszawa, co-director of the Section of History of Modern Philosophy at the Institute of Philosophy and Sociology of the Polish Academy of Sciences, and an independent member of this Institute. He is the editor of the periodical *Archives d'histoire de la philosophie et de la pensée sociale* and the editor of *Pensées et Hommes* (*série philosophie moderne*). During student unrests in 1968 (see note 67), he was accused of revisionism and dismissed from his position at the university. Presently he lives and works in Switzerland. Major works: *Filozofia francuskiego oświecenia* (*The Philosophy of the French Enlightenment*) (1961), *Jan Jakub Rousseau: Samotność i społeczeństwo* (*J. J. Rousseau: Solitude and Society*) (1964), *Człowiek i światopoglądy* (*Individual and World Views*) (1965).

62. *SANACJA*   In the early 1920s, Poland was besieged by instability, political infighting and procrastinating parliamentary policies of the right-centrist groups. In view of this, Piłsudski (see note 99), who in 1922 retired from politics, staged a military coup d'état and ousted the president (Stanisław Wojciechowski) and prime minister (Wincenty Witos, see note 100). Although he did not formally assume the powers of a dictator, Piłsudski remained the major power-broker of the new regime called *sanacja* (return to/political/health). The regime sought a broad basis of support through the so-called Non-Party Block for Cooperation with the Government (BBWR), but upon failing to secure such support, resorted to absolutist methods through another organization called the Camp of National Unification (OZoN). The regime quelled opposition from both the left-center (*Centrolew*) and the right (the Camp of Great Poland, OWP). The leaders of the opposition were arrested and tried (1930–33) and many of them emigrated from Poland. The new constitution (1935) permitted an arbitrary rule of the regime. However, one must note that the regime, although introduced by illegitimate and violent means, can hardly be compared to totalitarian systems of other countries (Nazism in Germany or Communism in the Soviet Union). Indeed, it exercised a rather benevolent dictatorship and permitted a veritable explosion of scholarship, science, and education. Second, it represented a valiant, though often misguided and futile, effort to save

Poland's existence in the face of the growing threat from both Germany and the Soviet Union and a lack of cooperation by the Western democracies.

63. KROŃSKI, TADEUSZ (1907–58)   Marxist philosopher and historian of philosophy. He was professor and chairman of the Department of History of Modern Philosophy, in Warszawa University (1955). Major works: *Wykłady z filozofii starożytnej* (*Lectures in the History of Ancient Philosophy*) (1955), *Koncepcje filozoficzne mesjanistów polskich w połowie XIX w* (*Philosophical Concepts of Polish Messianists in the Mid—19th Century*) (1955), *Hegel i jego filozofia dziejów* (*Hegel and His Philosophy of History*) (1958).

64. DESCARTES, RENÉ (1596–1650)   French scientist and philosopher. He was educated at the University of Poitiers. At the age of twenty-nine, he left France and settled in Holland. Although his major interest was in mathematics (analytical geometry, negative roots, exponent notations), he also made significant contributions in optics, physiology and psychology. In his scientific pursuits he primarily followed rationalization and logic rather than empiricism. However, his greatest achievements are in the field of philosophy, where he developed his own system based on the assumption that everything should be doubted but doubt itself. Using this tenet, he arrived at the proof of existence (*cogito ergo sum*), proof of God and then proof of the physical world. He is often called the father of modern philosophy and certainly he strongly influenced Spinoza (see note 138). Major works: *Compendium musicae* (1628), *Discourse on Method* (1637), *Principia philosophiae* (1644), *Traité des passions de l'âme* (*Treatise on the Passions of the Soul*) (1649).

65. WILHELMIAN YEARS AND WEIMAR PERIOD   At the victorious conclusion of the Franco–Prussian War (1870–71), the German princes assembled in Versailles proclaimed King Wilhelm I of Prussia German emperor and ushered in the era of the German constitutional monarchy. The conservative government, led by Chancellor Bismarck (1815–98), instituted several political and social measures that made of Germany a European and world power, but also led unavoidably to conflicts with other powers (Russia, England and France). These conflicts culminated in World War I (1914–18). At the end of the war, Emperor Wilhelm II was forced to abdicate and Germany was transformed into a republic by the constitution adopted at Weimar (1919). The country was headed by a president (Ebert and then Hindenburg) and the government was run by a chancellor (Marx, Luther, Brunning, Papen, Schleicher). The great depression and the rise of the Communist and Nazi movements

halted the process of reconstruction and created the conditions for Hitler (see note 151) to ascend to power; soon thereafter, Hitler put an end to the Weimar Republic by abolishing the presidency (1934).

66. ZHDANOV, ANDREI ALEKSANDROVICH (1896–1948)   Soviet politician and general, a leading figure in the Stalinist era. Zhdanov was the first secretary of the Party in Leningrad (1934), a member of the Politburo (1939), a general during the Finnish–Russian War (1939–40) and then World War II. In 1940, Zhdanov was Soviet ambassador to the pseudogovernment of Estonia, before that country was annexed by the Soviet Union. He organized the Communist Information Bureau (Cominform) in 1947 to control the Communist parties outside Russia. A loyal and devoted supporter of Stalin (see note 69), Zhdanov represented the extreme nationalistic and represssive attitudes of the Soviet Union after World War II. His death was blamed, in a perverted way, on Jewish doctors who allegedly were part of a conspiracy against Stalin and his regime. These accusations, part of state-sponsored anti-Semitism, were retracted after Stalin's death.

67. MARCH 1968 (STUDENT UNREST)   In 1960–68, there was increasing disenchantment with the economic and political situation in Poland, and especially with the arbitrary policies of the Party which, under the leadership of Gomułka (see note 57), had taken the neo-Stalinist course and was exercising severe censorship. A political crisis was precipitated by the intervention of the Soviet ambassador in Warsaw, who demanded the closing of the play, *Dziady* (*Forefather's Eve*, by the romantic era poet Adam Mickiewicz), for its purportedly anti-Soviet elements (sic!). This closing, in January 1968, elicited the official protest of the Polish Writers Association and sparked student protests and public demonstrations in Warszawa, Kraków, Poznań, Łodź, Wrocław, Gdańsk, Toruń, and Katowice. Students also protested brutal intervention by police and dismissal from the university of intellectuals such as Kołakowski (see note 70) and Baczko (see note 61), as well as protesting students, among them Adam Michnik (see note 156). Against these protests, the Minister of the Interior, General Mieczysław Moczar, directed police and groups of belligerent workers in an attempt to provoke a clash between workers on one side and students and intellectuals, described as revisionists and Zionists, on the other. This attempt to fan anti-Semitism and quell opposition backfired and led to protests in the ranks of workers, as well as in the army (even earlier, in 1967, a group of Polish officers celebrated the "triumphs of our Jews over their Arabs" during the Arab–Israeli War). The anti-Jewish campaign was soon called off and a call for national unity was issued by Gomułka. However, at

the same time, several intellectuals (Kołakowski (see note 70), Jan Paweł Jasienica) were ostracized and Gomułka acceded to Polish participation in the infamous Soviet invasion of Czechoslovakia (October 1968).

68. HEIDEGGER, MARTIN (1889–1976)   A leading German exponent of existentialism. He studied Catholic theology and medieval Christian philosophy at Freiburg, and was for a time a Jesuit novice. He was influenced by pre-Socratic philosophers, Nietzsche (see note 148) and Husserl (see note 24). He taught at Freiburg (1915, and 1928–52) and at Marburg (1923–28). Before World War II he praised Hitler (see note 153) and gave pro-Nazi speeches, but later lost his enthusiasm for the Nazi movement. Nevertheless, he was investigated after the war, but was found innocent. In his philosophical work he sought the meaning of being as the principle of reality. He considered its close linkage with temporality. Finally, he ascribed the crisis of Western civilization to the forgetfulness of being. His philosophy is expressed in a strange and difficult vocabulary which cannot be properly translated into the usual philosophical terms. This contributes much to the problem of frequent misunderstanding of his writings. He strongly influenced Sartre (see note 74). Major works: *Sein und Zeit* (*Being and Time*) (1927), *What is Metaphysics?* (1929), *An Introduction to Metaphysics* (1953), *The End of Philosophy* (1956).

69. STALIN, JOSIF VISSARYONOVICH (DZUGASHVILI) (1879–1953) Soviet dictator of Georgian origin. He studied at the theological seminary (1894–99), but was expelled. Early in his career, Stalin embraced Marxism and first joined the Russian Social Democratic Labor Party and then its Bolshevik faction led by Lenin (see note 80). Active in the revolutionary movement in the Caucasus and later St. Petersburg (Leningrad), he was repeatedly arrested and finally in 1913 exiled for life to Siberia, but was soon pardoned by the Kerensky government (1917). On his return from Siberia, he and Kamenev edited the Communist newspaper *Pravda*. After the November revolution, Stalin slowly gained influence and power until, in 1922, he became the General Secretary of the Central Committee. Lenin, who highly regarded Stalin as an organizer, at the same time sharply criticized his conduct and advised against his becoming the leader of the Soviet Union. Nevertheless, immediately after the death of Lenin, Stalin formed a triumvirate with Kamenev and Zinoviev to oust Trotsky (1925) and later, with help from Bukharin (see note 146), eliminated his former allies (Kamenev and Zinoviev) and seized unlimited power. As dictator, Stalin proceeded to dismantle the relatively liberal NEP (see note 152) and took drastic steps

toward industrialization and collectivization. With ruthless premeditation to break national resistance, he precipitated the infamous Ukrainian famine in which millions perished. In the political sphere, Stalin abandoned the idea of world revolution and pursued the goal of entrenching the Communist dictatorship as a stable and legitimate system. To this end, he returned to the traditional concept of the state and reintroduced many aspects of prerevolutionary czarist Russia. He carried out his plans and policies by unmitigated terror and physical elimination of his real and even alleged opponents. In the purges of the 1930s, almost all Stalin's former collaborators, viewed as potential rivals, were accused, tried and executed, regardless of their previous merits. With only a brief interruption (1933–34), Stalin pursued the policy of friendship and alliance with Germany that culminated in the Ribbentrop–Molotov pact (1939), in which the two countries agreed to the division of the spoils of World War II that was just about to begin. In fact, this pact triggered the war and assured Germany of its initial successes.

The Nazi attack on the Soviet Union in 1941 surprised Stalin and almost led to the collapse of the Soviet Union if it had not been for massive aid from the West. Stalin covered up deficiencies in strategic and tactical experience with forceful leadership and diplomatic skills. Turning to his advantage the errors of the Nazis, who terrorized otherwise friendly Ukrainians and Georgians, as well as the gullibility and naiveté of the Western powers, Stalin not only kept the gains guaranteed by the Ribbentrop–Molotov pact, but actually increased them. With the concessions granted to Russia at the Tehran, Yalta and Potsdam Conferences, he achieved for the Soviet Union unprecedented and undeserved influence in global politics. Suspicious of any independence, Stalin scorned the Chinese and Yugoslavs for their independent policies and terrorized other countries into submission.

The last years of his life consisted of paranoia-fueled repressions reminiscent of the purges of the 1930s. Stalin's excesses were denounced in 1956 at the Twentieth Congress of the Soviet Communist Party in a secret speech by Nikita Khrushchev; the text of this speech remained secret in the Soviet Union until 1961. It was, however, broadly publicized in Poland and precipitated the events of October 1956 (see note 73). Khrushchev's successors moderated anti-Stalinism and, in fact, partially exonerated him as a great leader. Major works: *Leninism* (1928–33), *Problems of Leninism* (1934), *The Great Patriotic War of the Soviet Union* (1945) and collected articles and speeches.

70. KOŁAKOWSKI, LESZEK (1927–)   Philosopher, writer and publicist. He studied at the University of Łódź (1945–50) and Warszawa University, where he received a doctorate (1953) and from 1964 on was

professor. He also was professor at the Institute of Philosophy and Sociology of Polish Academy of Sciences (PAN). In 1945, he became a member of the Communist Party (PPR) and often was the vocal exponent of its narrow and dogmatic views. Beginning in 1954, he was accused of revisionism for his criticism of Stalinism. In 1966, he was expelled from the Party and in March 1968 (see note 67) was dismissed from his professorial post. He left Poland in 1968 to become professor at McGill University, Montreal; the University of California, Berkeley; Yale University; and finally, Oxford University. Even though he resided abroad, he was intimately involved in Polish affairs and was a member of the Committee for Defense of Workers (KOR). He is a member of many international societies and academies, as well as the recipient of several prizes. His writings, which are widely translated, are forbidden in Poland, and even citation of his name in scholarly works is not allowed. During the Solidarity era (1980–81), Warszawa University attempted to annul his expulsion, but the request was ignored by the Communist authorities. Major works: *Szkice z filozofii katolickiej* (*Sketches on Catholic Philosophy*) (1955), *Der revolutionaere Geist* (*The Revolutionary Spirit*) (1972), *Husserl and the Search for Certitude* (1975), *Main Currents of Marxism* (1976–79), *Igraszki z diabłem* (*Frolics with Devil*) (1982).

71. FEUERBACH, LUDWIG ANDREAS (1804–72)   A German philosopher. He studied theology and philosophy at Heidelberg and Berlin. Unlike his master, Hegel (see note 59), who undertook to explain man by a superhuman, immaterial "idea," Feuerbach based his explanation on man's concrete, material reality. He considered man as his own God, gradually moving more and more toward materialism, and became the first philosopher openly to defend humanistic atheism. He influenced the development of Marx (see note 54) more than any other thinker except Hegel. Major works: *Geschichte der neueren Philosophie* (*History of the New Philosophy*) (1833–37), *Das Wesen des Christenthums* (*The Essence of Christianity*) (1844), *Gottheit, Freiheit and Unsterblichkeit* (*Divinity, Freedom and Immortality*) (1866).

72. SÈVE, LUCIEN (1926–   )   French philosopher and writer. He received a degree in philosophy from the University of Paris (1949), and taught philosophy (1950–70) at the French Lycée in Brussels, until dismissed for Marxist–Leninist propagandizing. Presently, he is a director of the publishing house Editions Sociales, Paris. A member of the Central Committee of the French Communist Party (1961). Major works: *La différence* (*The Difference*) (1960), *Contemporary French Philosophy* (*La philosophie française contemporaine et sa genèse de 1789*

à nos jours) (1962), *Man in Marxist Theory and the Psychology of Personality* (*Marxisme et théorie de la personalité*) (1978).

73. OCTOBER 1956 (POLISH OCTOBER, POST-OCTOBER ERA)   The process of Stalinization in Poland was inhibited after the death of the dictator in 1953 (see note 69). Collectivization of agriculture was slowed (1953), the Ministry of Security was disbanded (1954), some Communists who were accused of revisionism were released from jail (1954), and censorship was somewhat relaxed (1955). A political crisis in Poland was sparked by a secret speech delivered at the Twentieth Congress of the Soviet Communist Party (February 1956) by Khrushchev, who denounced Stalin's excesses, and by the coincidental sudden death of Bierut (see note 116), while attending the same congress. Edward Ochab, Bierut's successor as the First Secretary of the Polish Communist Party, removed some compromised Party bosses (Sokorski, Berman), but at the same time the workers in Poznań rioted under banners reading "Bread and Freedom" and "Russians go home." The riot was mercilessly suppressed by the police, who shot more than fifty people. Marshal Konstanty Rokossowski, serving as the Commander–in–Chief of the Polish Army, planned a coup d'état that was foiled. On October 21, 1956, Gomułka (see note 57) was elected First Secretary of the Party without regard for Soviet opinion. In spite of the military threat from the Soviets and the opposition of dogmatic Communists called the Natolin group (from the Branickis' palace in Natolin where they held meetings), Rokossowski was dismissed and Gomułka's selection was confirmed, with the understanding that the Polish Communist Party would maintain control of the state. Many at that time mistook these changes for a true liberalization and reform of Communism, while in fact they only reflected political convenience, since Gomułka was, like his predecessors (and his successors), a Communist bent on the subjugation of Poland to the Soviets. He promptly reached an understanding with other Communists, renewed repressions, and reasserted the submissive and loyal position of the Polish Communists toward the Soviets. Gomułka's post-October period ended, as it began, in the cruel suppression of workers' protests in December 1970 (see note 102) in Gdańsk, where an unknown number of workers were shot by troops.

74. SARTRE, JEAN-PAUL (1905–80)   French existentialist, writer and playwright. During World War II, Sartre served in the French Army, was taken prisoner of war, and after being released became a leader in the anti-Nazi resistance. In his works he considers the human being as a responsible but lonely creature. At some point he became interested in Marxism and attempted to replace its historical materialism with an

existentialist interpretation. In 1945, he founded the periodical *Les temps modernes*. He was awarded the Nobel Prize in literature (1964) but declined it, believing that it exaggerates the significance of a writer's work. Major works: philosophical treatises: *Being and Nothingness* (1943), *Saint Genet* (1952), *The Ghost of Stalin* (trans. 1968), *On Genocide* (1968); novels: *Nausea* (1938), *Intimacy* (1939); plays: *The Flies* (1943), *No Exit* (1944), *The Respectful Prostitute* (1947), *Dirty Hands* (1948), *The Devil and the Good Lord* (1951).

75. CAMUS, ALBERT (1913–60)   Algerian-born French novelist, playwright, moralist, and political theorist. He was briefly a member of the Communist Party. His writing centered around the themes of the isolation of man in an alien universe, estrangement of the individual from himself, the problem of evil and the finality of death. He defended such humanistic values as truth, moderation and justice. He received the Nobel Prize in literature (1957). Major works: philosophical essays: *The Myth of Sisyphus* (1942), *The Rebel* (1954); novels: *The Stranger* (1942), *The Plague* (1948), *The Fall* (1956); plays: *Caligula* (1949), *Cross Purpose* (1948), *State of Siege* (1958), *The Just Assassins* (1958).

76. DE BEAUVOIR, SIMONE (1908–86)   French philosopher (existentialist) and writer. She taught philosophy until 1943, but afterward concentrated on writing. She was a socialist by conviction and a devoted feminist. For many years she was closely associated with Sartre (see note 74). Major works: philosophical treatises: *The Second Sex* (1949–50), *The Coming of Age* (1970), *Ethics and Ambiguity* (1947); novels: *All Men are Mortal* (1946), *The Blood of Others* (1946), *The Mandarins* (1955), *Memoirs of a Dutiful Daughter* (1958), *Force of Circumstances* (1963).

77. KLISZKO, ZENON (1908–)   Polish Communist activist. He entered the ranks of the Communist Party of Poland (KPP) in 1931 and edited its official paper *Kronika tygodniowa*. He was arrested and imprisoned (1933–1934) by the *sanacja* regime (see note 62). During World War II, he remained in the Nazi-occupied territories and organized the Communist Party (PPR) and its military units—first, the People's Guard (GL, see 1) and then the People's Army (AL)—as well as the Communist dominated National Homeland Council (KRN) that opposed the democratic resistance. He quickly advanced in the Party hierarchy, becoming a secretary of the Central Committee (1945) and deputy to the diets (1947). Subsequently, he fell victim to Stalinist purges and in 1949 was, together with Gomułka (see note 57), removed from the Central Committee for allegedly rightist–nationalist deviations and then im-

prisoned. He was "rehabilitated" in October 1956 (see note 73) and again became secretary of the Central Committee, a member of the Politburo (1957) and deputy to the diets. He was the chief ideologue of the Party and confidante of Gomułka. The tragic events of December 1970 (see note 102) occurred in great part at his insistence and under his personal direction. In 1970, he was dismissed from the Party leadership, which was by that time dominated by Edward Gierek (see note 117).

78. KUCZYŃSKI, JANUSZ LUCJAN (1930–   )   Philosopher and publicist. Professor of philosophy at Warszawa University since 1975 and member of the Polish Academy of Sciences (PAN). He was chief editor of the quarterly *Dialectics and Humanism: The Polish Philosophical Quarterly* and published articles in many periodicals (*Po prostu, Argumenty*). Major works: *Urok wiary* (*Charm of Faith*) (1957), *Chrześcijaństwo i sens życia* (*Christianity and the Sense of Life*) (1959), *Porzadek nadchodzącego świata/katolicyzm–laicyzm–humanism* (*The Order of the World to Come/Catholicism–Laicism–Humanism*) (1964), *Żyć i filozofować* (*To Live and to Philosophize*) (1969), *Homo creator: Wstęp do dialektyki człowieka* (*Homo Creator: Introduction to the Dialectic of the Human Being*) (1976), *Christian–Marxist Dialogue in Poland* (1979).

79. SZEWCZUK, WŁODZIMIERZ (1913–   )   Psychologist, professor of psychology at Jagiellonian University in Kraków (see note 91). Cofounder of the Central Psychopractical Institute of the Smelting Industry. Major works: *Teoria postaci i psychologia postaci* (*Theory of Form and Psychology of Form*) (1951), *Psychologia za-pamiętywania* (*Psychology of Memorizing*) (1957), *Psychologia* (*Psychology*) (1963/66).

80. LENIN, VLADIMIR ILYICH (1870–1924)   Born Vladimir Ulyanov, he studied law at Kazan University and for a brief period practiced as an attorney. He propagated Marx's teachings among workers and was sentenced to exile in Siberia (1887). After his release (1890), he emigrated abroad, where he stayed until 1905. While abroad, he formulated the radical policies for the Russian socialist movement by declaring the crucial role of the highly disciplined and professional party. Upon the split of the Russian Social Democratic Labor Party (1903), Lenin took the helm of the Bolshevik faction. He returned to Russia at the time of the 1905 February Revolution, but emigrated again (1907) to stay in Switzerland until World War I.

During World War I, he argued against the involvement of the proletariat and called for civil war in the belligerent countries. With the tacit approval and actual help of the Germans, he traveled across Europe in a sealed train to Russia (1917) to instigate revolution and thus disrupt the Russian war effort. After the initial failure of the revolutionary movement (July 1917) aimed at the democratic government headed by Kerensky (which had taken power after Czar Nicholas II's abdication in April 1917), Lenin fled to Finland, only to return the same year to lead the Soviet revolution (or as some historians call it, the Bolshevik putsch) in November 1917. This revolution overthrew the only democratic government Russia ever had and replaced it with the Communist dictatorship of Lenin, Trotsky, Stalin (see note 69), Rykov, and Feliks Dzierzyński (see note 114). Since in the first election to the national assembly the Bolsheviks gained only twenty-five percent of the votes, the assembly was immediately dissolved by the Communists. One of the first acts of this dictatorship was to fulfill the earlier promise given by Lenin to the Germans. Lenin signed a separate peace with Germany (Brest–Litovsk, 1918) and withdrew Russia from the war. Although the Communists professed a break with the imperial policies of the czars, they soon tried to reconquer the imperial domains that strove for independence—the nations of the Caucasus (Georgia, Armenia, Azerbedzan), Ukraine, and Poland. The internal policy was guided by terror enforced by the secret police under Dzierzyński, forced expropriations, and nationalization of the economy and trade. These policies soon threatened the total collapse of the Russian economy and, to counteract it, the relatively relaxed New Economic Policy (NEP) (see note 152) was introduced. Before his death, Lenin warned against Stalin and urged his expulsion from the leadership of the Party. Lenin's testament was suppressed and Stalin took the reins of power. Lenin was a theoretical dogmatist, but at the same time a pragmatist who did not shrink from abandoning his idealistic principles for temporary political gains. Major works: *What Is to Be Done?* (1902), and a collection of writings and speeches.

81. RICOEUR, PAUL (1913–) French philosopher. He studied under Marcel (see note 124), but has been influenced by Husserl (see note 24). His development as a philosopher proceeded in two stages—structural phenomenology and hermeneutic phenomenology. He is particularly interested in questions dealing with human will and freedom that he studied through rational philosophy, as well as the language of symbols and myths. He teaches philosophy in Paris and in Chicago. Because of his insights into the problem of evil and its symbolic expressions, his teachings are of particular interest to religious thinkers. Major works: *Philosophy of the Will* (1950–60), *Freedom and Nature: the Voluntary and the Involuntary* (1950), *History and Truth* (1955), *Freud and Phi-*

losophy: An Essay on Interpretation (1956), *The Living Metaphor* (1975), *Semantics in Action* (1978).

82. OWEN, ROBERT (1771–1853)   British socialist and social re-former, who pioneered cooperatives. Self-taught, he ventured into the textile business and created in New Lanark, Scotland and in Harmony, Indiana utopian socialist communities that could be considered fore-runners of the welfare state. He believed that an individual is formed by his environment and can be changed through the influence of others, hence he called for peaceful transformation rather than reformation of society. He was deeply concerned with child labor, public schools, and work time; he proposed several statutes none of which was passed. However, he was instrumental in passing the Factory Act of 1819. Al-though he was initially supportive of trade unionism, in later years he disassociated himself from it because of its advocacy of class struggle. He was a proponent of Anglo–American federation. Major works: *Essays on the Formation of Character* (1813–14), *Report to the County of Lanark* (1821).

83. THOMPSON, EDWARD PALMER (1924–   )   British historian and political activist. He was lecturer in history at Cambridge University, where he belonged to the Communist Party Historians' Group. He founded with John Seville the journal *The Reasoner* (1956) and its suc-cessor *The New Reasoner* (1957) as a platform for criticism of Stalinism and promotion of "socialist humanism." Because of his views, Thomp-son is considered a dissident Marxist. He began political activity as a member of the peace movement against the Korean War, and is still active today within the Campaign for Nuclear Disarmament. Major works: *William Morris: Romantic to Revolutionary* (1955), *The Making of the English Working Class* (1963), *Protest and Survive* (1980), and numerous essays.

84. CYWIŃSKI, BOHDAN (1939–   )   Catholic thinker, scholar and writer. He studied philosophy at Warszawa University and received a doctorate (1973) from the Academy of Catholic Theology in Warszawa. Initially, he worked at the Institute of Books and Readership of the National Library (1962–64) and then as an editor of the periodical *Znak* (1966–73). He was cofounder and lecturer of the Society of Scholarly Courses (TKN). Always deeply involved in the struggle for human rights and dignity, he served as a counselor to striking workers in August 1980 (see note 4). During the Solidarity era he was editor of *Tygodnik So-lidarność* and after the imposition of martial law (1981), he represented Solidarność in the International Labor Organization in Geneva. He

delivered the acceptance speech, on behalf of Wałęsa, at the ceremony in Oslo for the Nobel Peace Prize. He taught at the University of Geneva and presently teaches at the University of Fribourg, Switzerland. Major works: *Rodowody niepokonanych* (*Genealogies of the Undefeated*) (1971), *Korzenie tożsamości* (*Roots of Identity*) (1982), *Doświadczenie polskie* (*Polish Experience*) (1984).

85. PKWN MANIFESTO (LUBLIN MANIFESTO)   A manifesto prepared and proclaimed in Moscow on July 20, 1944 by a group of pro-Soviet Polish Communists who called themselves the Polish Committee of National Liberation (PKWN, also known as the Lublin Committee). The manifesto was issued with total disregard for the Polish people and even of Polish Communists active in Poland under the German occupation. The manifesto was dated July 22, 1944 in Chełm and Lublin, but in reality it was prepared in Moscow. The manifesto arrogated the role of provisional government for the Committee and outlined its plans, in the form of a decree, to subjugate Poland to Soviet domination (see note 1).

86. MAYAKOVSKY, VLADIMIR VLADIMIROVICH (1893–1930) Russian poet and writer. He was the leader of the futurist school (1912) and the main poet of the Soviet revolution (1917). After the period of uncritical glorifying and propagandizing of the Communist revolution in Russia, he gradually became disillusioned and increasingly critical of the revolution. Ultimately, he committed suicide. His writings are unique in rhythm, rhyme, and metaphoric expressions. Major works: *The Cloud in Trousers* (1915), *Mystery Bouffe* (1918), *The Bedbug* (1928) and *Bathhouse* (1929).

87. SAINT MAKSYMILIAN KOLBE, O.F.M. CONV. (1894–1941) Rajmund Kolbe assumed the name Maksymilian when in 1910 he became a member of the Franciscan Order of Minor Conventual Friars. During his studies in Rome, Father Kolbe organized a group of Knights of Mary Immaculate (Marian Sodality). Ordained in 1918, Kolbe returned to Poland and, in spite of a serious bout with tuberculosis, he carried out missionary and teaching works in Kraków and then in Grodno. He formed a community of friars that built its own friary, called Niepokalanów. From there he published the magazine, *Rycerz Niepokalanej* (*Knight of the Immaculate*), a children's magazine, and a Catholic daily, and also broadcast a radio program. In 1930, he and some Franciscan brothers departed for Japan, where they built a Japanese friary in Nagasaki and published a magazine in Japanese. Upon his return to Poland in 1935, Father Kolbe worked again in Niepokalanów until he

was arrested and imprisoned in Amtitz by the Germans (1939). Released from prison, he worked with the anti-Nazi resistance between March 1940 and February 1941 under the pseudonym Korajmak. Arrested again on February 17, 1941, he was sent to the Auschwitz concentration camp (see note 88), where he still carried on his mission by teaching and comforting other inmates. In a striking act of Christian love in July 1941, he offered his life for that of another prisoner (Franciszek Gajowniczek), who with ten others was selected for death by starvation. After two weeks of slow agony in the hunger bunker, during which he ministered to his companions, he was killed by an injection of carbolic acid on August 14, 1941. After the end of World War II the two Franciscan communities, in Niepokalanów and Nagasaki (the latter spared from A-bomb destruction), continued their activities. The Catholic Church recognized the sanctity of the life and death of Father Kolbe and, in 1982, Pope John Paul II canonized him with a feast day on August 14. Gajowniczek, the prisoner saved by Father Kolbe, was present at the canonization ceremony. Father Kolbe was accused by some of anti-Semitism, but Jewish scholarly centers declared these accusations false and unfounded.

88. OŚWIĘCIM   An industrial town in Southern Poland (population ca. 50,000). After September 1939 the town was incorporated into Germany and renamed Auschwitz. Here, in June 1940, a concentration camp was built as an internment center for about 10,000 political prisoners, but in fact it became an extermination camp in which the life expectancy of the inmates was about three months. The original camp was expanded in 1941 to nearby Brzezinka (Birkenau) to hold up to 200,000 prisoners. Until early 1942 the majority of the inmates and victims of the camp were Poles (including many Gypsies), but on May 4, 1942 the first Jewish victims of the holocaust perished in the newly constructed gas chambers. From this time onward, daily train loads of Jews (up to 20,000 per day) from all corners of Nazi-occupied Europe were brought in, killed within a few hours of arrival and their bodies burnt in crematoria or pits. During its existence the infamous Auschwitz–Birkenau camp became the place of death for over 4,000,000 human beings, among them approximately 3,000,000 Jews (including Polish Jews) and close to 1,000,000 Poles of non-Jewish origin. On January 27, 1945 only 7,500 live inmates were found by the advancing Soviet Army. During his visit to Auschwitz in 1979, John Paul II (see notes 2 and 3) said that it represents the "Golgotha of a contemporary human being."

89. SAINT STANISŁAW, BISHOP (1030–79)   Stanisław of Szczepanów (Szczepanowski) was archbishop of Kraków during the reign of King

Bolesław Śmiały (the Brave) (1058–79). During the king's campaign against Kiev, Archbishop Stanisław criticized the king's conduct and incurred the royal wrath. The conflict reflected the mounting tension between secular and clerical authorities, but its details are unknown. Sentenced by the king to death, he was allegedly killed at the steps of the altar. His death precipitated a crisis and resulted in the abdication (1079) of the king, who died (1081) as an exile, probably in Osjak, Carynthia. Archbishop Stanisław, whose remains are entombed in the main altar of the Krakow cathedral, was canonized in 1235 and is considered one of the patron saints of Poland. His feast day is April 11.

90. BLESSED QUEEN JADWIGA (1374–99)   The daughter of the Hungarian and Polish King Louis (1370–82) of the House of Anjou and granddaughter of the last king of the Piast dynasty, Kazimierz Wielki (the Great) (1333–70) was betrothed at the age of four to Wilhelm Hapsburg of Austria. The betrothal was broken when she was elected Queen of Poland (1384) and then married to the Grand Duke of Lithuania, Jagiełło (1386). This marriage was instrumental in the conversion of Lithuania to Christianity and began the Jagiellonian dynasty (1386–1572) in Poland. Jadwiga coreigned with Jagiełło and undertook some political actions on her own (the conquest of Red Ruthenia, mediation between Poland and the Teutonic Knights). She died after delivery of her only child and in her last will bequeathed her gems and valuables to renovate and reform Kraków University (see note 91), known ever since as Jagiellonian University. Her virtues as a human being and Christian were recognized soon after her death, but only recently was she officially beatified by the Roman Catholic Church. Her remains are interred under the floor of the Kraków cathedral.

91. KRAKÓW OR JAGIELLONIAN UNIVERSITY   The second oldest university in East-Central Europe was founded (1364) in Kraków by King Kazimierz the Great (1330–70) primarily as a law school. The university declined progressively until in 1400 King Władysław Jagiełło undertook its reorganization and renovation, using the jewelry of his late wife Queen Jadwiga (see note 90). The renovated university, since then known as Jagiellonian, became a center of higher education and culture for this part of Europe. The university was reformed again by Hugo Kołłątaj on the orders of the Commission of National Education (see note 96). Over the centuries it produced many internationally prominent scientists, scholars and statesmen.

92. JAN KAZIMIERZ (1609–72)   Son of King Zygmunt III Vasa and half brother of King Władysław IV, Jan Kazimierz was the third and

last king of the Vasa dynasty (1587–1672) in Poland. Initially, he pursued a military and later a church career, becoming a cardinal. Elected king (1648–68), he was released from his priestly vows. During his reign, Poland experienced the most dramatic period of her history fighting wars with the Cossacks and Tartars (1647–57), Russians (1654–67), Swedes (1655–60), and the Hungarians (1657), as well as a civil war (1666). In 1656, upon his return from temporary exile where he had been driven by the advancing Swedish invaders, Jan Kazimierz made solemn vows in Lwów cathedral, making the Blessed Virgin the perpetual "Queen of the Crown of Poland," and promised to improve the lot of the peasants by abolishing serfdom. While the first part of these royal vows was fulfilled (in fact, the vows were renewed in 1966 by Stefan Cardinal Wyszyński, see note 7), the second was not. Jan Kazimierz, upon conclusion of all the wars, and after the death of his wife Marie Louise Gonzaga, abdicated and left for France, where he stayed at the abbey of Nevers until his death. His remains were brought to Poland and interred in Kraków cathedral, but his heart is inside a tombstone in the church of St Germain-des-Prés, Paris.

93. Lwów   Lwów (in Ukrainian, Lviv) is a city founded in 1256 by the Ruthenian prince Daniel Romanowicz. It became a center of commerce and culture. Lwów was conquered and destroyed by the Tartars (1259). After the death of the last prince of the ruling house, the city was captured by the Poles in 1340. It remained part of Poland until 1772, when it was taken by Austria (see note 165). While in Polish hands, Lwów was rebuilt and became an outpost for the struggle against the invading Tartars and Turks. Inhabited predominantly by Poles, Lwów had a significant population of Ukrainians, Armenians and Jews. In 1919, it was occupied by the forces of the Western Ukrainian Democratic Republic, but was retaken by the Polish population and the Polish Army. In 1920, in accordance with the convention between Semen Petlura and Józef Piłsudski (see note 99), the Ukrainian claim to Lwów was abandoned and the city remained in Poland until 1939. The Soviets occupied Lwów in 1939–41 and again in 1944; in the intervening period, it was held by the Nazis. Both occupiers ruled with ruthless brutality, directed against Poles and Ukrainians alike. After the war, Lviv was incorporated into the Ukrainian Soviet Socialistic Republic and most of the Polish population was either expelled to Poland or deported into the interior of the Soviet Union. During its history, Lwów has been the seat of three archbishoprics (Latin, Ukrainian, and Armenian) as well as the site of the third Polish University (University of Jan Kazimierz).

94. PAWEŁ WŁODKOWIC (1370–1435)   Paweł Włodkowic, also known as Paulus Vladimiri, was a jurist and rector of Jagiellonian Uni-

versity in Kraków (see note 91). He was a member of the Polish dele-
gation to the Council of Constance (1414–18), where he argued the
Polish case against the Teutonic Knights. He weakened his argument
by claiming that the Teutonic Knights were heretics and their leaders
should be punished by death. Włodkowic was the author of thirty-five
treatises that rested unknown in various archives for almost 500 years;
the major treatise was published for the first time in 1878. His ideas
were forerunners of modern international law and exerted a strong influence on its creators, Grotius and Vittore. Włodkowic addressed several crucial social and political issues in his works and his views were
surprisingly progressive. Specifically, he claimed that pagans, as well as
nations of other religions, Islam and Judaism, have the right to exist
and to their religious freedom. Consequently, they should not be converted by force but by persuasion. Perhaps his most revolutionary idea
was the concept that the international community must follow the principles of law upheld by an international tribunal under the aegis of the
pope and the emperor. He redefined the concept of a just war, stating
that such a war must be carried out by legal authority, for just cause
and in a decent manner. The presence of these factors must be decided
by an independent judicial power. His ideas exerted a strong influence
on the legal, political and moral debates of Western Europe in the years
that followed.

95. KOPERNIK, MIKOŁAJ (1473–1543)   Mikołaj Kopernik (Nicolaus
Copernicus), priest, physician and astronomer was the son of a Toruń
burgher. He studied at the Jagiellonian University in Kraków (see note
91) and then at the University of Padua, Italy. Upon completion of his
studies, he settled at Frombork in the province of Warmia, where he
was a cathedral canon. Comparing his own observations with those of
Ptolemy, Kopernik formulated his heliocentric concept of the solar system. His monumental work *De revolutionibus orbium coelestium* was
published in 1543 and was dedicated to Pope Paul III. Although in some
respects the Copernican system was incorrect, it provided the basis for
the more advanced concepts of Kepler and Newton.

96. COMMISSION OF NATIONAL EDUCATION   After the suppression
of the Jesuit Order by Pope Clement XIV (1773), the property of the
order was allotted by the Polish Diet of 1773 to the newly created
Commission of National Education, under the chairmanship of first,
Bishop Michał Poniatowski, and then Ignacy Potocki. The Commission,
considered to be the first ministry of public education in Europe, was
supposed to replace the Jesuit educational system with a new system.
It elaborated a program of national education at primary and university

levels, under the influence of the Piarist Order. The program strove to prepare students for their civic duties and gave priority to moral and practical instruction. The work of the Commission, supported strongly by the last Polish king, Stanisław August Poniatowski (1764–95), played a significant role in the Polish national revival in the second half of the eighteenth century.

97. NATIONAL UPRISINGS   After the second partition in 1792, Polish patriots repeatedly raised arms against the partitioning powers. The major uprisings occurred in 1794 (Kościuszko Uprising), 1830–31 (the November Uprising or the Polish–Russian War), 1848 (the Spring of Nations), 1863 (the January Uprising). Although all of them ended in military defeats, they kept the flame of the spirit of independence burning. In the tradition of the eighteenth century uprisings, the resistance forces and population of Warszawa in 1944 took up arms against the Nazis. Since most of these military efforts were aimed directly or indirectly against Russia's intention to dominate Poland, the interpretation of the events and their aims was often perverted by pro-Soviet Communist historians.

98. WILNO UNIVERSITY   The University of Wilno, one of the oldest in Central Europe, was founded in 1579 by King Stefan Batory (1576–1586) from the Jesuit College that was founded in 1570. The university was reformed and expanded (1780) by the Commission of National Education (see note 96) and became a center of education. It produced many outstanding teachers and disciples (Jędrzej Śniadecki, Karol Szajnocha, Adam Mickiewicz, Marian Rose). In the wave of repressions after the 1830–31 uprising (see note 97), the university was closed by the Russians and later opened as a Russian institution. Reopened immediately after World War I, it prospered until Wilno was occupied first by the Russians and then by the Germans. In 1939, when Wilno was given to the Lithuanians, the university was temporarily closed as a symbol of Polish culture.

99. PIŁSUDKI, JÓZEF (1867–1935)   Chief of state, marshal and statesman. Early in his career Piłsudski was active in a terrorist conspiracy against the Russians, for which he was exiled to Siberia (1887–92). Upon his return from Siberia, he joined the socialist movement and edited a journal *Robotnik* (*Worker*), but he subjugated his social aims to the patriotic struggle for Polish independence. During World War I he organized paramilitary and military organizations (Legion, Strzelec, POW) under Austrian auspices, to fight against Russia, but at the same time he refused allegiance to Germany and was imprisoned in Magdeburg

(1917–18). Upon release, he obtained virtually unlimited civil and military authority as the chief of state (a title granted earlier only to national hero Tadeusz Kościuszko in 1794). He proclaimed Poland's independence on November 11, 1918. Soon after, he concluded an agreement on collaboration with independent Ukraine (1919) and won the Polish–Soviet War (1920) that ended in the Treaty of Riga (1921). In accordance with the Constitution, Piłsudski resigned as chief of state and retired to private life. He led the military coup d'état (see note 62) in 1926 that overthrew the elected government, and assumed the authority of prime minister and minister of war, with almost dictatorial powers. While his actions were in violation of the then valid Constitution and impinged on civil rights, they were motivated by patriotic feelings and a deep concern for the safety of Poland. He tried to establish a balance between excessive freedom, perceived as a danger to the existence of free Poland, and strong executive power, by which to provide Poland's safety. His death in 1935 was genuinely mourned by the majority of Poles, especially since his successors did not match up to the marshal's stature and may be blamed for the outcome of the 1939 campaign. Major works: *Pisma* (*Writings*), consisting of memoirs, articles and speeches.

100. WITOS, WINCENTY (1874–1945)   Peasant (agrarian) activist, journalist, politician. Member of the Galician Diet (1908–18), member of the Austro–Hungarian parliament (1911–18), chairman of the Polish Peasant Party–Piast (1913), member of the Polish Diet (Sejm) (1919–33), prime minister of Poland (1920–21, 1923, and 1926). Arrested and imprisoned after Piłsudki's coup d'état (1926) (see notes 62 and 99), he also was arrested in 1930 at the time of the crackdown on the opposition to the Piłsudski regime. Upon release, he fled to Czechoslovakia and joined other politicians (e.g., Ignacy Paderewski) in the so-called Morges Front concerned with the foreign policy of Poland. He was imprisoned by the Nazis (1939–40). At the end of the war, he was approached by the Communists to join their government but flatly refused.

101. SIKORSKI, WŁADYSŁAW (1881–1943)   Civil engineer, general and statesman. Associated with the Polish Democratic Party. Organizer of Polish paramilitary units in Galicia before World War I. Chief of staff of the Przemyśl Region, commanding officer of Polish troops that relieved Lwów from the siege by Ukrainian forces (1919), commander of the Fifth Army (1920), chief of the general staff (1921–22), minister of military affairs (1922–23, 1924–25), prime minister and commander in chief of Polish Army in exile (1939–43). He was instrumental in negotiating the resumption of diplomatic relations between Poland and

the Soviet Union after they had been severed when the Soviets and Nazis attacked and partitioned Poland in 1939 (see note 1). He was killed in an air crash in Gibraltar under suspicious circumstances (1943). Major works: *O polską politykę państwową* (*For Polish State Policy*) (1923), *Polesie jako węzeł strategiczny wschodniego frontu* (*Polesie as a Strategic Zone of the Eastern Front* (1924), *La Campagne Polono–Russe de 1920* (*Polish–Russian Campaign of 1920*) (1928), *Przyszła wojna* (*Future War*) (1934).

102. DECEMBER 1970   The announcement of the sharp rise in prices of basic food articles sparked widespread protests by workers, especially in seaside cities (Gdańsk, Gdynia, Elbląg, and Szczecin). The riots, during which workers attacked and burnt Party headquarters, were brutally quelled by police and troops led by General Grzegorz Korczyński and ordered by the Party under Gomułka's leadership (see note 57) and government of prime minister Józef Cyrankiewicz. An undetermined number of workers (several eye witnesses of masacre died under suspicious circumstances) was killed when they arrived at their work place after being assured by Communist authorities that there would be no reprisal for the protests. The protests also bridged the gap between students and workers which had developed during the events of March 1968 (see note 67). Public outrage forced the dismissal of Gomułka and his replacement by Gierek (see note 117). Similar food price rises in 1976 sparked another outburst of protest, especially violent in Warszawa and Radom. These riots were followed by many arrests. To defend and help the arrested workers, a group of intellectuals organized the Committee for Defense of Workers (KOR) to which Michnik (see note 156), Kołakowski (see note 70) and many others belonged. Furthermore, workers began organizing themselves into the Free Trade Unions (WZZ). In August 1980 (see note 4), striking workers, and later the Solidarity Trade Union, demanded that honor be given to the victims of police and army brutality, and saw to it that in 1981 a monument was erected in front of the Gdańsk shipyard.

103. LETTER OF THE EPISCOPATE   In connection with the approaching thousandth anniversary of the conversion of Poland to Christianity, Polish bishops attending Vatican Council II (see note 8) issued invitations to fifty-six episcopates around the world and to the Orthodox Patriarch of Constantinople. A letter to the German episcopate dated November 18, 1965, giving an analysis of the history of Polish–German relations, contained the following lines: "We stretch our arms to you seated on the benches of the now concluding Council and we forgive and ask for forgiveness. And when you German bishops and Council

Fathers take our hands as brothers, only then will we be able to celebrate our millennium with a clean conscience in the most Christian way." The letter elicited a furious reaction from the Communist regime, which feared that Polish–German reconciliation might deprive them of a powerful tool for the intimidation of the Polish people. In a memorandum, the regime accused the episcopate of meddling in political affairs and the authorities refused a diplomatic passport to the Primate of Poland, Stefan Cardinal Wyszyński (see note 7), who was about to visit Rome and the United States in connection with the millennium celebrations. In contrast, the Polish people followed the appeal of the cardinal, when thousands of worshipers at an open air Mass responded in unison: "We forgive." The invitation was accepted on December 5, 1965 by the German bishops, who stated in their reply: "and we ask you to forget, even more—we ask for forgiveness."

104. KULAK   Derisive name (originating from the Russian word meaning "fist") for independent farmers possessing large and medium-size farms, who resisted forced collectivization in the Soviet Union during the 1930s. Stalin (see note 69) defined kulaks as a distinct social class that must be eliminated. Thus, being classified as a kulak usually meant an automatic sentence to Siberian exile and often death. The term kulak (kułak) was adopted by Polish Communists after 1945, but while being considered a kulak in Poland meant harassment, it did not result in imprisonment or death.

105. MICHURIN, IVAN VLADIMIROVICH (1855–1935)   This mostly self-taught Russian horticulturist is recognized for work on cross-breeding of fruit plants with the aim of adapting them to the adverse climatic conditions in Northern Russia. He subscribed to the Communist Party criticisms of modern genetics and expanded them into theories of the inheritance of acquired traits (Michurinism). These theories were embraced by the political opportunist Lysenko (see note 106).

106. LYSENKO, TROFIM DENISOVICH (1898–1976)   Russian agronomist and disciple of Michurin (see note 104). He achieved a position as a leading biologist and virtual dictator in biological sciences in the Soviet Union through political means, e.g., contributing to the accusations and Siberian exile of renown biologist Vavilov. After becoming a deputy to the Supreme Soviet (quasi parliament) in 1937, he was named head of the Institute of Genetics of the Soviet Union Academy of Sciences and president of the All-Union Academy of Agricultural Sciences. With the approval and support of the Party, he negated theories of heredity and propounded the concept of the inheritability of environ-

mentally induced changes. This concept was enshrined as Marxist orthodoxy by the Party and caused long-lasting stagnation of Soviet biology. Even worse, Lysenko's pseudoscientific theories were also forcibly imposed on the scientists in the countries politically dominated by the Soviets. The opponents of Lysenko's theories were often harassed and even overtly persecuted by the authorities. Even after Stalinism was denounced (1956) and Lysenko was relieved of the presidency of the Academy of Sciences, it was not until 1965 that he was removed from the Institute of Genetics. Major works: *Heredity and its Variability* (1943) and *The Science of Biology Today* (1948).

107. PAVLOV, IVAN PETROVICH (1849–1936)   Russian physiologist. Pavlov was professor and chairman of the Institute of Experimental Medicine in Leningrad. He studied the functions of the gastrointestinal tract and their nervous control. His work on conditioned reflexes laid the foundation of modern behaviorism and profoundly influenced other branches of medicine (neurology, psychology). He received the Nobel Prize in medicine and physiology (1904). Unfortunately, his concepts were forced on Soviet medicine by Party ideologues, often to the detriment of scientific analysis. Major work: *Conditioned Reflexes* (1926).

108. KOSTOV, TRAJCZO (1879–1949)   Communist activist, member of the Bulgarian Communist Party and its Central Committee. Editor of the party newspaper *Workers' Deed* (*Roboticzesko Delo*). Vice-premier and minister of electrification of the Bulgarian People's Republic. During the Stalinist era, he lost in an intraparty power struggle and was arrested, tried, convicted, and executed. He was rehabilitated posthumously in 1962.

109. CZERVENKOV, VYLKO (1900–?)   Bulgarian communist activist and politician since 1919. He was involved in the coup of 1923, in which Prime Minister Stambolijski was killed by the Macedonian Revolutionary Organization, and in a terrorist bomb attack in 1925, in which hundreds of people gathered in the main church of the city of Sofia were killed. In 1925, he emigrated to the Soviet Union, where he resided until 1944. On his return to Bulgaria and after the death of Georgi Dimitrov, he became first secretary of the Central Committee of the Bulgarian Communist Party (1944–54) and prime minister (1950–55). He gained these two positions after eliminating his former comrade Kostov (see note 108). As prime minister, he issued draconian laws (ten years of labor camp and later even death) against people and their families who attempted to flee Bulgaria, which was at that time undergoing intensive Stalinization. Accused of fostering a personality cult, he

was removed from the Politburo and government (1961) and then expelled from the Party (1962).

110. FRITZHAND, MAREK (1913–)　Marxist philosopher and member of the Communist Party (1944). He studied at the University of Lwów (1937). He is professor (1954) and chairman (1956) of the Department of Ethics at Warsawa University and Dean of Philosophy Faculty. He is a member of the Polish Academy of Sciences and chairman of its Philosophical Committee. He founded the periodical *Etyka* (1966). Major works: *O pochodzeniu i istocie norm moralnych* (*On the Origin and Essence of Moral Norms*) (1950), *Człowiek, humanism, moralność* (*Man, Humanism, Morality*) (1961), *O niektórych właściwościach etyki marksistowskiej* (*On Some Features of Marxist Ethics*) (1974), *Fakty a wartości* (*Facts and Values*) (1982).

111. KOZYR-KOWALSKI, STANISŁAW (1936–)　Marxist philosopher, sociologist and member of the Party (1956). He studied at Warszawa University and worked in Toruń (1960–69) and Poznań (since 1969), where he is a professor (since 1974). Major works: *Od Mojżesza do Armii Zbawienia* (*From Moses to the Salvation Army*) (1966), *Max Weber a Karol Marks: Socjologia Maxa Webera jako "pozytywna krytyka materializmu historycznego"* (*Max Weber versus Karl Marx: Max Weber's Sociology as "Positive Criticism of Historical Materialism"*) (1967), *Klasy i stany: Max Weber a współczesne teorie stratifikacji* (*Classes and Estates: Max Weber versus Contemporary Theories of Stratification*) (1979), *O ideologii* (*On Ideology*) (1982).

112. ŁADOSZ, JAROSŁAW (1924–)　Professor at the Faculty of History and Philosophy, and director of the Institute of Philosophy, Sociology and Logic at the University of Wrocław. He is also the chairman of the Department of Philosophy at the Medical Academy in Wrocław and at Śląsk University in Katowice. Major works: *Marksistowska teoria walki klas* (*Marxist Theory of Class Struggle*) (1969), *Przedmiot filozofii i jej rola społeczna* (*Subject of Philosophy and Its Social Role*) (1975).

113. ŚLIPKO, REV. TADEUSZ (1918–)　A member and the dean of the Faculty of Christian Philosophy at the Academy of Catholic Theology, Warszawa. He is chairman of the Department of Ethics and teaches ethics and moral philosophy. Major works: *Zarys etyki ogólnej* (*Fundamentals of General Ethics*) (1974), *Życie i płeć człowieka* (*Life and Sex of the Human Being*) (1978).

114. DZIERZYŃSKI, FELIKS (1877–1926)　Born to a family of the Polish gentry, he renounced his Polish origins and became a Soviet

citizen. He organized and led (1917–21) the dreaded Soviet secret police CHEKA (acronym for All-Russian Extraordinary Commission for the Suppression of Counterrevolution and Sabotage) and its successors, GPU and OGPU. Particularly cruel toward Poles, Dzierzyński and his secret police were responsible for murdering countless thousands of people. He was succeeded by the likes of Jezhov, Beria, and Andropov. In 1920, together with two other Polish renegades, Marchlewski and Kohn, Dzierzyński formed the provisional government of Poland under the auspices of the invading Soviet Army. It is particulary offensive to Poles that the Communists erected a monument to Dzierzyński and named a major square in Warszawa for him.

115. STACHANOV MOVEMENT   Movement begun in 1935 by Aleksey Grigorevich Stachanov, a coal miner in Donets Basin, to increase production through labor division. While production did indeed increase up to sevenfold, labor was not proportionately compensated. Instead, to the chagrin of workers, ever higher requirements were instituted. Stachanovism was also introduced in Poland by coal miners Pstrowski and Markiewka. The movement was strongly criticized by free trade unions as a means of exploitation by the state.

116. BIERUT, BOLESŁAW (1892–1956)   Socialist (1912) and then Communist (1918) activist and member of the Central Committee of the Polish Communist Party (1925–27). He emigrated from Poland to the Soviet-occupied zone, where he was indoctrinated in the School of the Communist International and delegated to organize the Communist movement in Bulgaria, Czechoslovakia and Austria. He returned to Poland in 1933 and was active in the Communist movement. In 1939, he fled to the Soviet Union, where he participated in pro-Soviet organizations (see note 1). In 1943, he returned to Nazi-occupied Poland and organized the Polish Workers Party (PPR), even though officially he did not belong to the Party. In 1947, he was made president of Poland. After the removal and imprisonment of Gomułka (see note 57), he became general secretary of the PPR and after its unification with the Polish Socialist Party (PPS) (see note 141), he became the chairman (1948) and then first secretary (1954) of the Polish United Worker Party (PZPR). He also was prime minister of Poland (1952–54).

117. GIEREK, EDWARD (1913–)   Communist activist and politician. Resided in France and Belgium (1923–48), where he was a member of the corresponding Communist Parties. After his return to Poland (1948), he was member and secretary of the Central Committee of the Polish United Workers' Party (Communist), as well as the first secretary of the Regional Committee of this Party in Katowice (Silesia). He re-

placed Gomułka (see note 57) as first secretary of the Party (1970) and de facto ruler of Poland. In the wake of the Solidarity era (1980), he was removed from his position and then expelled from the Party. He was criticized for misguided and authoritarian policies that saddled Poland with enormous debts and led to the economic crisis and near bankruptcy of the Polish economy.

118. PIWOWARCZYK, REV. JAN (1889–1959)   Thomistic philosopher. He taught social ethics at the Jagiellonian University. He was the first editor of the Catholic weekly *Tygodnik Powszechny*. Major works: *Socjalizm i chrześcijanstwo (Socialism and Christianity)* (1924), *Współczesne kierunki społeczne (Contemporary Social Currents)* (1927).

119. KELLER, JÓZEF (1911–)   Polish philosopher. He studied at the Warszawa University. He taught at the Catholic University of Lublin and the Warszawa University. He is director of the Section of History and Theory of Religion at the Institute of Philosophy and Sociology of the Polish Academy of Sciences. He is editor of the periodical *Studia religioznawcze (Studies of Religion)* and a member of the editorial board of an international scholarly publication, *Ost und West in der Gesichte des Denkens und der kulturellen Beziehungen*. Originally, he was a proponent, but later he became a critic of Catholic ethics. Major works: *Etyka (Ethics)* (1954), *Etyka katolicka (Catholic Ethics)* (1957), *Zarys dziejów religii (Outline of History of Religion)* (1968), *Katolicyzm jako religia i ideologia (Catholicism as Religion and Ideology)* (1969), *Zwyczaje, obrzędy i symbole religijne (Religious Customs, Ceremonies and Symbols)* (1974), *Kultura a religia (Culture and Religion)* (1977).

120. CATHOLIC UNIVERSITY OF LUBLIN (KUL)   A Catholic University was founded in Lublin immediately after World War I. Some of its original faculty came from the Roman Catholic seminary in St. Petersburg. The university was closed during World War II, but reopened before the Communists seized power and remains today the only Catholic institution of higher education in East–Central Europe. It is a center of independent thought and inquiry, with its own periodicals, e.g., *Spotkania*. The University has counted among its faculty Stefan Cardinal Wyszyński (see note 7) and Karol Cardinal Wojtyła (now Pope John Paul II, see note 3). The Communist regime has tried to suppress the university's activities by the unprecedented move of levying a tax on it.

121. POLONAISE   This Polish national dance originally was a popular processional dance among peasants, but then became the court dance. The moving description of the polonaise given in Book Twelve of the

epic poem *Mister Thadeus,* by Mickiewicz, is the basis of Tischner's text on page 105.

122. LACROIX, JEAN (1900–   )   French philosopher and exponent of personalism. He earned advanced degrees in the humanities, law and philosophy and was a professor of philosophy. He writes a regular column in *Le Monde* and is the editor of the series *Initiation Philosophique.* Major works: *Personne et amour (Person and Love)* (1956), *Maurice Blondel* (1968).

123. BERGSON, HENRI (1859–1941)   Leading French philosopher of the early twentieth century. He was a professor at the Collège de France (1900). He defended humanistic and spiritual values against a narrow scientific interpretation of reality. His philosophy underlines the presence of the two opposing tendencies—life force and the resistance of matter. The latter is known to human beings through the intellect. He elaborated a process philosophy that stressed the flow of time, i.e., duration that is demonstrable by memory. A writer with a clear and gracious style, he received the Nobel Prize in literature (1927). Major works: *Time and Free Will* (1889), *Matter and Memory* (1896), *Creative Evolution* (1907), *Introduction to Metaphysics* (1908), *Two Sources of Morality and Religion* (1932–1939).

124. MARCEL, GABRIEL (1889–1973)   French philosopher and writer who called himself a "concrete philosopher." A Christian existentialist, he saw philosophy as a personal reflection on the human situation and considered a close personal involvement centered in God and characterized by mutual fidelity and hope as the basic fulfillment of human existence. Major works: *Being and Having* (1935), *The Mystery of Being* (1950), *Philosophy of Existentialism* (1961) and the play *Un Homme de Dieu (A Man of God)* (1925).

125. SCHELER, MAX (1874–1928)   German philosopher strongly influenced by Husserl (see note 24) and Franz Brentano. He taught in Jena (1901–07), Munich (1907–10), and after World War I in Cologne and Frankfurt. In his works he was concerned with values in human personality and action. He considered love as a divine gift and prime mover behind human association. Major works: *Formalism in Ethics and Non-formal Ethics of Values* (1913–16), *On the Eternal in Man* (1921), *Man's Place in Nature* (1928).

126. ST. THOMAS AQUINAS, O.P.(1225–74)   Italian philosopher and theologian. Born into a princely family, he entered the Dominican order

(1244). He studied in Paris (1245–48) with Albertus Magnus and became professor there (1252–59 and 1269–72), with some time spent as an adviser to the papal court in Rome. He retired to Naples and died on his way to the second Council in Lyons (1274). Although being slow and stout gained him the nickname "Dumb Ox," his worth was soon recognized and shortly after his death he was canonized (1323). Later he was proclaimed Doctor of the Church (1567) and Pope Leo XIII declared (1879) his teaching the official Catholic philosophy and named him the patron saint of schools and education (1880). He is often called the Great Synthesizer since he developed Scholasticism (Thomism), in which he rejected concepts of both Averroists (separation of truth and faith) and Augustinians (making truth a matter of faith). His philosophical system is complete, all-embracing, and applicable to every aspect of human life (neo-Thomism represents an attempt to apply his philosophy to modern conditions). Briefly, he proposed that truth (reason) and faith are both divine gifts and complement each other, but reason has its autonomy. The affirmation of being is a first step, followed by the acquisition of knowledge through the senses (realism). The latter perceive the form (universals) that exists in three ways: in things, in the mind, and in God. God can be discovered by reason and, using concepts of potency and act (Aristotle), one can prove the existence of God as pure act in which essence (form) and being (existence) form a unity. Being may be characterized according to modes (transcendentals)— unity, truth, and goodness—that are convertible. Since there are no opposites of being, and goodness is identical with being, it follows that evil is the absence of good. Major works: *Questiones disputatae* (1256– 72), *Summa contra Gentiles* (1258–60), *Summa theologica* (1267–73), and beautiful hymns for the feast of Corpus Christi.

127. PROTAGORAS (CA. 490–421 B.C.)   Greek Sophist philosopher of Abdera. He taught in Athens but had to flee when threatened with prosecution for agnosticism. His tenet was that truth is relative (subjective), i.e., depends on who holds it, and that "man is the measure of all things." He denied the distinction between senses and reason. None of his writings are extant.

128. KANT, IMMANUEL (1724–1804)   German philosopher. Studied theology in Koenigsberg (1740), but later became interested in philosophy and mathematics. After graduation (1755) he was for a while a tutor, but subsequently was given the chair of logic and metaphysics at Koenigsberg University (1770–96). Kant, who called himself a "critical philosopher," can well be called a genius who attempted to form a synthesis between sense knowledge and intellectual knowledge—be-

tween the theoretical and practical activity of human beings or between rationalism (Leibniz, see note 137) and skepticism (Hume). He proposed that reality is known to the extent of its conformity to the mind. Thus, phenomena may be known, but things behind them (things in themselves), although existing, are unknowable. He asserted that the great questions of metaphysics—God, freedom, and immortality—are unsolvable by speculation and their existence can neither be proved nor denied. His doctrine exerted a strong influence on numerous philosophers. Major works: *The Critique of Pure Reason* (1781), *The Critique of Practical Reason* (1788), *The Critique of Judgment* (1790), *Religion within the Limits of Reason Alone* (1793).

129. JOHN XXIII (1881–1963)   Angelo Giuseppe Roncalli was ordained a priest (1904), consecrated bishop (1925), and elevated to cardinal (1953). Early in his career he was Apostolic Visitor to Bulgaria, Apostolic Delegate to Turkey and Greece, and Nuncio to France. Upon leaving diplomatic service, he was made patriarch of Venice (1953) and after the death of Pius XII (see note 163), he was elected pope (1958) and assumed the name John XXIII. His brief pontificate marked the beginning of deep reforms (*aggiornamento*) within the Roman Catholic Church. In 1962, he convened Vatican Council II (see note 8) that instituted many changes. Throughout his life, John XXIII was a staunch supporter of ecumenism and collaboration among people, regardless of their faith; for example, during World War II he saved many Jews by procuring Portuguese passports for them. His most famous encyclical—*Pacem in Terris*—outlines his position toward the modern world. His death was mourned by millions, non-Catholics as well as Catholics. In 1968, the process of his canonization was initiated.

130. PAUL VI (1897–1978)   Giovanni Battista Montini, after being ordained (1920), entered the diplomatic service of the Vatican where he worked for thirty years (1922–52), exerting a great deal of influence on Pope Pius XII. Upon leaving the Vatican service, he became archbishop of Milan (1954–63) and cardinal (1958). After the death of Pope John XXIII, he was elected his successor and assumed the name Paul VI. He reconvened the recessed Vatican Council II (see note 8) and put the Council's reforms into practice. In addition to pressing the Council's reforms in the face of opposition and turmoil, he internationalized the focus of the church and the papacy. He was the first pope (since Pius VII) to travel far from Rome, with visits to the Holy Land (1964), India (1964), United Nations headquarters in New York City (1965), Africa (1969), and the Philippines (1970). While upholding a strict doctrinal position on such issues as the celibacy of the clergy, birth control,

and papal infallibility, Paul VI worked to improve relations with Communist states and other churches and religions. His best known encyclicals are *Populorum Progressio* (on social issues) and *Humanae Vitae* (on birth control).

131. TEILHARD DE CHARDIN, S.J., PIERRE (1881–1955)   French philosopher and paleontologist. Ordained a Roman Catholic priest (1911), he studied paleontology and received a doctorate from the Sorbonne (1922). Initially, he taught theology at the Catholic Institute in Paris (1920–23 and 1924–26), but was dismissed from his post because his views were deemed incompatible with the church's magisterium. Forbidden to publish theological works, he left for China and devoted his time to paleontology (1926–46) and discovered (1929) fossil remnants of *Homo pekinensis*. He tried to unify his positive scientific work with philosophical pursuits and arrived at the concept of cosmic evolution. According to this concept, both the living and the inanimate cosmos undergo changes that lead to the "omega point" that frequently is interpreted as the Christian parousia (see note 38). Although in this concept the human being constitutes a central point, Teilhard never rejected his deep Christian faith. Even though suspected and distrusted by the church, Teilhard's works gained broad popularity when published posthumously. Major works: *The Phenomenon of Man* (1955), *Letters from a Traveler* (1956), *The Divine Milieu* (1957), *The Future of Man* (1959), *Hymn of the Universe* (1964).

132. JAROSZEWSKI, TADEUSZ, M. (1930–   )   Marxist philosopher. He is director of the Section of Dialectical Materialism of the Institute of Philosophy and Sociology of the Polish Academy of Sciences, chairman of the Department of Philosophy at the Central Party School, and a member of the Institute of Basic Problems of Marxism–Leninism. He is also vice-president of the Polish Society of Religious Studies. Major work: *Osobowość i wspólnota* (*Personality and Community*) (1970).

133. KĘPIŃSKI, ANTONI (1918–72)   Noted psychiatrist and humanist in Kraków. He was one of the intellectuals and scientists who formed a circle around Karol Cardinal Wojtyła (see note 3), archbishop of Kraków. He proposed a concept of a threefold metabolism—energy metabolism, biological metabolism and information metabolism. It is the last one that determines a true human existence and its disturbances may be a primary cause of mental disorders. Major works: *Rytm życia* (*Rhythm of Life*) (1972), *Schizofrenia* (*Schizophrenia*) (1972) and several medical treatises (*Psychopathology of Neuroses, Melancholy,* and *Fear*).

134. KRAJEWSKI, WŁADYSŁAW (1919–)   Marxist philosopher. He is professor at the University of Warszawa and Łódź and director of the Institute of Philosophy and Sociology of the Polish Academy of Sciences. He is a member of the editorial board of the periodical *Studia filozoficzne*. Major works: *Teoria i doświadczenie* (*Theory and Experience*) (1966), *Związek przyczynowy* (*Causative Association*) (1967), *Engels o ruchu materii i jego prawach* (*Engels on Laws of Motion of Matter*) (1973).

135. DUHEM, PIERRE MAURICE MARIE (1861–1916)   French physicist and philosopher of science. He studied at the Ecole Normale Supérieur and taught in Lille (1887–93), Rennes (1893–94), and Bordeaux (1894–1916). His major interests were physics and the history of sciences. He extended thermodynamics into chemistry. In his writing he emphasized the continuity in the development of science. He propounded the concept that physics and metaphysics should be viewed separately, but still he understood the significance of the latter. Major works: *La théorie physique; son objet et sa structure* (*Aim and Object of the Theory of Physics*) (1906), *Traité d'energetique générale* (*Treatise on General Energetics*) (1911), *Etudes sur Leonard de Vinci* (*Studies on Leonardo da Vinci*) (1906–13), *Le système de monde* (*The System of Universe*) (1913–59, several volumes published posthumously).

136. LE ROY, EDOUARD (1870–1954)   French philosopher and mathematician. He developed the evolutionary philosophy of Bergson (see note 123). Some of his thoughts are reflected in the ideas of his friend Teilhard de Chardin (see note 131).

137. LEIBNIZ (ALSO SPELLED LEIBNITZ), GOTTFRIED WILHELM (1646–1716)   German philosopher, logician, mathematician and politician. He studied at Leipzig, Jena, and Altdorf, but never accepted an academic position. Instead, he served as a diplomat in France (1672–76) as well as councilor to the elector of Hanover. He proposed the formation of the Academy of Science in Berlin and became its first president (1700). After early interest in mathematics, where he developed (1684), three year before Newton, infinitesimal calculus, he became involved in philosophical studies. In his rationalistic system, the universe consists of related occurrences that are the results of a divine plan. This universe is the best of all possibilities, even though evil is its necessary ingredient. The ultimate constituents of the universe are immaterial and nonacting monads that are nevertheless capable of interaction due to a preestablished harmony. All monads have consciousness, but those that are rational also have self-consciousness. The interaction between monads

is continuous since "nature makes no leaps." He also makes a distinction between "truth of reason" and "truth of fact." Major works: *Nouveaux essais sur l'entendement humain* (*New Essays on Human Understanding*) (1704), *Essais de Théodicée sur la bonté de Dieu, la liberté de l'homme et l'origine du mal* (*Essays of Theodicy on the Goodness of God, Freedom of Man and the Origin of Evil*) (1710), *Monadology* (1714).

138. SPINOZA, BARUCH (1632–77)   Dutch philosopher. He was a lens grinder by trade and refused an academic post in Heidelberg. Educated in Judaism, he was excommunicated from synagogue (1656) for his independent thought. His rationalistic and monist philosophy was influenced by Descartes (see note 64), whose works he rephrased. However, in contrast to Descartes, he assumed that there is no conflict between ideas and the physical universe—both being two aspects of the same thing, called either God or Nature. God is Nature in its fullness. In his thought he adheres strictly to the principles of logic according to which an idea must represent a coherent and properly related physical experience. The ideas compel us to act. As an exponent of ethics, Spinoza accepts that human beings strive for self-preservation, and the power that is needed to accomplish this, i.e., knowledge of necessity, represents virtue. Thus, powerful (that is, virtuous) man acts because he knows it is necessary to do so. When one has confused ideas, one is unaware of causes and is not free to act. In the field of sociology, Spinoza assumes that there is a possibility of community providing all members full satisfaction. Such a community is possible as long as there is freedom of inquiry, permitting one to escape deleterious desires through understanding such desires. Major works: *A Treatise on Religions and Political Philosophy* (1670), *Ethics* (1677), *Opera posthuma* (1677).

139. HERACLITUS (CA. 535–475 B.C.)   Greek philosopher from Ephesus. The expression *panta rei* summarizes the heart of his doctrine, according to which there is constant change or becoming, which occurs throughout reality. The process of change is circular and nature is always dividing and uniting. Although his thought was profound and the language bold and figurative, his style was careless to such an extent that his writings are difficult to understand. This earned him the nickname "the Obscure," together with another, "the Weeping Philosopher," which reflects his tendency to gloominess. His major work, *On Nature,* represents the oldest Greek prose of which original fragments have been recovered.

140. PIASECKI, BOLESŁAW (1914–79)   Member and activist of the Polish Fascist and anti-Semitic group called Falanga (Phalanx). The

group was spawned by the repression of the right-wing opposition by the *sanacja* regime (see note 62). After World War II Piasecki was arrested by the Soviet secret service (NKVD), but soon released, most likely after he promised collaboration with the Communists in an attack against the church in Poland. In 1947, he formed a pseudoreligious organization called PAX, with the aim of driving a wedge between some clergy and lay Catholics on the one side and the church hierarchy on the other. Although discredited, he remained at the helm of PAX, which was built into his private empire, even after October 1956 (see note 73), and the periodical *Po prostu*, which requested his removal, was closed by the authorities.

141. MICEWSKI, ANDRZEJ (1926–)   Political writer, publicist and lay Catholic activist. He studied law at Warszawa University, became involved in church-sponsored activities of lay Catholics (Club of Catholic Intelligentsia, KIK) and published articles in many periodicals. Editor of the publishing house *Verum* and the Catholic weekly *Tygodnik Powszechny* (since 1974), he is presently a member of the Social Council for the Primate of Poland. Communist authorities tried to involve him in political activities, nominating him for parliament in 1985, but he refused. Major works: *Z geografii politycznej II Rzeczypospolitej* (*Of the Political Geography of the Second Commonwealth*) (1965), *W cieniu Marszałka Piłsudskiego* (*In the Shadow of Marshal Piłsudski*) (1968), *Roman Dmowski* (1971), *Współrządzić czy nie kłamać* (*Co-rule or not to Lie*) (1978), *Kardynał Wyszyński, Prymas i mąż stanu* (*Cardinal Wyszyński, Primate and Statesman*) (1982), *Polityka staje się historią* (*Politics Becomes History*) (1986).

142. POLITICAL PARTIES   Before World War II, there were four major political parties in Poland—the Polish Peasant Movement (PSL, and later SL), the Polish Socialist Party (PPS), National Democracy (ND) and the Labor Movement or Christian Democracy (SP), as well as a score of minor parties, including the Polish Communist Party (KPP), which was dissolved (1938) by decision of the Comintern. During the Nazi occupation, the major parties—Peasant Movement (SL), National Movement (SN), Polish Socialist Party (PPS, also known as Liberty, Equality, Independence (WRN)) and Labor Movement (SP)—formed a coalition both abroad (Government–in–Exile) and within the country (consecutively, Main Political Council (GRP), Political Committee of Accord (PKP), Home Political Council (KRP), Council of National Unity (RJN)) to coordinate military resistance and political struggle by the Underground State (see note 1). The coalition formed the Underground Government (Home Delegature), which was presided over by

the home delegate (consecutively, Jan Skorobohaty, Cyryl Ratajski, Jan Piekałkiewicz, Jan Jankowski and Stefan Korboński). By the end of World War II, Communist sympathizers, with the help of the Soviet and Polish Communists, formed several small "front" parties that assumed names similar to or identical with those of the legitimate parties of the coalition. For example, leftist socialists formed a party called at first the Polish Socialists, and then renamed Worker's Polish Socialist Party (R-PPS). This was done to create an impression that the conditions of the Yalta decisions (see note 1) stipulating involvement of all parties in a new postwar government of Poland, were being fulfilled. From the very beginning, these "fake" parties were totally subjugated to the control of the Communists, but still many of them were dismantled by arranging so-called unification, e.g., the union of the Socialist and Communist parties (1948).

143. SERTILLANGES, O.P., ANTONIN-GOLBERT (1863–1948) French Dominican preacher, apologist, philosopher, and moral theologian. After receiving his doctorate (1890), he taught moral theology at Corbara, Corsica and later became professor of philosophy and moral theology at the Catholic Institute in Paris (1900–20). He was secretary of the periodical *Revue Thomiste*. He preached widely during World War I, but his political views led to his suspension from the faculty (1922) and exile to Jerusalem, Holland and Belgium. He was permitted to return to France in 1939. Major works: *Les sources de la croyance en Dieu* (*Sources of the Faith in God*) (1903), *La politique chrétienne* (*Christian Politics*) (1904), *Socialisme et christianisme* (*Socialism and Christianity*) (1905), *S. Thomas d'Aquin* (1910), *La vie héroique* (*Heroic Life*) (1914–18), *La vie intellectuelle* (*Intellectual Life*) (1921).

144. BEBEL, AUGUST (1840–1913)   German Marxist socialist, instrumental in the formation of the German Social Democratic Party (1869). He was a deputy to the German parliament (Reichstag) from the opposition to Chancellor Bismarck. He was tried and sentenced to two years in prison on false charges of treason. Major works: *Women and Socialism* (1883) and an autobiography (1910–14).

145. KAUTSKY, KARL JOHANN (1854–1938)   Austrian Marxist socialist who set the German Social Democratic Party on a Marxist course (Erfurt program). He was a leading personality in the Second International (Socialist). He opposed the German involvement in World War I and was also a sharp critic of the Soviet revolution, considering it undemocratic and contrary to Marxist principles. Together with Hugo Haase, he organized the Independent Social Democratic Party of Ger-

many. Major works: *The Economic Doctrines of Karl Marx* (1925), *Ethics and the Materialist Conception of History* (1907), *Bolshevism at a Deadlock* (1931). He also edited and published the fourth volume of Marx's *Capital* under the title *Theorien ueber den Mehrwert* (*Theories of Surplus Value*) (1905–10).

146. BUKHARIN, NICOLAI IVANOVICH (1888–1938)   Russian theoretician of communism, member of the Bolshevik faction of the Russian Social Democratic Labor Party. Bukharin spent several years (1911–17) in New York City, editing the revolutionary newspaper *Novy Mir* (*New World*). After the November 1917 revolution, he was a leader of the Third International (Communist), also known as the Comintern, and editor of the newspaper *Pravda,* a job that he inherited from Stalin (see note 69). As member of the Politburo (1924), Bukharin allied himself with Stalin against Kamenev and Zinoviev, but then his economic views favoring slow collectivization were defeated and he lost his position in the Politburo. Accused of treason, he was tried, sentenced and executed in 1938 during the Stalin purges.

147. NIEDZIAŁKOWSKI, MIECZYSŁAW (1893–1940)   Theoretician and publicist of the Polish Socialist Party (PPS), politician, member of the Polish Socialist Party (1914), member (1916–19) and vice-chairman (1924–27) of its Central Committee. Active participant in the defense of Warsaw against the Nazis (1939) and a member of the patriotic underground resistance; he was vice-chairman of GRP (see note 142). Arrested by the Gestapo, he was executed in 1940. Major works: *Organizacja pośrednictwa pracy* (*Organization of Labor Exchange*) (1916), *Teoria i praktyka socjalizmu wobec nowych zagadnień* (*Theory and Practice of Socialism in Light of New Problems*) (1926), *Demokracja parlamentarna w Polsce* (*Parliamentary Democracy in Poland*) (1930).

148. REIFF, RYSZARD (1923–)   Politician and publicist. During World War II, Reiff participated in the patriotic underground movement. After the war, he worked as a journalist, and was a founder and editor of the newspaper *Słowo powszechne.* He was cofounder of PAX, its deputy director (1976–79) and president after 1979. His attempts to change the political platform of PAX failed, and he was removed from the presidency of PAX after the imposition of martial law (see note 4). Reiff was a deputy to the Polish parliament in 1964–68 and again since 1980. He was the only member of the State Council who had the courage to vote against the imposition of martial law.

149. EILSTEIN, HELENA (1922–)   Marxist philosopher. She studied philosophy at the Warszawa University. She taught Marxist philos-

ophy in the department of dialectical Marxism at the same university. She was director of the Research Center of Historical Materialism at the Institute of Philosophy and Sociology of the Polish Academy of Sciences. She was editor of the periodical *Studia filozoficzne* (1950–55). She emigrated to the United States and taught at the University of New Mexico, Albuquerque. Major works: *Jedność materialna świata* (*Material Unity of the World*) (1961), *Wartości i oceny* (*Values and Evaluations*) (1967).

150. NIETZSCHE, FRIEDRICH WILHELM (1844–1900)   German philosopher of half-Polish origin. He studied at Bonn and Leipzig and became professor of philology at Basel (1869). In the later years of his life, he became insane. He was more a moralist than a philosopher, and rejected Western and Christian civilization as being based on a decadent and slave morality. He proposed instead a superhuman being (Übermensch) whose morality, affirming life and its values, would set him above the rest of humanity. Nietzsche despised both egalitarism and absolutism (especially German), and it is ironic that his thoughts were taken up and distorted by Nazi ideologues to justify their doctrines of German superiority and anti-Semitism. Major works: *The Birth of Tragedy* (1872), *Thus Spake Zarathustra* (1883–84), *Beyond Good and Evil* (1886), *The Genealogy of Morals* (1887), *The Anti-Christ* (1888), *Ecce Homo* (1888), *Twilight of the Idols* (1889).

151. CATHREIN, S.J., VICTOR (1845–1931)   Leading neo-Thomist philosopher, ethician, and theologian. He stood strongly against positivistic influences in ethics and jurisprudence. He also opposed the notion that morality can be separated from religion. He was a strong critic of socialism. Major work: *Socialism: Its Basis and Practical Application* (1904).

152. NEW ECONOMIC POLICY (NEP)   An economic program introduced in 1921 by Lenin (see note 80) to halt the declining economy and increasing deprivation of people caused by the policies (forced requisitions, nationalization of industry, confiscation of capital, control of labor) of early communism in the Soviet Union. The introduction of NEP was probably prompted (at least partially) by the Kronstadt insurrection, which was brutally suppressed, with almost 20,000 killed. NEP consisted of a partial return to the capitalist economy (free trade of excess agricultural products, private operation of small business, abolition of compulsory labor). Although NEP significantly improved the economy, it was abolished in 1928 by Stalin (see note 69), who returned to the totally state-controlled economy.

153. HITLER, ADOLF (1889–1945)   German dictator and founder of National Socialism. Austrian-born Hitler lived in Vienna (1907) and Munich (1913), and developed vicious anti-Semitic and strong anti-Communist convictions. After World War I, in which he participated as a corporal and won the Iron Cross for bravery, Hitler blamed the defeat of Germany on Jews and Communists. Soon he joined the German Workers' Party which in 1920 was renamed the National Socialist Party of Germany (NSDAP or Nazi). The Nazi Party was reorganized under Hitler's authoritarian rule and was transformed into a paramilitary organization known also as "brown shirts." After the unsuccessful "beer-hall putsch" (1923) aimed at overthrowing the Bavarian government, Hitler was sentenced to five years in prison, but was released after only nine months. While in prison, he wrote (actually dictated to Rudolf Hess) his book *Mein Kampf (My Struggle)*, which was to become the "bible" of the Nazi Party. The Nazi Party, led by Hitler, Strasser, Goebels, and Goering gained the mass support of the German people during the depression era (1929–33) by promising the despoilage of Jews to the poor, job security to workers, and control over the trade unions and Communists to financiers and industrialists. The Party won a majority of seats in parliament in 1932 and after civil riots and the resignation of Chancellor Schleicher, Hitler was named chancellor (1933) by President Hindenburg. While chancellor, Hitler used Machiavellian politics to solidify his power and after the 1933 elections attained dictatorship through parliamentary decree. As Fuehrer, he eventually united in his hands the power of the chancellorship and presidency, after the death of President Hindenburg (1934). Hitler proclaimed the formation of the Third Reich (*Grossdeutsches Reich*), eliminated his former allies and supporters, and instituted policies of terror and anti-Semitism. He subjugated the army by appointing his cronies to command positions. On the international scene, through skill and deceit, Hitler succeeded in annexing Austria (1938) after the assassination of Austrian Chancellor Dolfuss, and in occupying the western part of Czechoslovakia (1938), as sanctioned by the Munich Pact signed by the Western powers. In preparation for war, he signed alliances with Italy, Spain, the Soviet Union, and Japan, as well as with many smaller countries such as Bulgaria, Rumania and Hungary.

On September 1, 1939 Hitler, assured of Soviet cooperation in the partition of defeated Poland, ordered the German Army to attack Poland. In 1941, he assumed the supreme command of the German Army and, against the better judgment of military leaders, continued the war to its disastrous end. During World War II Hitler survived several plots on his life. At the end of the war Hitler gave a great share of power to Himmler and the dreaded services—Gestapo and SS (see note 159).

Just before the end of the war, he resigned his position in favor of Admiral Doenitz and committed suicide (April 30, 1945). It is believed that Hitler suffered from paranoic fears of plotting and persecution—possibly due to quarternary syphilis.

154. "SHORT COURSE . . ." *Short Course of History of the All-Union Communist Party (Bolshevik)* was prepared by an anonymous Party committee and published in 1938. Only after World War II was the authorship of the book ascribed to Stalin (see note 69). Despite omissions, distortions and falsifications of data, the book achieved record editions of millions of copies in virtually all languages. It became the "bible" of Soviet communism and a tool for propaganda and indoctrination both in the Soviet Union and in any country that fell under Soviet influence. The book presented communism and its practice uncritically and in the best possible light. In the late 1940s and early 1950s, the book was a mandatory text in high schools and universities in Poland, where courses in Marxism were compulsory, regardless of the field of studies.

155. STRZELECKI, JAN (1919–   )   Sociologist and writer. He studied law, but eventually received his degree in sociology. During World War II, he participated in the patriotic resistance; he published socialist newspaper *Płomienie* and fought in the Warsaw Uprising. After the war, he worked in the Institute of Philosophy and Sociology of the Polish Academy of Sciences. He was a member of the Expert Commission of Solidarity Trade Union. Major works: *Zapiski (Notes)* (1957), *Amerykańskie niepokoje (American Anxieties)* (1962), *Kontynuacje 1 (Continuations 1)* (1969), *Próba świadectwa (Attempt at Testimony)* (1971), *Kontynuacje 2 (Continuations 2)* (1974).

156. MICHNIK, ADAM (1946–   )   Historian and human rights activist. Son of prewar Communist activist Ozias Schechter, he studied at Warszawa University, but was expelled for his participation in the events of March 1968 (see note 67), arrested, and imprisoned. After release from prison he had to work at a blue-collar job and was permitted to continue his studies only as a part-time student in Poznań, where he received his doctorate (1975). Cofounder of the Committee for Defense of Workers (KOR, see note 102) and lecturer in the independent university called the Society of Scholarly Courses (TKN), he was an editor of the independent periodicals *Znak, Krytyka,* and *Biuletyn informacyjny.* During the Solidarity era (see note 4), he served as adviser to the leadership of the trade unions. Interned after Jaruzelski's coup d'état

(1981) and accused with several others of treason, he was held in prison for several years until released under the pressure of public opinion in Poland and abroad. Arrested again in 1985, he was given a "show trial" and sentenced to three years in prison and released in 1986. His activities in defense of freedom are widely recognized in Poland (although his writings are banned in Poland and published only abroad) and elsewhere. He received the *Prix de la Liberté* of the French Pen Club, an honorary doctorate from New York's New School for Social Research, and the Robert Kennedy Award. Major works: *Kościół—lewica—dialog (The Church—the Left—Dialogue)* (1977), *Szkice (Sketches)* (1981), *Penser la Pologne (Thinking of Poland)* (1983), *Szanse polskiej demokracji (Chances of Polish Democracy)* (1984).

157. WESTERPLATTE   This small penninsula north of Gdańsk at the mouth of the Wisła River was ceded in 1925 to Poland by the Free City of Gdańsk under the conditions of an agreement sponsored by the League of Nations. Westerplatte, a military transit storage area for war material imported by Poland between 1925 and 1939, was guarded by a detachment of Polish armed forces. On September 1, 1939 the Polish garrison, consisting of about 182 soldiers and sailors armed with 3 field guns, 4 mortars and 43 machine guns, was attacked by the German Army, Navy and Air Force (the German forces included 2300 soldiers armed with 30 field guns, 12 howitzers and 60 machine guns, the battleship *Schleswig–Holstein* armed with 18 guns, and 40 planes of the Luftwaffe). The Polish soliders, commanded by Maj. Henryk Sucharski and Capt. Franciszek Dąbrowski, fought against these overwhelming odds until September 7, 1939, when they surrendered after inflicting at least 300 casualties on the Germans and losing 16 of their own soldiers. Among them were Sgt. Wojciech Najsarek, the first Polish casualty of World War II, and Sgt. Kazimierz Rasiński, killed after the surrender for refusing to disclose the military code. The heroism and devotion of the defenders of Westerplatte received recognition even by their enemies in a 1940 article in the Italian newspaper *La Voce di Bergamo* entitled "I leoni della Westerplatte" ("The Lions of Westerplatte").

158. BONHOEFFER, DIETRICH (1906–45)   Leading German Protestant theologian, studied in Berlin, Tübingen and New York. He insisted on the role of Christianity in the modern world and urged following Christian teaching in its most ideal form of committing oneself to the service of others. He was active in the ecumenical movement. He was strongly opposed to the Nazi movement and as a part of his resistance activity was involved in an unsuccessful plot to assassinate Hitler (see note 153), leading to his arrest and execution by the Nazis. Major works:

Cost of Discipleship (trans. 1948), *Prisoner of God: Letters and Papers from Prison* (trans. 1953), *Ethics* (trans. 1965).

159. SS-MEN   SS is an acronym for the Security Department (*Schutzstaffel*), an elite Nazi party storm troop created in 1925 and originally limited in number. SS grew in 1929 to 50,000 and became under Himmler a security force for the Nazi party. In 1934, the SS was instrumental in eliminating, during the so-called "night of long knives," the original Nazi street fighters led by Ernst Roehm. With the passing of time the SS infiltrated the state police, security forces (*Gestapo*) as well as military, political, and economic circles of Hitler's Germany. During World War II, the SS, by then 240,000 strong, became a tool of racist and anti-Semitic policies and was responsible for operating concentration and extermination camps. As early as 1939 part of the SS formed military units (*Waffen–SS*), with the chain of command independent of the regular army (*Wehrmacht*). Ultimately, the Waffen–SS comprised 38 divisions with 900,000 men, of whom 200,000 were foreigners, e.g., the Belgian Legion of Walloons or the French Charlemagne Brigade. These units were the most ruthless and brutal force, as exemplified by the massacres of Oradour–sur–Glane (France) and Lidice (Czechoslovakia).

160. WEIL, SIMONE (1909–43)   French writer and mystic. She studied philosophy and logic at the Ecole Normale Supérieur (1928–31), but never had a formal academic position and published her works in rather obscure trade union and Communist publications. Having strong convictions about justice and human duties, she joined the republican cause during the Spanish Civil War (1934), worked as a farm hand during the Nazi occupation of France (1940–42), and ultimately died of self-starvation after she emigrated from France to the United States and Britain. She believed that she had experienced a revelation of Christ and felt obliged to transmit it to others. She was strongly attracted to Catholicism. She considered goodness as a sacred part of the person and believed that basic frustration is caused by the contradiction between rigorous necessity and the expectation of good. She also believed that a person can "decreate" itself by relinquishing the particulars and "annihilating" itself in a divine love. Major works: mostly published posthumously from essays and articles, *Selected Essays* (1934–43), *La pésanteur et la grace* (*Gravity and Grace*) (1946), *Cahiers* (*Notebooks*) (1951–56), *Oppression and Liberty* (1958).

161. KISIELEWSKI, STEFAN (1911–   )   Writer, journalist, politician, and composer. He studied at Warszawa University (1927–31), as well as

at the Warszawa Conservatory (1934 and 1937). In 1939, he participated in the defense of Warsaw and then joined (1942–45) the patriotic underground resistance as member of the Home Delegature (see notes 1 and 142). After the war, he taught music theory in the School of Music and at the same time published essays in several periodicals (*Polityka, Tygodnik Powszechny, Kultura*). He was elected a deputy to the Polish parliament (1957–65) and was a member of the Catholic deputies' caucus (*Znak*). Because of his outspoken criticism of Marxism, he was repeatedly barred by the censors from publishing and was finally dismissed from his teaching post. At present, he writes mostly for underground (uncensored) publishing houses in Poland or publishes abroad. Major works: *Sprzysiężeni* (*Conspirators*) (1947), *Miałem tylko jedno życie* (*I Had Only One Life*) (1958), *Widziane z góry* (*Seen from the Top*) (1967), *Podróż w czasie* (*Time Travel*) (1982), *Walka o świat* (*Struggle for the World*) (1982). Kisielewski has also composed four symphonies and musical scores for plays and movies.

162. ZABŁOCKI, JANUSZ ZBIGNIEW (1926–)   Publicist and Catholic activist. He studied political science at the Jagiellonian University (see note 91), and during World War II was a member of the patriotic resistance (Home Army). For a while (1950–55), he joined the PAX movement (see note 140), but eventually left it after October 1956 (see note 73) and became (1957–76) a member of the Club of Catholic Intelligentsia (KIK) and founder of the Center for Social Documentation and Studies (ODiSS). He was a press correspondent at Vatican Council II (see note 8). A president of the Polish Social-Catholic Association (1981–84), he always gravitated toward collaboration with the Communist regime in Poland and was for many years a deputy to parliament, where he led the so-called pseudo-*Znak* (see note 161). He published in many periodicals (*Słowo powszechne, Dziś i jutro, Więź*) and founded (1969) the monthly *Chrześcijanin w świecie* (*A Christian in the World*). Major works: *Kościół i świat współczesny* (*The Church and the Contemporary World*) (1967), *Na polskim skrzyżowaniu dróg* (*At the Polish Crossroad*) (1972), *Tożsamość i siły narodu* (*Identity and the Forces of the Nation*) (1978).

163. PIUS XII (1876–1958)   Eugenio Pacelli was ordained in 1899 and began work in the diplomatic service of the Vatican as undersecretary of state (1912) and then nuncio to Bavaria (1917–1929). Made a cardinal (1929) and secretary of state (1930), he negotiated a concordat with Nazi Germany (1933) that was ignored by Hitler. Elected pope in 1939, he assumed the name Pius XII. Although he sharply criticized totalitarianism both as diplomat (the encyclical *Mit brennender Sorge*

was drafted by then Cardinal Pacelli for Pius XI) and as pope (the encyclical *Summi Pontificalis*), he believed that the papacy could be most effective by maintaining neutrality during World War II and by declaring Rome an open city. He was strongly criticized for his position, especially for not standing in defense of the Jews. This criticism disregarded the fact that both the church and the Pope unequivocally condemned the extermination of the Jews and gave them considerable help during and after the war. After World War II, Pius XII assumed an intransigent posture toward Communism and its sympathizers, both in Italy and in the world. Conservative and legalist, he was genuinely concerned with reform in the church and was the first to use the concept of *aggiornamento* in his attempts to foster biblical studies and the reform of the liturgy and monastic life. Still, his insensitive stance toward Protestant and Orthodox churches did nothing to foster the ecumenical movement.

164. CZĘSTOCHOWA   Częstochowa is a city in Southern Poland (pop. about 200,000) on the Warta River. Its most notable feature is the ancient monastery of the Paulines, Jasna Góra (Bright Mountain). In the monastery church is the famous icon of the Black Madonna, which legend says was painted by St. Luke on a table top made by St. Joseph. The same legend says that the picture was brought from Jerusalem to Constantinople by St. Helen, mother of the first Christian Roman emperor, Constantine the Great (307–337). During the Crusades it passed through Red Ruthenia to the hands of prince Władysław (Naderspan) of Opole and Kujawy, who established the monastery (1382) and entrusted the icon to the Paulines. The monastery became a national shrine, richly endowed by kings, dukes and magnates, as well as by the common people. In 1655, a handful of Poles successfully defended the monastery against a superior force of Swedes and reversed the tide of a Swedish invasion. This defense prompted King Jan Kazimierz (1648–68) (see note 92) to proclaim the Virgin Mary the Queen of Poland. Today, Częstochowa and Jasna Góra are the destination of annual pilgrimages by millions of the faithful.

165. PARTITIONS   Poland's eighteenth century neighbors—Russia, Prussia and Austria—in pursuit of their expansionist policies, conceived a plan to dismember Poland. The internal strife and progressive weakness of the outdated political system of elective monarchy facilitated this plan. The first partition (1772) resulted from four years of war waged by Russia against the so-called Confederation of Bar, which deposed King Stanisław August Poniatowski (1764–95), elected under pressure from Catherine the Great (1762–96), empress of Russia. The second

partition (1793) occurred after Russia first instigated civil disturbances and then intervened on behalf of the Confederation of Targowica, which was signed in St. Petersburg and demanded repeal of the recently proclaimed (1791) constitution of May third. The third and final partition (1795), which erased Poland from the European map for 123 years, ensued after the defeat of the national uprising (see note 97) led by General Tadeusz Kościuszko. The insurrection erupted in an attempt to regain territorial losses and to reinstate the constitution.

166. BŁONIA   Błonia is a large common in Kraków. At this location, a mass celebrated by Pope John Paul II during his first visit to Poland (see note 2) was attended by an estimated crowd of 3,000,000 faithful.

167. NOWA HUTA   A city in the vicinity of Kraków. Nowa Huta (pop. ca. 250,000) was built to provide living facilities for the builders and employees of the huge steelworks. Conceived and built in the early years of the six-year plan (see note 10), it was to be a model socialist city without religion or places of worship, inhabited by loyal citizens of the Communist state. Ironically, Nowa Huta became the symbol of defiance and its workers actively participated in the protests of 1968 (see note 67), 1976, and 1980 (see note 4). The inhabitants demanded construction of a church that, after a lengthy struggle with state authorities, was actually erected (1977) under the patronage of the then archbishop of Kraków, Karol Wojtyła (see note 3). Many foreign groups (*Suhnezeichen, Bauorden*) participated in the construction work. This church of Our Lady Queen of Poland, often referred to as Arka (the Ark), was visited by John Paul II during his second visit to Poland in 1982 (see note 2). At present, four new churches are under construction in Nowa Huta.

VI.
Bibliography

Baczko, Bronisław. "O poglądach filozoficznych i społeczno-politycznych Tadeusza Kotarbińskiego" (On the philosophical and sociopolitical views of Tadeusz Kotarbiński). *Myśl filozoficzna* 1951 (1–2).

Cywiński, Bohdan. *Zatruta humanistyka* (Poisoned humanistics). Warszawa: Nowa 2. ND.

Engels, Friedrich. *Ludwig Feuerbach and the Outcome of Classical German Philosophy*. New York: International Publishers, 1941.

Fritzhand, Marek. *O niektórych właściwościach etyki marksistowskiej.* (On some features of Marxist ethics). Warszawa: PWN, 1974.

Heidegger, Martin. "Letter on 'Humanism'." In *Basic Writings*. New York, Hagerstown, San Francisco: Harper & Row, 1976.

Jankowski, Henryk. "Moralność jako forma świadomości społecznej" (Morality as the form of social consciousness). In J. Banaszkiewicz, J. Grudzień, H. Jankowski, eds., *Filozofia marksistowska* (Marxist philosophy). Warszawa: PWN, 1971.

Jaroszewski, Tadeusz M. *Osobowość i wspólnota* (Personality and community). Warszawa: Książka i Wiedza, 1970.

Jasińska, Aleksandra, and Renata Siemieńska. *Wzory osobowe socjalizmu* (Personal models of socialism). Warszawa: Wiedza Powszechna, 1978.

Klaus, Georg, and Manfred Buhr. *Philosophische Woerterbuch* (Dictionary of philosophy). Leipzig: Bibliographische Institut, 1964.

Kliszko, Zenon. "Report from the Meeting of the Central Committee." *Nowe Drogi* 1965 (199).

Kłósak, Konstantyn. *Materializm dialektyczny* (Dialectical materialism). Kraków: Wydawnictwo Mariackie, 1948.

Kłósak, Konstantyn. "Dialektyczne prawo jedności i walki przeciwieństw" (Dialectical law of the unity and struggle of opposites). *Przegląd powszechny* 1949 (9).

Kłósak, Konstantyn. "Próba oceny" (Attempt at evaluation). *Życie i myśl* 1956 (3).

Kolendo, Janina. "Czytając roczniki czasopism katolickich 1945–1950" (Reading the annals of Catholic periodicals 1945–1950). *Życie i myśl* 1955 (1).

Kołakowski, Leszek. *Szkice z filozofii katolickiej* (Sketches on Catholic philosophy). Warszawa: PWN, 1953.

Kołakowski, Leszek. "Kapłan i błazen" (Priest and jester). *Twórczość* 1959 (10).

Kołakowski, Leszek. "Jezus Chrystus—prorok i reformator" (Jesus Christ—prophet and reformer). *Argumenty* 1965 (51/52).

Kołakowski, Leszek. *Kultura i fetysze* (Culture and fetishes). Warszawa: PWN, 1967.

Kołakowski, Leszek, and Stuart Hampshire, eds. *The Socialist Idea: A Reappraisal.* New York, Basic Books, 1974.

Kołakowski, Leszek. *Main Currents of Marxism,* Vols. 1–3. Oxford: Clarendon Press, 1978.

Konwicki, Tadeusz. *Kalendarz and klepsydra* (Diary and hourglass). Warszawa: Czytelnik, 1976.

Kroński, Tadeusz. "Świat w klamrach ontologii" (The world in the shackles of ontology). *Myśl filozoficzna* 1952 (1).

Kroński, Tadeusz. "Recenzja z 'Historii filozofii' W. Tatarkiewicza" (Review of *History of Philosophy* by W. Tatarkiewicz). *Myśl filozoficzna* 1952 (4).

Kuczyński, Janusz L. "Personaliści w Polsce, czyli nowe doświadczenia katolicyzmu w Polsce" (Personalists in Poland or new experiences of Catholicism in Poland). *Studia filozoficzne* 1952 (2).

Kuczyński, Janusz L. *Homo creator. Wstęp do dialektyki człowieka* (Homo creator: Introduction to the dialectic of man). Warszawa: Książka i Wiedza, 1976.

Kuczyński, Janusz L. "Marksizm—laicyzm—chrześcijaństwo" (Marxism—laicism—Christianity). *Studia filozoficzne* 1978 (5).

Kuczyński, Janusz L. "Dźwignąć świat" (To lift up the world). *Studia filozoficzne* 1979 (1).

Marx, Karl. *Capital,* vol. 1. New York: Modern Library/Random House, 1936.

Marx, Karl. *The Economic and Philosophic Manuscripts of 1844.* New York: International Publishers, 1964.

Marx, Karl, and Friedrich Engels. *Basic Writings on Politics and Philosophy.* Garden City, N.Y.: Anchor Books–Doubleday & Co., 1959.

Michalik, Mieczysław. "Etyka marksizmu i moralność socjalistyczna" (Ethics of Marxism and socialist morality). In: H. Jankowski et al., eds., *Etyka (Ethics).* Warszawa: PWN, 1973.

Michalski, Konstantyn. *Pisma wybrane* (Selected writings). Kraków: Znak, 1964.

Michnik, Adam. *Kościół—lewica—dialog* (The church—the left—dialogue). Paris: Instytut Literacki, 1977.

Miłosz, Czesław. *The Captive Mind.* New York: Vintage Books, 1953.

Mysłek, Wiesław. "Zwrot w katolickiej interpretacji pracy" (Change in the Catholic interpretation of work). *Studia filozoficzne* 1977 (4).

"Od Redakcji" (From the editorial board). *Myśl filozoficzna* 1951 (1–2).

Piasecki, Bolesław. "Zagadnienia istotne" (Essential issues). *Zycie i myśl* 1954 (3).

Reiff, Ryszard. "Umacnianie ideowe, społeczne i organizacyjne stowarzyszenia PAX—warunkiem twórczej kontynuacji i normalnego rozwoju" (Ideological, social, and organizational strengthening of the PAX association—a condition of the creative continuity and normal development). Manuscript of speech delivered Feb. 23–24, 1979 (for internal use).

Reiff, Ryszard. "Doskonalić rzeczywistość i służyć człowiekowi—oto platforma współdziałania i dialogu" (To improve reality and to serve the human being—this is a platform for cooperation and dialogue). *Wrocławski tygodnik Katolików* 1979 (26).

Reiff, Ryszard "Czas próby" (Time of trial). *Słowo powszechne:* 1980 (232).

Richta, Radovan et al. *Civilization at the Crossroad: Social and human implications of the scientific and technological revolution.* White Plains, N.Y.: International Arts and Science Press, 1969.

Schaff, Adam. "Poglądy filozoficzne K. Ajdukiewicza" (Philosophical views of K. Ajdukiewicz). *Myśl filozoficzna* 1952 (1).

Schaff, Adam. *Marksizm a jednostka ludzka* (Marxism and the human individual). Warszawa: PWN, 1965.

Sève, Lucien. *Man in Marxist Theory.* Atlantic Highlands, N.J.: Humanities Press, 1978.

Stalin, Josif V. *Zagadnienia leninizmu* (Problems of Leninism). Warszawa: Wydawnictwo Książka, 1949.

Strzelecki, Jan. *Kontynuacje 2* (Continuations 2). Warszawa: PIW, 1974.

Szewczuk, Włodzimierz. *Psychologia* (Psychology), vol. 2. Warszawa: PZWS, 1962/66.

Szewczyk, Jan. "Ideologia alienacji czy alienacja ideologii" (Ideology of alienation or alienation of ideology). *Życie literackie* 1965 (46–47).

Szewczyk, Jan. "O istocie filozofii marksistowskiej" (On the essence of Marxist philosophy). *Studia filozoficzne* 1969 (1).

Ślipko, Tadeusz. "Pojęcie człowieka w świetle współczesnej antropologii marksistowskiej" (Concept of the human being in the light of contemporary Marxist anthropology). *Zeszyty naukowe KUL* 1967 (2).

Tatarkiewicz, Władysław. *Historia filozofii* (History of philosophy), vol. 3. Kraków: Czytelnik, 1948/50.

Thompson, Edward, P. "Socialist Humanism: An Epistle to the Philistines." *The New Reasoner* 1957 (1).

Wójcik, Przemysław. *Marksowsko–engelsowska koncepcja dezalienacji pracy* (Marx–Engels concept of the unalienation of work). Warszawa: PWN, 1978.

VII.
Subject Index

VIII.
Name Index